Margaret Addison

Margaret Addison

Margaret Addison

❧

A Biography

❧

JEAN O'GRADY

McGill-Queen's University Press
Montreal & Kingston · London · Ithaca

Legal deposit second quarter 2001
Bibliothèque nationale du Québec

Printed in Canada on acid-free paper

This book has been published with the help
of a grant from Victoria University.

McGill-Queen's University Press
acknowledges the financial support of the
Government of Canada through the Book
Publishing Industry Development Program
(BPIDP) for its activities. It also acknowledges
the support of the Canada Council for the
Arts for its publishing program.

Canadian Cataloguing in Publication Data

O'Grady, Jean, 1943–
Margaret Addison: a biography
Includes bibliographical references and index.
ISBN 0-7735-2152-6
1. Addison, Margaret, 1868–1940. 2. Deans of
women – Ontario – Toronto – Biography.
3. Victoria College (Toronto, Ont.) –
Biography. 4. Victoria College (Toronto, Ont.).
Annesley Hall – History. I. Title.
LE3.T618A335 2001 378.1'94'092 C00-900975-2

Typeset in Palatino 10/12
by Caractéra inc., Quebec City

For my husband, Walter

Contents

Illustrations

Credits for Illustrations

Addison family collection:
Frontispiece, pages 19, 27, 32, 40,
81, 82, 83, 152, 222, 223.
Rephotographed in recent years
by Ernest Lewis

United Church of Canada/Victoria
University Archives, Toronto:
page 29 91.161P/738N;
page 31 91.161P/353N;
page 85 87.240P/11N;
page 88 89.113P/2;
page 106 91.161P/413;

page 120 91.161P/419N;
page 129 76.002P/16;
page 151 89.147P/2;
page 153 91.161P/599

The principal and fellows of
Newnham College, Cambridge:
page 76

The principals and fellows of
St Anne's College, Oxford:
page 77

Victoria University: page 200

Acknowledgments

In preparing this biography I have been assisted greatly by the Addison family. The late Louise Lewis, Margaret Addison's eldest niece, gathered together many documents relating to Addison's life and the family history. She was unfailingly helpful and charming, and I wish she could have lived to see her Aunt Margaret's life receive the recognition she felt it deserved. For further details I am indebted to William Addison, Elizabeth McGregor, Edward Addison, Christine Dow, and Ann Lewis. Among those who shared their memories of early days were Julia, George, and Ottelyn Addison; Celia Corcoran; Kingsley Joblin; Laure Rièse; Helen Langford; Irene Rinch; Jean Cameron; Dorothy Carver Nicholson; and Dora Wattee. Other details have come through the kindness of Elizabeth McLeod, Judith Grant, Heather Murray, John Court, Jay Macpherson, Susan McDonald, and Ken Thompson. I am also grateful to the two anonymous readers at Carleton University Press for their suggestions and comments.

The staff of the Victoria University / United Church Archives have been most patient and helpful, as have the staff of the Victoria University Library and the archivists at Trinity College (Toronto); the National Archives of Canada; the town of Whitby; Trafalgar Castle School; the University Women's Club; Havergal College (Toronto); Newnham College, Girton College, Homerton College, Hughes Hall, the Cambridgeshire County Record Office, and the Central Library in Cambridge; and St. Hugh's College, Lady Margaret Hall, St. Anne's College, and St. Hilda's College in Oxford. I thank the Massey family for permission to quote from several Massey letters.

At home, my mother has been a constant help, and my three daughters have been their usual selves – supportive in general, blissfully ignorant of details. This book is dedicated to my husband Walter, who has gone over every aspect of it with me. Without his encouragement I certainly could never have brought it to fruition.

Abbreviations

AA   Alumni Association Fonds

AHCOM   Annesley Hall Committee of Management

AO   Archives of Ontario

DCB   Dictionary of Canadian Biography

DOW   Dean of Women Fonds

MA   Margaret Addison

MAP   Margaret Addison Papers

NAC   National Archives of Canada

OISE   Ontario Institute for Studies in Education

UCA   United Church Archives

UTA   University of Toronto Archives

VUA   Victoria University Archives

VUL   Victoria University Library

VWREA   Victoria Women's Residence and Educational Association

Note: References to documents in VUA generally give box and file number. The files of letters in MAP, box 1, are not numbered, but letters can easily be found by date.

Margaret Addison

Introduction

As dean of residence at Victoria University, Margaret Addison had the habit of welcoming the incoming class of first-year women with a speech that began, "Women of the university." For new students such as Gertrude Rutherford in 1917 and Esther Trewartha in 1920, it was an awesome moment – a gesture emphasizing their entry into a splendid intellectual community with all its challenges, privileges, and responsibilities. They and many of their classmates retained throughout their lives something of the vision of the socially committed and fruitful life of the educated woman that Addison had tried to impart. As Rutherford wrote years later, "With unwearying zeal, Miss Addison worked with us and for us – but mostly with us – to help us achieve the full stature of maturity."[1]

Addison thus holds an important place in the history of the higher education of Canadian women. She was herself one of the small first wave of university-educated women in Ontario. As well, she presided over the living arrangements of a second wave of women who were being integrated in increasing numbers into college life. In 1903 she was named dean of residence, in charge of the newly erected Annesley Hall; thus she became the first, and until 1919 the only, female staff member at Victoria. In 1920 she was made dean of women, responsible for commuters as well as residents. Until she retired in 1931 – for a period of twenty-eight years – her policies set the tone and defined the expectations for female students at Victoria.

Addison remains, however, little more than a name to most people, even at her own university. And that name is current only because the second women's residence, erected in 1959, was called Margaret Addison Hall – now popularly known, with a familiarity that would have startled the dean, as "Marg. Add." Part of the reason for the lack of knowledge may be that her papers did not make their way to the Victoria University Archives until 1984 and access was restricted until 1989. But also, as a figure from the recent past, she had a mindset that is not very congenial to most people in the early twenty-first century. Although far enough removed to have embraced some "old fashioned" views that many are still reacting against, she remains too close to have acquired an aura of quaint historicity.

In three particular areas relevant to her educational work, Addison's beliefs show a theistic and moralistic orientation that has gone completely out of favour. First, though she dedicated her energies to expanding the social role of women, she never ceased to maintain that women were endowed by the Creator with a distinctive "womanliness" that precluded their simply mimicking the activities of men. Secondly, she held the unfashionable notion that education should form the character and improve morality, as well as train the intellect. And lastly, she was a Christian who prayed daily for the spread of righteousness and peace, who tried to ascertain God's design for her life, and who believed that God was calling individuals to work to improve the world. Unlike her contemporaries such as Nellie McClung, Addison did not have the populist touch that could make such beliefs palatable to a modern sensibility.

It is not easy, then, to enter sympathetically into Addison's point of view. The effort to do so, however, brings rich rewards. She was an articulate woman, and the thoughts expressed in her many letters and reports offer insight into the matrix of ideas and expectations governing the lives of women in the early twentieth century – both her own and those of her students. Her beliefs were held not as rigid doctrines but as nuanced and constantly evolving positions. Moreover, although she appears to be that unpopular figure – a member of the establishment – she was actually a visionary who worked for change from within the existing social and intellectual framework. Her position as a woman within a male-dominated institution turns out to be a subtle and fascinating balancing act – an instructive story of tact and compromise, struggle and repositioning. Early in her career as dean she wrote to one of her close friends about the need for a diplomatic approach:

Probably people in every age think they are living in critical times, but it would seem as if now we are in a transition stage of the woman question, waging war against the very old notions, yet with a certain conservatism in our hearts, and finding it difficult not to be aggressive and still to be aggressive enough, not to offend, and also to be brave enough to step out of the beaten track because it is to the interest of the world we should.[2]

Because she respected popular opinion and held many of the values shared by her society, she could do more to free women from traditional bonds than could many of her more flamboyant sisters.

The notion of the innate differences between men and women was embedded deeply in Addison's culture and religion. The Methodist Church in which she was raised looked upon the two sexes almost as distinct species, with complementary interests and abilities. Man was held to be practical and active by nature, while woman was thought to be spiritual and reflective. He was rational and dominated by interest and ambition; she was intuitive and led by her affections. It followed that women were credited with the unique ability to build a family home to which a man could retreat, as into a sanctuary, after the toil and struggles of business life.[3] This ascription of specific abilities to the sexes was not confined to religious circles; it permeated society. As late as 1891, for instance, one finds in an Ontario school inspector's report discussing whether women should be teachers the assertion that "woman is essentially more a religious being than man, and is therefore possessed of more love, goodness and kindness. She approximates very closely to the divine ..."[4]

Fortunately, although women were believed to have a special competency in human relations and in the moral sphere when Addison was growing up, it did not automatically follow that they must remain intellectually impoverished. There existed, of course, a fear of educated women that has been studied extensively and become the stuff of legend – a fear that was partly doctrinal and partly attributable to a fear of change, and that has made every advance of women in the educational sphere an adventure and a challenge. Many Methodists nevertheless held that Christian education entailed the drawing out of all faculties and that women's high calling as wives and mothers demanded no less. As one enlightened writer in an Episcopal Methodist newspaper put it in 1876,

A proper education aids to give man the full use of all the powers that God has given him, not only that he may act well his part in this state of probation, but that he may be prepared for the full enjoyment of eternal life beyond. Woman, too, has a physical nature to be cared for, intellectual powers to be developed, moral faculties to be directed and trained, and a spiritual nature to be cultured and adorned. She is as capable of a liberal education in all the arts and sciences as man. Why should she be debarred? ... One day, equally with man, she will be called upon to account for the use of the talents committed to her. Why should she make answer, "My father, my husband and my brother forced me to bury them under the dull routine of kitchen drudgery, and never afforded me the opportunity to put them to usury, or make them shine as the day."[5]

This was the attitude of Margaret Addison's family, who encouraged her to go to university, and of Addison herself. Their God was vitally involved in human history, orchestrating the gradual development of a just society peopled by a higher type of humanity.

Margaret Addison was quite within her religious tradition, then, in maintaining that women had the potential to be more than homemakers – that, given training and experience, they could play a valuable role in national life. One of her strengths was that she kept an open mind about the form their contribution might take. "If only one could foresee what a woman will do in the future," she mused with regard to the women's movement, "whether she will be in a home of her own, or whether she will follow a profession."[6] She encouraged her residents to explore the new careers opening up in such fields as nursing, librarianship, business, and journalism. But more importantly, she sought to awaken in them an ability to respond to whatever the future might bring, by developing their talents and by learning to situate themselves in reference to history and to God.

Addison's second seminal notion – that education must involve the whole character – had its roots both in Canadian Methodist practice and in the English tradition, especially as elaborated by nineteenth-century thinkers such as Jowett and the two Arnolds. Newman's *Idea of a University*, which assigned to the university the role of forming intelligent and capable members of society, was a favourite of hers. This ideal was by no means universally held even then; for example, some contemporary women's educators championed a purely intellectual education. Following the example of Emily Davies in England, they believed that any attempt to take women's characters into account would result in a gendered – and probably inferior – curriculum for women. On these grounds, Mary Woolley, president of Mount Holyoke in the United States from 1901 to 1937, resisted the introduction of a course in domestic science, since it suggested special vocations for women.[7] Addison championed domestic science on educational and vocational grounds, but not in a discriminatory spirit: her ideals of education for life extended to both sexes. Curriculum, though, was not her main concern. The residents of Annesley Hall already took classes with the men and, in general, followed the same courses of study. The responsiblity for character development was the chief burden resting on her shoulders, and she was always conscious of its great weight.

At one time Addison spoke of the tremendous consequences any fault on her part might have: "With how much levity we look upon life, and how little we seem to think about the stray words and the stray acts, which are indelibly stamped upon some soul. It is useless to think about one's influence – that belongs very much to youth; but one does feel how much each one of us who has to deal with young people should keep a pure and deeply Christian life."[8] Like a small-town minister, she was conscious that all eyes were upon her. Fortunately, she was also aware of the tremendous potential for good that her position entailed. She once defined her vocation in terms that combine the widest social influence with personal and individual concern: "To have a vision of the possibilities of the higher education of women, and to seek to make it more than a vision, yet not to neglect the personal contact of Dean and student, to be interested in great and earnest things, but to be sympathetic toward all that concerns the woman undergraduate in play, work, or in spirit – this is the high mission of the Head of a woman's college residence."[9]

Finally, Addison's beliefs as a practising Christian offer insights into the assumptions that shaped our society. Christianity gave Addison her ultimate perspective, providing a context in which she could see her work as dean as part of a wider civilizing movement, destined to transform the world. She was perhaps deficient from a multicultural point of view, in that she hoped for the spread of Christianity throughout the world, but she was no narrow sectarian and took a lively interest in other cultures and societies. What she revered most in the life of Christ was altruism, the quality that enabled people to work together for the common good. In this she was typical of her generation – a generation that gave birth to progressive and co-operative political parties and to the League of Nations.

Addison's Christianity also has a significant consequence for her biography, or at least for her biographer. Though never loath to talk about religion – she had a parable for every occasion – she said and wrote very little about the private dimension of her religious life. Probably, her life for her had a very different shape and meaning from the one developed here. She thought of it, one suspects, as a story of spiritual crises – as a record of temptations and occasional victories, of alienations from God, and of moments of vision and communion. All this, though, is a closed book to others. The only possible biography is a public one, detailing her relationships with other people, her acts, and her innovations and ideas. This focus has its compensations, of course, for it means that her story is, to some extent, the story of the women of Victoria College during her tenure there as dean.

Even in relation to her own time, Margaret Addison could not be labelled with any precision as a feminist. She did not talk much about "women's rights" in the abstract. Like the "maternal feminists" of her time, who believed that women should contribute to the public sphere specifically because of their genius for family life,[10] she believed that women had something to contribute to society as women, not as imitation men. She differed from the maternal feminists, however, in that she emphasized women's intellectual abilities as much as their nurturing and caring qualities. She resembled even less most modern feminists, in that she had very little sense of oppression by the patriarchy. Of course, the articulation of this oppression is a recent phenomenon, but even during Addison's time women such as Virginia Woolf were starting to resent a male-dominated society. Addison's perspective was quite different, and more traditionally Christian. To blame the imperfections of the social system on one sex would have seemed to her unfair, and in any case she was not inclined to view the shortcomings of people's lives chiefly in terms of the social system. For her, men and women were equally struggling pilgrims in an imperfect world.

There is a psychological dimension, as well, to Addison's ability to live with the patriarchal symbols of her religion and the existing constitution of society. Whereas Virginia Woolf's memories of her demanding father, Leslie Stephen, must have contributed to her increasing resentment of the male hegemony, Margaret Addison, as far as I have been able to determine, had a good relationship with her father – a man who expected much but was basically very proud of her. Her reflections when he died suggest a shadowy crossover in her mind between his image and that of God the father, and help to explain why she was not in overt rebellion. "It was not merely losing him [she wrote to her sister], but it seems as if unconsciously I had depended so much upon him to keep things straight that I have had to go in a new way back to that source of power which made his life so strong, so beautiful and so good."[11]

But if Addison was not against the patriarchy, she was nevertheless very much for the women's movement. Like many of the deans and professional women of the time, she never married; she was of the generation that set out to show that women could have a career, rather than of the subsequent generation that tried to show that a career could be combined with marriage.[12] A great deal of her time was devoted to women's institutions, clubs, and societies, which were just being formed or were breaking new ground. Having a sense that her generation was making history and suspecting that at some time her experience might be of interest to future historians of the women's movement, she kept a number of her papers, which are now available in the Victoria University Archives. She also collected material on the early experience of women in universities for an article, and once she even contemplated writing a history of Annesley Hall (at that time all of seventeen years old). Finding that no one was in charge of keeping memorabilia regarding women in higher education, she assumed that responsibility herself, "for some day, these items will be of interest."[13] It is thanks to her, then, that it is to some degree possible to piece together the experience of women as reflected in her life.

Towards the end of her life especially, she felt a solidarity with women that contains the germs of a feminist perspective. Part of the maturing of women, she felt, involved their taking control of their own lives and, thus, resisting the interference of men. After a prolonged struggle with the administration in 1920–21, for instance, she protested in her diary against "the autocracy of men in the affairs of women"; she maintained that "Victoria College should lead in the idea that women know better how to manage women's education than men."[14] When she first thought of retiring, in 1926, she recommended setting up a separate women's department in the college, with a dean to direct it. She argued that women should "develop their own particular gifts, that life may be enriched by variety, not hampered by uniformity. This is the reason why we desire that women shall be responsible in the largest measure for the education of their own sex, that they may have freedom to work out their own genius."[15]

Addison's increasingly separatist attitude is much easier to understand in the 2000s than it would have been in the 1960s and 1970s, during the most strident equality-seeking phase of the women's movement. The work of recent feminist essentialists has shown, though in a radically different key from Addison's, that to cherish an essential difference in the sexes is not necessarily to sell out to the patriarchy. With today's renewed interest in such questions as separate schools for girls, her views take on a new cogency.

Many biographers of women besides myself have been perplexed about how to refer to their central character – using her surname alone seems curt, yet using only her first name could possibly be judged as patronizing. In any case, Margaret Eleanor Theodora Addison had many names. She was "Maggie" as a child (in her father's brogue it sounded more like "Muggie"). As she grew up she became "Margaret" to many, although for a while she signed her letters to her brother "Marguerite." Later, around the college, she was known as "Miss Addison," though behind her back the students referred to her as META (from her initials), and this was the name she used to sign some youthful essays. Finally, much to her satisfaction, she metamorphosed into "Dr. Addison." Although I have opted generally for "Addison," I have varied the name according to circumstances.

The other women of the time are almost invariably referred to as "Mrs So-and-so," or even "Mrs George So-and-so" in such documents as the minutes of the committee of management; Addison,

herself, did the same, though she knew them well. I have frequently
followed this practice, although the index gives their full names
when it was possible to ascertain them. The index also contains the
life dates of the principal characters. I frequently use the commonly
used term "Victoria College," though after 1884 it was officially
known as "Victoria University," not becoming a separate college
again until 1928. As well, as in the usual Toronto fashion, I identify
the University of Toronto students by their graduating year; for
example, "2T1" refers to the class of 1921. As for the Annesley residents, Addison was careful to refer to them as "young women," but
because they often called themselves "girls," I have sometimes done
so, meaning no disrespect.

CHAPTER ONE

Growing Up

Margaret Addison was not born into the urban and intellectual milieu she later inhabited. On the contrary, like many Canadians in the newly formed Dominion of Canada, she was a pioneer's child: her birth on 21 October 1868 took place at Horning's Mills, Ontario, a mere clearing in the woods. Her first impression was perhaps the sunlight filtered through the rustling boughs. Her mother was a warm presence, nurturing and soft, crooning hymns to her first-born. Her father was out on the trail when she was born, and he came and went, perceptible as the sudden wind in the trees, smelling faintly of sweat, his leather travelling clothes stiffened by the rain. Their first home was a miserable wooden hovel, her father said later, with two main rooms – one serving as kitchen, living and dining rooms; the other as a bedroom – and three tiny rooms upstairs, under the eaves.[1] Water was pumped from a well; the surrounding forest hid a rustic privy, where clouds of mosquitoes hovered.

But this was no ordinary family of settlers, content to eke out a subsistence from the bush. The cabin was a centre of spiritual activity. Margaret's father, Rev. Peter Addison, was a Methodist preacher, her mother a former school-teacher. Both were on a pilgrimage, guided by the Word of God, and they were convinced it was God's will that they should labour in this corner of his vineyard and play their part in his evolving plan. For God had a plan, they believed, whereby, in the fullness of time, this sinful world would be transformed into the Kingdom of God and loving kindness would replace strife. The Addisons believed deeply in the responsibility of each individual to contribute to this hoped-for consummation – by prayers, exhortation, and selfless labour. Literally from her cradle, Margaret was surrounded by this religious atmosphere; it was to colour all she did.

Margaret's parents provided a formidable example of strength and piety. Although they were the products of different strains in the evolution of Methodist life, the stories collected about them in the family history binder suggest that they both constructed the narrative of their lives in terms of service to a larger whole.[2] The Rev. Peter Addison came to Methodism in his young manhood and, after a dramatic conversion, directed all his immense natural energy and physical stamina to the one end of serving God. He was some six feet tall, with a bush of hair, piercing blue eyes, and a stern face that could crinkle into a smile of amazing warmth. Born in England on 20 December 1831, he lived in the village of Beathwaite Green (now the town of Levens), not far from Kendal, Westmorland. His father, Thomas Addison, worked partly as a farm labourer and partly at home as a basket weaver. He had six children, of whom Peter was the fifth. They had little formal education but much native intelligence, and the local rector constantly lent them books of a sober and thoughtful cast. In the evenings, while the whole family wove baskets by the light of a peat fire, one member would lie on the floor with a book catching the light of the fire, and read aloud. Afterwards, their father commented on what had been read and answered questions before family prayers and bed.

Respect for learning, one of the chief traits preserved in family lore, was thus to become an important inheritance for Margaret. According to tradition, the Westmorland Addison family included a number of parsons and doctors. Joseph Addison, of the *Spectator*, was said to be a distant relation, although the distance may have been considerable. Joseph's father Lancelot was born in the village of Maulds Meaburn, Westmorland (near Shap), but his relation to the Levens branch is not clear – there were a number of Addisons in the county. More closely related was Robert Addison (1754–1829), Peter's great-uncle, a graduate of Cambridge; after emigrating to Canada in 1791, Robert had a distinguished career as founding minister of St. Mark's in Niagara-on-the-Lake, chaplain of the Province of Upper Canada, and confidant of Bishop Strachan.

Peter's uncle Robert, who had also emigrated to Upper Canada the year Peter was born, settled in South Norwich township, Oxford county. In 1848, when he was sixteen, Peter was allowed to follow him, accompanied by his older brother James, now about twenty-five. They were strong and hard-working young men who had little trouble finding work in the lumber mills and farms of what was then Canada West. Eventually they saved up $1200 and bought a 200-acre farm from a Quaker near Avon, a village south of London in South Dorchester Township, Elgin County, some twenty-five miles from the Norwich Addisons.

Though Peter had worked hard before, it was nothing compared to the labour of clearing and farming the land. In Peter and James's onslaught on the virgin forest, they brought mighty oaks, walnuts, maples, and hickory crashing down and piled up huge branches, which they burned at night in an inferno that would make a modern ecologist weep. Then the stumps had to be pulled, crops planted, and the farm stocked. Sometimes Peter found the work heartbreaking: "We had 19 acres of fall wheat and some spring wheat and the midge came and destroyed it so that we did not get even our bread and had nothing to sell for two years, and we had not a hundred dollars for our work, two men. These were the hardest times that I ever saw."[3]

Peter and James were still Anglicans at this time, but most of their neighbours attended the Methodist church nearby and sometimes invited the Addisons along. According to one anecdote, the brothers once went to pass an evening at the local tavern, after which the following exchange took place: "Not our kind, James." "No, not our kind, Peter." Later they spent an evening at a Methodist revival meeting, and the ensuing homeward-bound conversation went: "Not our kind, James." "No, not our kind, Peter." "More our kind than the other lot, James." As it happened, the Methodists did become Peter's kind, but not without a struggle. "The opposition he put up was real, intelligent and whole-hearted," wrote his son Arthur in his memoir. "He was impatient and violent in his likes and dislikes. And his conversion was a violent affair." Indeed, it followed the classic pattern laid down by Wesley for those trying to flee from the wrath to come. One night, crossing his own fields after a revival meeting, Peter was overwhelmed with a sense of his sin and worthlessness and fell to his knees on the spot, praying and mentally wrestling in the darkness until he came to a sense that his sins were forgiven.

From then on Peter was a man under discipline, who tried to lose his self-will in the will of God. It was not easy to tame his headstrong nature – to exchange turbulence of spirit for meekness, impetuosity for patience, and stubbornness for quiet persistence. According to those who knew him later as a minister, "There was something fierce in his labor; he tolerated nothing that interfered with his work and by his will he was driven into strange places, and made great demands on the powers of a body that was willing and very strong. He had it in him to be intemperate and fanatic almost were it not that he was kept gentle in all things by his persistent habits of prayer."[4]

Peter's induction into the Methodist ministry was involuntary. He and his brother continued to attend the Anglican church until the minister objected to their going to Methodist meetings, at which point they left and joined the local Methodist Society. Here Peter revealed unexpected powers of exhortation and preaching in class meetings – the early Methodist version of support groups, in which a dozen or so members met to discuss their spiritual life and to buck up those who were backsliding. Peter became a class leader, but, conscious of his lack of education and his thick North-of-England accent, resisted suggestions that he consider the ministry. He did agree to become a lay local preacher, however, giving sermons in outlying churches when the minister could not be present. So successful was he that in 1859, at the age of twenty-seven, he accepted his fate and became a candidate for the ministry.

Then came the difficult task of getting educated for the position. At that time spiritual gifts were esteemed more highly than formal education in a Methodist preacher, and there was no requirement for a theological degree or, indeed, any means of obtaining one in Canada. Nevertheless, applicants for a probationary position had to demonstrate a reasonable general education on a high-school level, as well as some knowledge of biblical and ancient history and Methodist doctrine. Once accepted as a probationer, they were assigned to a circuit where, for several years, they trained under the supervision of an experienced minister and studied the theology, biblical work, church history, moral philosophy, languages, and literature on which they would be examined by their conference before being ordained.[5] At first, Peter continued to farm while studying English grammar and Latin and preaching; eventually, he spent two academic years at the Wesleyan Methodist Victoria College in Cobourg (1862–64). The college, not wishing to risk its government grants by any appearance of sectarianism, was still innocent of a theological faculty or even of courses in theology.[6] Nonetheless, it did give Peter a grounding in metaphysics, morals, logic, chemistry, Latin, and Greek[7] and instilled in him a love of books that he passed on to his daughter; in fact, in later years, his theological collection was superb. In 1864, Peter was received into full communion and ordained.

This was the time of the Methodist itinerancy, when ministers spent a maximum of three years in one place and then were moved on; their ministerial year began on 1 July and ran to the following 30 June. As a probationer, Peter served for a year each at Belmont (near his home at Avon), and at the even less settled outposts of Durham (a village in Grey County with only sixty Methodists) and St. Vincent (a township on Georgian Bay). After ordination he went to the larger and more settled Bradford (1864–65). Methodist ministers in the early days were also itinerant in the sense that they travelled widely in the course of their duties. Assigned to a "circuit" that consisted of up to fifteen scattered appointments or preaching places – some of which were staffed by local preachers in the minister's absence – they were expected to visit them all in regular rotation. Often a minister would spend two weeks away from home covering one segment of his circuit. Before his marriage Peter travelled on horseback; with a few spare clothes, his Bible, and his notes in two leather saddlebags, he would make his way down the forest's narrow blazed trails, doused on rainy days with icy water from overhanging boughs. To repel the rain he wore buckskin, lined with homemade flannel dipped in linseed oil, and high leather boots. Sometimes dusk overtook him, and his pace necessarily slowed as he peered about anxiously for the lights of a settlement or even an isolated cabin.

In the early years, services in outlying areas were often conducted in people's houses, and the building of churches here and there on a circuit became a priority. Peter was a mighty church builder – quite literally, according to his son's biographical memoir, which describes him as an "axeman" who "helped build the church during the day and preached to them at night."[8] If the overtones of log church construction are somewhat anachronistic here, the axe-work might be taken to refer to preliminary clearing of the site. Every circuit Peter was on benefited from his zeal; no doubt it served, too, as a release from the tensions of forbearance.

Besides visiting his churches, Peter conducted revival meetings, practising a type of old-style Methodism that was already being put aside in the more populous districts.[9] The winter form of these was the "protracted meeting," in which the minister would move into a central town for a period of weeks and conduct nightly meetings at which the Gospel was proclaimed amid much singing, prayer, and testifying. During the day, the minister and church members would canvass the townspeople, discuss religious concerns, and issue invitations to the meetings. Frequently a fervent atmosphere built up and dramatic conversions (such as Peter's own) occurred. Somewhat less common, but equally characteristic of early Methodism, were the outdoor camp meetings, held in summer during the brief periods between haying and harvest or harvest and seeding. These took place in a clearing in the bush area of some farm, with felled trees for benches. From miles around the settlers would trek in for the services, which included sessions held at night by the light of huge pine fires. In an atmosphere of heightened expectation, amid groans and pious ejaculations and outcries of "Hallelujah" and "Lord answer prayer," many souls were, in the language of the day, "won for Christ."[10]

These meetings had both the strengths and the weaknesses of early Methodism. As well as providing an expression of religious commitment, they were a focus for community life, attracting a wide circle of participants and spectators to what were, in effect, high points of the social year. They engendered bonds of sympathy and concern. But they could also be overemotional and, in seeking to avoid the dry formalism of established religion, risked falling into the opposite extreme of mass hysteria. For one thing, early Methodists could be fanatical in their concentration on the one question, "Are you saved, brother?" Focusing on this supreme goal of life, they were all too prone to identify salvation with outward signs of piety – chiefly the avoidance of strong drink – and to condemn minor amusements such as card playing or novel reading which, since they did not positively help the Christian life, were denounced as entrapments of the devil.[11]

Fortunately, Peter Addison seems to have been free of the sanctimoniousness and closed-mindedness that could be associated with such a creed. He was a powerful preacher, but not what might be termed a ranter. He was certainly gifted with a stentorian voice, so that he had no difficulty being heard over the crackle of pine fires. But according to his son, his preaching avoided rhetorical and emotional excesses – the practice of "firing red-hot balls at the conscience"[12] – and was logical to a fault. In fact, his parishioners sometimes said that they valued his opening prayers even more than his sermons.[13] Peter spent part of every day in private prayer and meditation, from which he drew his strength and conviction, and his public prayers were powerful and moving. They were not petitions for particular things, but a search for communion that lifted the spirit temporarily into a more spacious realm.

One particular anecdote from around the time of Margaret's birth in Horning's Mills suggests Peter's moral authority. Previous revival meetings had been plagued by a group of young toughs, who came to sit at the back and interrupt with hoots and catcalls. When Peter held the first meeting of his own campaign, they gathered ominously in a phalanx; by the third night, they were out of hand. After trying to ignore them and carry on, Peter finally raised his tremendous voice: "If you think you are going to trample these services under foot you are very much mistaken. If you keep this up I'll put you as far as British law will send you."[14] Unused to active resistance, the toughs were cowed and the service proceeded. Afterwards, Peter sought out the ringleader, a one-eyed youth, and probed into the sources of his hostility. Although not, at first, an easy conversation, it ended with the two praying together. There was no further heckling at meetings.

Methodists at that time were deeply concerned with the spiritual state of their fellows, as the class meetings show. In the Methodist *Discipline*, members were exhorted not to take any step towards matrimony without first consulting with the most serious of their brethren. When Peter neither stepped nor consulted, one of the brethren took it upon himself to sketch the fitting course – not only recommending matrimony, but also pointing out the ideal candidate, one Miss Campbell of Dundas. And so Margaret's mother entered the picture.

It may be trite to say that Margaret's father evoked ideas of strength, energy, and intelligence, while her mother suggested those of intuition, nurturing, and compassion, but it is not surprising, given the ideals of the time. Even their pictures fit the stereotypes: Peter Addison, fierce, proud, angular, his hair shooting up in a huge coif, his whiskers luxuriant; Mary, smaller and more tentative, with a broad, calm face made broader by hair parted in the middle and pulled down tightly into a bun. Later, she wore circular steel-rimmed glasses that added to her round, twinkling quality and decorated her hair with rows of sausagelike curls. Mary did not lack strength, but it was of a quality different from that of her husband. She was better educated than he, more cultured, and her religious experience was that of one who had grown up in the faith.

Mary Campbell was born in Canada, but her ancestry was Irish. Both her mother and grandmother, like herself, had been teachers. Her grandmother, Mrs Cross, was an emigrant whose husband had died tragically on board ship, leaving her to land and settle in an unknown country with a huge family that may have numbered twelve children. She set up house near L'Orignal, a village on the Ottawa River between Ottawa and Montreal, and opened a school. Although her daughter Margaret Cross, Margaret Addison's grandmother, was to keep it going for some time, she eventually married another Irish immigrant, John Campbell, and moved to Hamilton, Upper Canada.

John Campbell, like his future son-in-law Peter Addison, was an immigrant willing to turn his hand to any honest work. Though without training in cooperage, he managed to secure a job making flour barrels in Dundas, Ontario. Eventually he established his own business, making barrels and producing potash, soap, and candles. He and Margaret had nine children, of whom Margaret Addison's mother Mary was the oldest. In 1859, when business slumped and proved insufficient to support a family of eleven, he bought a farm near Fergus, moved his equipment there, and combined farming with the cooperage and potashery. Margaret, true to her early calling as a teacher, used to read aloud to neighbouring farmers while they ate their dinner at the farm after threshing bees.

The Campbells were a Wesleyan Methodist family, where religion had pride of place. John was a class leader who went so far as to nurse one of his class members during a cholera epidemic in 1854 when no nurse could be found, confining himself in her house and living on food left for him at the gate in order not to infect his own wife and children. Margaret Campbell lived an intense spiritual life. The language in which her son Wesley describes her in a family memoir gives a good idea of the prevailing ethos:

At about twenty years of age she had a definite enriching spiritual experience that left its mark on all her after life, what the Methodists know as Sanctification of the Spirit ... Her public prayers led her hearers into intimate contact with God. Very many have testified how greatly they were edified and encouraged by listening to them in prayer and class meetings. Her relation to the heavenly Father was so intimate and joyous that her religion was a most natural expression of life. Her life interest in every detail belonged to God. No matter what might be employing her hands, her spirit would be in conscious fellowship with the Father.[15]

Not surprisingly, two of her three sons became ministers and her eldest daughter married one; the other son and four sons-in-law were all lay officers in the Methodist church. There is no record of even one black sheep.

Margaret Addison's mother Mary Campbell, as the eldest of nine children, was undoubtedly used to work and responsibility from an early age. She inherited her mother's respect for learning and also, apparently, a kind of intuition akin to second sight. While she was training to be a teacher at the Toronto Normal School in 1864, she had an experience of a type not uncommon to herself and her mother. The Methodist Conference of that year was held in the church she attended, the Elm Street Church in Toronto. On the Friday of the conference, a service took place at which the candidates for ordination spoke in public about their conversions and calls to the ministry. Among them was the thirty-two-year-old Peter Addison. While listening to him, Mary speculated (in a reverent manner) on the possibility of marrying him and experienced "a strange confidence that that union would sometime be compassed within the will of God."[16] But for now, she said and did nothing about it. After qualifying as a teacher, she obtained a post at the little public school at Dundas.[17] One day while she was teaching, there was a knock at the schoolroom door; Peter Addison, without preliminary introduction or explanation, had come to see the bride recommended by his fellow minister. "I know who you are and I know why you've come," she said when she opened the door and saw him standing there. At least so went the story handed down in the family and told to the young Margaret. Whether or not it is true in every detail, it encapsulates Mary's sense that her life was under the direction of a higher power.[18]

Within a few months these extraordinary young people were married, convinced they were propelled
by the will of God. Obviously, in
their raising of a family they would
exert an influence even stronger
than that of the average parents.
Their children would be left in no
doubt that they were put on earth to
help others and to do good according to God's ordinance. Although
this evangelistic creed could easily
have provoked a reaction in their
children, it seems, in fact, to have
provided a bedrock. One of the
interesting features of Margaret
Addison's life is the way in which
she was able to reinterpret her
inherited Christianity, dropping
some strictures and shibboleths
while preserving its core values as
circumstances changed. Though
she continued to express herself
in traditional religious language,

Peter and Mary Addison around
the time of their marriage

she used it to convey new meaning in the very different intellectual
climate of the twentieth century.[19]

After their marriage in 1866, Peter and Mary Addison began housekeeping in a modest way: they were assigned two chilly, unfurnished
rooms on the second storey of a house in Alliston, some forty miles
north of Toronto, to live in while Peter travelled the Cookstown
circuit (1865–67). The talents of both husband and wife were used in
the ministry; Peter used to say that "Mary and I are a team. I preach,
she teaches." Mary always had a Sunday school class and Bible
classes for girls and women; she was also a class leader, again for
groups of women. Very musical, she could lead the singing as well.
With some money saved from her teacher's salary she had bought a
melodeon, a kind of miniature organ powered by bellows inflated by
the player's feet; on this she accompanied hymns.

In the summer of 1868, a few months before Margaret's birth, the Addisons took up a new charge at Horning's Mills. This was a small village in Melanchthon Township, Grey County (now in Dufferin County), about six miles from the present Shelburne. It was an isolated posting compared with the Cookstown circuit they had left. The Mills had been founded as a lonely outpost, some forty miles in advance of the main wave of settlement, by Lewis Horning in the early 1830s. Horning's visions of a flourishing community never really materialized, and he and most of his family left in 1838 after three children wandered into the bush and were lost. The settlement provided the basis for W.F. Munro's *The Backwoods' Life*, a realistic warning and invitation to prospective settlers, in which Munro admits that the hamlet "remained for many a weary year a sort of Ultima Thule of backwoods life."[20] Settlement increased with the coming of the road (the Toronto Line) around 1848, but it was not to reach its zenith of 350 inhabitants until the late 1880s.

The journey to Hornings Mills must have been a difficult one, especially as Mary was pregnant. As Peter wrote to a friend of their comfortless arrival: "[We] reached Horning's Mills about eleven at night tired and weary, and the teams almost done out with the heat. We stretched out on the floor as best we could till morning. No one came near to ask how we did. If ever I felt the worth of kindness it was then, and my thoughts wandered back to the past happy three years and the many kind friends that we had left." The rest of his letter shows faith struggling with despondency:

I hope and believe that we shall see souls brought to God, and if so it will be much better than ease. I want to live and labour for this ... We held our quarterly on Saturday and Sabbath; at the quarterly board we had three present – one leader and two stewards. Sometimes in the past they have had as low as two. I think two others would have been there only for the fire. The returns from the whole Mission was five dollars and some produce, and for my comfort they told me I need not expect that the next quarter would be any better, but they would do better in winter, etc. We had a good meeting on the Sabbath – a good congregation. We had thirty-six for love feast and they thought there [sic] was a great many. But we felt it so different from anything we had been accustomed to that we thought it little ... I do hope that we shall see better times and that the Lord will turn the hearts of the people to Himself.[21]

His hopes may have been realized in terms of quality, but not of quantity. His circuit was never to exceed seventy registered Methodists.

On 21 October 1868, both Peter Addison and the settlement's doctor were out on the bush trails when Mary went into labour.

Margaret as a child, with her brothers
Arthur and William

Fortunately, she delivered her baby girl successfully, recording perhaps both her gratitude and her aspirations in the grand name bestowed on the mite: Margaret Eleanor Theodora Addison. Margaret in later years always insisted on a four-syllabled, sonorous El-é-an-ore. In the meantime, the baby was known as "Maggie."

Maggie was not long an only child. Her brother William Lockwood Thornton Addison was born a year and a half later at Horning's Mills, on 30 April 1870. After another year and a half, when the family had moved to Lloydtown, Arthur Peter Campbell Addison appeared (10 October 1871). The next posting, at Newcastle, brought forth a sister, even more magnificently named as Mary Agnes Charlotte Wallbridge Addison (10 August 1873), who was usually called "Lottie." Later, there was one more son who did not survive.

This family was tremendously important to Maggie, who never married. Her brothers eventually had four children each, providing her with the nieces and nephews in whom she could take a maternal interest. From birth, too, she was surrounded by an extended family of aunts, uncles, and cousins. Peter Addison's brother James had accompanied him to Canada, and later his older sister Elenor [sic] and brother William followed. Eventually, after the death of his mother in Westmorland, his father and younger sister Agnes emigrated as well, leaving only one brother behind. Though old Thomas Addison, Maggie's paternal grandfather, died about 1860, before Peter married, the others remained and raised their families in the area. On her mother's side, Mary Campbell's father, John Campbell, also died before Maggie's birth, in 1863, but the clairvoyant Margaret lived until 1886 (when Maggie was 17). Mary's five sisters and three brothers – all but one of whom married and settled in Ontario – along with Peter's siblings provided a copious supply of aunts and uncles to make up for the lack of even one grandfather.

The posting at Horning's Mills, where Maggie and Will were born, was probably the most spartan of Peter's career. During the first summer there, the family never once tasted meat. The meagre $5 that the quarterly board proffered for salary in the summer was eventually, that year, upped to the stipulated $500. But the next year, when frost killed the fall wheat, the settlers were reduced to penury and almost starvation, and the Addisons had to be paid in kind.

After that, though, their postings were on regular rather than missionary circuits, and they lived in substantial villages. First, they served for three years in Lloydtown, a village north of Toronto (1871–74). Then, when Maggie was nearly six, they moved to Newcastle (1874–77), on the shores of Lake Ontario. Newcastle was then the home of the Massey family, wealthy Methodist laymen, and of their thriving Newcastle Foundry and Machine Manufactory, and it was no doubt partly due to the Masseys that the Wesleyan Methodist church at Church and Emily Streets, the family's home church, was a handsome brick construction, completed in 1868. Hart Massey, whose benefactions were to be even more important later in Maggie's life, had also built a commodious parsonage onto the south part of the church's lot, which he apparently sold to the church trustees.[22]

The first recorded glimpses of Maggie, dating from this time, are characteristic. "My sweet Maggie is the angel of the household," wrote her mother in a letter; "she seems to know when to bear and when to amuse." Mary had been very active in the local temperance association, which served a large clientele, "some of them far gone." The perhaps unfortunately named J.P. Lovekin, one of its founders, was also among its most challenging clients. To reconstruct an incident, it appears that little Maggie, wearing the new bonnet and green gingham dress her mother had made for her, was playing around the front gate when Lovekin's buggy came into view. A far from sober Lovekin reined in his horse and invited her to come for a ride. What he had in mind is questionable and was certainly not apparent to Maggie; she only knew that something was not quite right. When she said nothing, he leaned closer. "Aw, come on little Maggie" came out on a blast of beery breath, and he made to catch her arm. Finally she summoned up the courage to run away and, some time later, her mother found her in the bedroom crying bitterly and lamenting over Mr. Lovekin: "Mama, all we can do is pray for him."[23]

The Addison children were brought up not only to act honourably, but also to strive for inner perfection. Daily family worship and grace before meals kept the ideal of a holy life constantly in view. Mary distrusted the dramatic extremes of sin and repentance, wild oats and conversion, at least for her own children; she kept them from the emotionalism of the revival meetings, thinking that their religious life could best be forwarded by the orderly development of Christian knowledge and a study of the Bible, not to mention the constant cultivation of virtues such as forgiveness and forbearance. On this point she was relentless: there was nothing in life that could not be made to serve the ends of spiritual development, either as a lesson or as an opportunity to exercise faith and virtue. And this attitude influenced Maggie throughout her life, for better and for worse. The habit of bringing all things to the test of ultimate truth is one that facilitates dedicated work and achievement and minimizes petty personal concerns. But it also allows little to be taken lightly. Every move is potentially problematical, every decision fraught with consequences; there is also a tendency to value things, not for themselves, but for the end they serve. In other words, it was difficult for Maggie ever to relax and take life as it came.

Two books survive that were inscribed to her in childhood.[24] The first, called *A Guide*, is a little leather pocketbook, some 2 inches by 3 inches, with "Maggie Addison" written in a childish hand on the inside cover. The opening words strike a grim note: "I take the liberty affectionately to put thee in mind, my dear reader, of what is known by most, yet properly thought of by very few, that we must shortly die. Our precious souls must soon appear before God's judgment-seat: either to be doomed with Satan to everlasting misery, or welcomed by Jesus Christ to eternal glory." Pointing out the path to eternal glory, the writer centres his discussion on original sin. Mankind's nature is totally depraved – mere filthy rags, "naturally destitute of every thing that is good in the Lord's sight," he asserts. Redemption comes only through faith in Jesus Christ, who paid the penalty for humanity's sin through his crucifixion. It is mainstream Protestant theology, but strong fare for babes and sucklings and not designed to encourage youthful insouciance. The book ends with "five dialogues on a preparation for death between the Rev. Mr. Barnabas Diligent and Mr. Careless, his sick parishioner." The other book, *The Young Christian's Pocket-Book; or, Counsels, Comforts, and Cautions, Conveyed in Short Striking Sentences*, put out by the Religious Tract Society in 1837, is inscribed "From Grandma to M.E.T. Addison"; although didactic, it is slightly less ferocious.

Of course, life was not all a struggle for salvation. In her earliest extant letter, a note to her grandmother written in Newcastle when she was six, Maggie talks of going to a tea party at Mrs Greenwood's. She writes proudly of her three houseplants, and also of her garden, where she grows lettuce and mignonette, corn, summer savoury, and melon. (Growing things was a passion with the family, and in every posting Peter began a garden.) Maggie talks, too, about learning the multiplication tables, and starting to write in cursive: "Mama says I write very nicely but I cannot write well enough to write a letter alone."[25]

Maggie had probably learned to write at home, under the tuition of her mother. Because of Peter's absorption in his work, Mary was the main force in the education of the children. She had achieved a first-class certificate herself as a teacher, and it was natural for her to envisage Maggie following in her footsteps, as well as those of her mother and grandmother. She made no invidious distinctions between her male and female children, expecting them all to go as far as they could in schooling. Quite early on, she encouraged Maggie to learn German from a Bible by following along in the German while the English was being read in church.

The school attendance laws of the time (the last years of Egerton Ryerson's long tenure as superintendent of education) in theory required schooling for seven- to twelve-year-olds for at least four months a year. Probably, then, Maggie's formal education began in the fall of 1875. The Ontario public schools offered a basic curriculum of reading, writing, arithmetic, spelling, composition, and geography sufficient to outfit most pupils for their life as workers and citizens. A heavy emphasis was placed on neatness, punctuality, and obedience, while the "Ontario Readers," the basic textbooks, inculcated further virtues; through story and song they preached honesty, thankfulness, submission to God's will, thrift, kindness, and admiration for heroic character.[26] It was taken for granted that the pupils were to be moulded into good Christians. Maggie's school would have been a small one, the back rows of its single room crowded in winter with overgrown and boisterous young men who worked on the farms as long as the weather held.

From 1877 to 1880, Peter Addison served in Trenton – a welcome appointment. The previous year, when the population of Trenton had reached about 2800, the Wesleyan Methodists, having decided that their church was too small, embarked on building a new one on King Street. The church was completed just as Peter arrived in July. A solid brick building with a soaring spire and a 1,100-lb. bell, its interior featured luxurious (for Methodists) appointments such as cushioned pews, five chandeliers, and stained glass windows. Its dedication on 6 September was a social event of such importance that special fares were extended by railroads and steamships to allow people from Toronto and other parts of the province to travel to Trenton to attend.[27]

Unfortunately, Maggie's mother had been suffering from poor health for some time; exhausted and lethargic, she had to lie down for part of each day. It was always a strenuous task for her to pack up the household every three years, and settle into whatever house the family was given. However, she would set to work to contrive comforts that could only be temporary, while Peter, adept with hammer and nails, always left their parsonages improved in some way. During the Trenton period, Mary gave birth to a third son, Watson, who lived for only three months. The family belief was that the local taverner, enraged at Peter Addison's attacks from the pulpit on the liquor business, had poisoned the family cow; when she sickened, the baby had to switch to a different milk which he could not tolerate and which led to his death. This sad story, if true, gives rise to many reflections, among them the thought that Mary must have been quite unwell if she was not breast-feeding the infant.

After the family had moved to Richmond Hill, just north of Toronto (1880–82), Maggie began high school, probably in 1881. Already she was part of an educated minority, for only about 5 per cent of Ontario children completed their four "books" in public school, sat the compulsory entrance exam, and began high school.[28] And an overwhelming number of those stayed for only one or two years.[29] In the high school at Richmond Hill in 1881, seventy-one pupils were in the two lower years, with only three in the two upper. Boys predominated, though there was no technical barrier to girls' attendance. Physically, the school was less than adequate. "The limit of the school accommodation was reached some time ago," noted an inspector's report of 1880, adding that "the privy is in a most filthy condition."[30] Intellectually, however, it was quite respectable, thanks partly to the labours of its headmaster, Thomas Carscadden, M.A., a gifted mathematics teacher. And, though female high-school teachers were a small minority (permitted since only 1872) and none had the benefit of a university education, his assistant was a woman, Miss Louisa Palmer, who had a first-class certificate and had passed the women's matriculation exam set by the University of Toronto with first-class honours. Perhaps she was an early role model.

In the midst of Maggie's high-school career, the family was posted back to Newcastle (1883–85), where Peter had served already. The high school was smaller than the one at Richmond Hill: it shared a building with the public school and had thirty-four pupils in 1883, only seven of whom were in the upper years. Once again there were two teachers, a male principal and a woman assistant. The school could not offer chemistry, botany, German, or music, and probably Maggie was not able to complete there the full Junior Matriculation exams set by Victoria University.[31] Nevertheless, she was glad to be back in Newcastle, where the family experienced what was the closest they came for many years to a settled home. In later years she often returned there for holidays, and at one time she planned to retire to Newcastle.

The family's dearest friends in Newcastle were the Beman family, who owned a farm with apple orchards some mile-and-a-half west of the town, on the lakefront. The two youngest Beman boys were particularly close to the two Addison boys. The fact that both families named their sons Arthur and William gives an added twist to an anecdote handed down in the family. On a Saturday, the four boys used to walk to the marsh near the farm, where there lived a blind man with a boat. The same dialogue regularly occurred. When the boys knocked at the door, the blind man would call out,

"Who's there?"

"The Beman boys."

"Come in."

"Can we borrow your boat?"

"Yes."

One Saturday, when Arthur and Willie had to stay home to work on the farm, Art and Will Addison went alone to the marsh. The temptation proved overwhelming.

"Who's there?" asked the man.

"The Beman boys."

Although they got the precious boat, a scandal ensued when word got back somehow to the Methodist congregation that the minister's sons had told a lie. They were punished, but perhaps Peter suffered more. "I don't know why it would have to be my boys," he groaned with head in hand.[32]

At this time the boys had a passion for roving around the countryside, collecting such things as birds' eggs, flowers, bugs, leaves, and stones. Only occasionally were they moved to slide off the lids of their pillboxes and let loose some of their interesting live insects among the rows of girls at school. Although Maggie and Charlotte would have been somewhat more decorous, they too were able to roam about in comparative freedom, to eat apples in the orchard and soak up the sunshine. Such youthful experiences laid the foundation for an abiding love of nature and the outdoors.

Not all was smooth in this second Newcastle period, as Peter became very ill and for some months the rest of the family had to

The Addison family

labour to make ends meet, meanwhile fearing superannuation or worse. But fortunately his health returned, and family life picked up again. They were a devoted group, loving but high-spirited, fiercely proud of the family name and ancestry, competitive, and with strong emotions. Photographs of Maggie as a young woman do not show a serene individual: she generally looks, as her niece Louise once put it, as though there is a bad smell under her nose. Though not quite a sneer, it is certainly a defensive look of unsmiling determination. But it is impossible to tell whether the camera truly captured her habitual outlook, or whether (as in later years) she disliked having her picture taken, and found her face awkwardly frozen as she tried to keep the same expression for the long exposure required.

The children were free-spoken and assertive. When their mother stayed with her sister Jennie's family in Sarnia, she wrote home reporting that "the manners of the children to one another are decidedly better than our own household – they don't flatly contradict eachother [sic]."[33] Maggie even apologized to her brother Arthur, years later, for her outspokenness: "Some of our family are so frank, I among them, that our feelings come very much to the surface. I have not always understood, as I do now, that deep feelings are buried sometimes, and that one hasn't any right to ferret them out."[34]

Arthur himself made his parents "gravely and continuously anxious" with his continual ill-health and lack of seriousness.[35] Charlotte, the youngest, had a stormy childhood and cried many a bout of tears into the comforting neck of her doll. Her life was not to become easier as her parents grew older and her siblings moved on. Her mother kept an ever-watchful eye on her; here is the note she sent with a Christmas present of a watch:

To Mama's Little *Pet...*

I want you my dear girl to keep this letter as well as the watch, and whenever you look at the timepiece remember that Mama – whether in this world or our home above – wishes you to study to be *always neat* in your *dress, manner,* and *general appearance* – and also study to be *always on time* – on time to your meals – on time at lessons – on time to everything – always on time.

Lovingly,
Mama.

An affecting letter, but odd considering that the recipient was now twenty-six years old![36]

Study and improvement were watchwords in the family. When Maggie was in high school, her mother instituted a "Family Literary Entertainment." Each family member, even their father, had to write an essay or other contribution in a large book; at the meetings each one would read his or her effort out loud, after which there was a special feast.[37] The compositions, which span the period from 1882 to 1890, give a good indication of family preoccupations. The adults' contributions fall mainly into the category of moral tales or observations, poems with a religious slant, and appreciations of nature, while the children as they grow older increasingly write of what they have learned about the world around them – pets, wild animals, history, mineralogy, and so on. Maggie as the eldest is the most ambitious, producing, for instance, an essay on the way Methodism came to Canada by the agency of Barbara Heck (a name to be significant later in her life) and translating Schiller's "The Diver" from German in a very Germanic syntax ("It the black mouth already has"). Throughout the book, God appears as the chief character in the household, and the next world is as much a neighbour as the United States. Towards the end, Mary Addison reports an extraordinary dream in which she sees herself in heaven, united with her children who have now grown into their full potential. With an almost coercive faith she spoke of Theodora, or Maggie: "Theodora had been to another circle what she had been to ours 'Gods gift' and still was to many others.

Uniting gentleness with great strength she reminded us now as she had often done on earth of the Master's pearl of great price."

These high ideals and the family solidarity and sense of responsibility kept Maggie hard at work. As she related later in a letter to Art, "Boys hardly know what an inspiration and help they may and can be to their sisters. I think it was the desire to be a companion for my brothers which first gave me a deep interest in my education. And many a time during it, when energy flagged, I said to myself, 'If you do not do well, how can you incite your brothers in their studies?'"[38] In another way, the perpetually strenuous and goal-directed Peter Addison was a

Margaret Addison
as a young woman

stimulus to achievement. A pioneer himself, he thought of the next generation as rather a soft lot, who did not know the meaning of real hardship.[39] It may have been emulation that caused Maggie to be, in her way, a pioneer too, advancing in territory that was strange to women. Though she did not inherit Peter's iron constitution, she had his tenacity and propensity to demand the utmost of herself. Pressures or expectations from all her family made it natural for her to plan to become a high-school teacher, and sent her, in the fall of 1885, to prepare for this career at Victoria University.

CHAPTER TWO

Student and Teacher

In 1885, Victoria University was a Methodist institution, open to all denominations, on the shores of Lake Ontario at Cobourg, Ontario. The college was a substantial, three-storey building with side wings and Grecian pillars, recently augmented by a separate science building known as Faraday Hall. Most of the students were studying for the Bachelor of Arts degree, though a sizeable group of theological students was in residence, and smaller contingents of students were in the science department and law school. In the arts faculty, nine professors supervised some 150 students. Many of these were housed in the college itself, on the upper floors, while others lived in boarding houses around town. A few – in protest against boarding houses "where you get nothing for breakfast, the same for dinner, and the bones for tea"[1] – even risked the severe displeasure of the authorities by putting up in the sin-laden precincts of the local hotels. In a small town of 5,000, they were not really in much moral danger.

This was an unsettled period in the college's history, for it was apparent that some change in its status was imminent. Since early 1884 the proposal to form one large provincial university from the various colleges had been under serious consideration. This scheme of federation, which had been put forward several times in different forms almost since the inception of the college, envisaged a University of Toronto or of Ontario in Toronto, with affiliated arts colleges: Victoria (Methodist), Trinity (Anglican), Queen's (Presbyterian), St. Michael's (Roman Catholic), Toronto Baptist College (soon to become McMaster), and the non-denominational University College separate from the university itself. Money considerations made the scheme attractive to Victoria. The college was supported entirely by voluntary contributions from the church and from fees, with virtually no access to public funds; its facilities were becoming increasingly cramped and inadequate. There was no gymnasium. A small college library did exist, but until Addison's graduating year it was virtually closed to students, having no librarian or provision for signing out

Victoria College at Cobourg

books. According to an 1885 letter in *Acta Victoriana*, the college newspaper (generally called *Acta*, and a fine reflection of the life of the college), few undergraduates had even seen the inside of the library. The editor, welcoming the freshman class, counselled them not to despair when they compared their college library with that in the Kingston Penitentiary, or when they further reflected that it was as hard to get into the library as it was to escape from the penitentiary.[2] In another manifestation of penury, exam papers were dictated to students instead of being printed. As well, it was becoming ever harder to afford the equipment for the science department, which had recently been founded to supply the needs of the province for engineers, scientists, and technicians. With federation, the university would undertake to teach the expensive science subjects, leaving the arts subjects to the individual colleges while giving them the benefit of the central library and special collections.

Supporters of federation also argued that Cobourg was something of a backwater, and that students needed the cultural resources of a large city, which Toronto (relatively speaking) could offer. Opponents of the move from Cobourg included the town of Cobourg, as well as those who liked the friendly, undistracting atmosphere of a small town and feared exposing the students to metropolitan haunts of vice. Others again, who did not wish Victoria to lose its independence as a degree-granting institution with university status and its ability to provide a complete education based on Christian principles, put forward the scheme of a "simple removal," as they called it, to Toronto or even Hamilton.

These competing schemes were bandied about in commencement addresses, in newspapers and the religious press, and in *Acta* for some years. In October 1886, after much debate, the General Conference of the Methodist Church endorsed the principle of federation; this meant that theoretically Addison's class, which was due to graduate in 1889, might be required to move to Toronto and perhaps to fulfil altered requirements for a Toronto degree. But, in fact, negotiations as to the terms of entry and countermoves by the opponents of federation continued throughout her undergraduate years and beyond. The town of Cobourg and its supporters (including the wealthy Hart Massey) even offered sizeable cash benefits to keep the college there and, in May 1889, after a site in Toronto and an architect had been selected, procured an injunction restraining Victoria from further work on the new college. The contention was that those who had given money or land to Victoria had done so on the understanding that it would stay in Cobourg in perpetuity. The suit was not tried until November 1889; settlement in Victoria's favour came only in August 1890. Such uncertainty over the fate of the college was bound to make sustained work difficult, and the wonder is, as President Burwash remarked in his history of the college, that so many of the students of those years did so well.[3]

The requirements for a Victoria B.A. at that time were surprisingly broad. There was one basic course, with an opportunity to specialize somewhat in upper years; honour students did all the pass work, plus extra work in the departments of their choice. All students were required to take mathematics in first and second year, and astronomy in fourth. They were given a thorough grounding in the sciences: biology in first year; physics and botany in second; inorganic chemistry in third, along with mineralogy and blowpipe analysis (particularly hated by students); and geology and paleontology in fourth. All students took English for at least two years, three years of philosophy (including Christian evidences), pass Latin for two years, and two other languages. The only history, however, was English and biblical. As a specialist in modern languages, Addison studied English, French, and German in all years, and Italian in her last two. Marks were low compared with those of today, so there is nothing too shocking in her 35 percent in first-year Latin or 37 percent in second-year math. Those who attained second-class honours (66–74%) were listed in the prize list, and Addison regularly appeared on those lists for her standing in English, French, German, and Italian.

The college, part of whose mandate was to train Methodist ministers, was obviously no hotbed of modernism; the students were nonetheless exposed to the new ideas that were shaking the Christian fabric at that time. These ran in two broad currents. One, "higher criticism," originally a German phenomenon, entailed studying the Bible critically and learning that many of its books were not written by the authors traditionally associated with them or at the date generally supposed. A similar methodology, when applied to the New Testament, brought into question its historicity and, as in the case of Strauss' *Leben Jesu* (1835), substituted a reduced "historical" Jesus for the Jesus of the Gospels. A second current of thought was given wings by Darwin's *Origin of Species* (1859) and particularly his *Descent of Man* of 1871, though grounded in earlier geological discoveries. The new theories of evolution brought into question not only the Genesis account of creation but also the general providential ordering of cosmic events, suggesting that they could be adequately explained by physical laws and the workings of blind chance.

Both presidents of the college during Addison's term – Samuel Nelles, and Nathanael Burwash, who succeeded him in 1887 – reacted with moderation to these challenges to traditional Christian thought. Burwash, it is true, did not strike Margaret's brother Arthur as particularly up-to-date when, as a theology student, Art attended Burwash's classes some years later. In his family memoir, he remarked somewhat enigmatically that Burwash was a saint, but that "his lectures on Systematic Theology I found very far from the thinking I had been doing. To the men trained in philosophy he was worse."[4] Nevertheless, Burwash was hospitable to the new tools of biblical criticism, believing that they could prove useful if applied in a reverent spirit; he had no difficulties with the notion of a progressive revelation fitted to humankind's developing knowledge.[5]

As a scientist, who had held the chair of natural science in the college for some years prior to the establishment of the Faculty of Theology, Burwash saw no irreconcilable conflict between Christianity and the doctrine of evolution. In the case of puzzling discrepancies, he advised his students not to reject out of hand what science revealed; in the end faith and reason would be reconciled.[6] The theology that he was working on, published in 1900 as *A Manual of Christian Theology*, was based on the inductive method of science. Its conclusions are adumbrated in his address to Margaret's graduating class, in which he maintained that personal experience of God is so real that it can sweep aside speculative and historical problems: "The personal attainment of this truth, that God is light, the light of supreme right in which is no darkness at all, and to walk in this light and to know that God is love and to dwell in this love – this is religion and it is nearer each one of us today than ever before."[7] He never lost the robust belief of his younger days that "this universe ... is but one vast display of the glory of God ... This it is which makes the researches of the laboratory, the examinations of the microscope, the ranging of the telescope all hallowed employment."[8] Presumably, this was the theme brought out on the "grounds of theistic and Christian belief" (part of the third-year philosophy course), which replaced the natural theology taught in earlier days. Margaret and her brother Will sometimes discussed the new and controversial ideas when they came home from college, perhaps hoping to provoke a reaction from their father; they were deflated when he only remarked with a yawn, "Well, it's bedtime. I think I'll turn in."[9]

In becoming a candidate for a degree, Margaret was going through a very narrow educational funnel indeed. Few Ontario youths pursued their education that far; university was mainly for those intending to become lawyers, ministers, or high-school teachers, and even these could do very well without a B.A. As a female student, Margaret was even more of a rarity. It was not until 1883 that Victoria conferred an M.D. from the Toronto School of Medicine, its affiliate, on Augusta Stowe – the first Ontario woman to receive a degree. In 1884, Victoria gave a B.Sc. to Nellie Greenwood, the first female graduate of the college, and the other Ontario universities began to accept a few women. In 1889, Addison was only the sixth woman to graduate from Victoria.

These figures do not, however, give a completely accurate picture of the number of women around the college.[10] The student body fluctuated, since students would join a class for a year or two and then leave to teach, to supply-preach (if they were men), or simply to help at home. Moreover, it was permissible to stay away for most of the year and then reappear to write the exams and move on with one's class, much to the annoyance of those who had stayed in Cobourg. And in addition to students enroled in degree programs, there was a category of "specialists," who seem to have been students who had not completed their junior matriculation but who attended some classes and hoped to transfer into the regular program. Discrepancies between the student lists in *Acta* and the Victoria University calendars make it even harder to determine the number of women in any particular class.

Mary Crossen seems to have been the first woman to attend some Victoria classes, in the early 1870s. In 1877 Barbara Foote was allowed to write the Victoria matriculation exam before attending classes, and for this reason she has been called the first co-ed in Ontario.[11] The women were both pupils at Mary Electa Adams's Brookhurst Academy in Cobourg, a Methodist women's academy with close ties to the college. Surprisingly, the first few women to proceed to a degree at Victoria were studying science: Adeline Shenick and Nellie Greenwood matriculated in 1880, and Clara Field and Carrie Munson joined them in 1881. All but Shenick were from the Cobourg area. They constituted four of the fourteen students in the science department and followed a different curriculum from that of the arts students, though they shared to some extent the same facilities. In the fall of 1882, Emma Woods enroled as the first woman in the freshman class of arts students. Two years later she retired temporarily, but her place was filled by Isabel Willoughby, who transferred to the junior year from another university. In October 1885, when Margaret arrived in Cobourg, Miss Willoughby was in her senior year, and would be the first woman to receive an arts B.A. in the spring. There were two women sophomores then, and at least one other young woman besides herself in first-year arts.[12] In addition, and less in evidence, were three of the original four women in the science department who had not yet graduated, and some six women specialists. Usually, Margaret was one of two women in the arts class of her year, which had about twenty members.

The calendar of the university, in stating unequivocally that "ladies are admitted to all the privileges of the University on the same terms as gentlemen," showed a commendable forwardness. At this time, University College in Toronto, under Daniel Wilson, was strenuously resisting the presence of women; even after the legislature had passed a resolution in 1884 compelling him to admit them, he continued to fight a rearguard action, arguing the obvious impossibility of having the required cloakrooms, lavatories, retiring rooms, and private staircases installed in time.[13] Members of the Methodist establishment, while not yielding their view that the sacred calling of woman was to make a home and to nurture the young, generally acknowledged that this role demanded a trained mind and enlarged views. How could one who was not enlightened teach and inspire the men who were to be future leaders? In fact Victoria in its early years as Upper Canada Academy (1836–41) had been one of the first seminaries in the province where young women could advance beyond the elementary subjects of the public schools and be exposed to science, philosophy, mathematics, history and languages at a high-school level.[14] Though women had been excluded when the academy was elevated to university status in 1841, provision had been made for their education in other Methodist institutions; it was therefore not too traumatic to welcome them back. An anonymous poem in *Acta* in 1887 celebrates their advent and ends prophetically:

Thus amid the future ages,
When philosophers and sages
Seek to find some old inscription
Which shall give the world our fame;
They might read in burning letters,
Here were loosened old-time fetters,
And each stone was made forever
Fragrant with a woman's name.[15]

With these views, at least among the more progressive, it was not entirely Victoria's fault that women were ill at ease at first. The university had evolved an intensely male culture, where the undergraduates were collectively known as "the boys," and individually urged to "be a man." The calendar was shot through with sexist language: the first year were "freshmen," and those who were not "honour men" were "pass men." The true life of the college was in its societies, the Literary and the Jackson, where debates were carried on far into the night; in class meetings and suppers; in athletics; and in that peculiar Victoria institution, the "Bob," where the sophomore class mercilessly ragged the freshmen through skits and songs and minstrel shows and then presented a purse to Bob the janitor. What with "tapping" (bodily immersion under cold water), shouting, scrumming, and stealing of lamp standards, it was a boisterous, adolescent male culture totally foreign to Methodist young women. And they were excluded from it all. Their intellectual development alone was provided for, and even there the immense benefits of informal interchange were curtailed.

According to one story, the two freshman women in Margaret's first year "received a written invitation to come to the first class meeting of the year. They were keen to go. However, it turned out that women were not welcome at class meetings or parties. The President of the class – who was a man, of course – wrote them a very nice little note to say that they wouldn't be expected to come, but would they please accept a basket of fruit."[16] There is gallantry and consideration here, as well as (from another perspective) a patronizing attitude to women. Civilized ideals, in which equality and fairness were gaining importance, warred with the equally strong taboo against dragging women into the common sphere. A cultural clash, it produced awkwardness as old manners failed to cover the new situations. One of the early college women remembers extravagant gestures: men parting their ranks like the Red Sea to let her through, and others vying to carry her books. Another recalls embarrassing footstamping as she entered the room, and unflattering songs such as "She Walks Abroad a Dandy with the Buttons off her Boots" sung *sotto voce* as she passed.[17]

One senses this uneasiness at times in the tone of *Acta*'s references to women students, particularly in the matter of the "freshman biographies." These were satiric and irreverent portraits of each member of the incoming class, designed to bring the newcomers down a peg. In 1887, when six women joined the freshman class, the local editor mentioned their presence at the end of his article, but declined to write their biographies. Presumably this was partly from delicacy, as he noted that if in future they did happen to be mentioned in *Acta*, owing to some childish mistake of theirs, they must take no offence; they are just college students like the rest.[18] But they seldom attained this sign of being considered "one of the boys." It is true that two years before this statement appeared, Margaret's fellow freshman Rachel Ellis had been greeted with a daring freshman biography: "You are *fresh*, Rachel, decidedly *fresh*; but when we say *fresh*, we mean 'not impaired by time' ... O-a-sis in the desert! How our editorial heart goes pitapat!" But the "O-a-sis" explains the daring: Rachel was the sister of one of the students in an upper year. Margaret, more typically, was greeted respectfully: "We have not had the pleasure of a personal acquaintance with Miss A. yet, but if we may be allowed to estimate from appearance, we do not take her to be one of the butterfly type, but a sensible matter-of-fact girl who will do faithful work, and honor her class in honoring herself."[19]

No, alas, there was nothing of the butterfly about Margaret. Did she ever wish that there was, or that she might cause an editorial or other heart to go pitapat? Impossible to say, since she has left no letters or diaries from this period. But however little is known of her inner life, the conclusion is inescapable that in her college days were sown the seeds of her later actions and beliefs. She must have come to realize, through the difficulties of integration and through partial exclusion, how important it was to participate fully in the college life. As she watched her classmates grow and prosper – Ed Pugsley carrying the Senior Stick, G.E.J. Brown becoming president of the Lit., Lewis Stevenson learning to be a little less obsessed with marks – she must have seen that education occurred not just in the classroom but also in extracurricular activities and informal exchanges, and that institutions were needed to embody this student life. In time, many of the male clubs would change in character sufficiently to admit women and to benefit from their new perspective; but in other cases, parallel female institutions might serve the purpose. Surely a dream of helping to bring them about began even then.

The women of the college must have developed some community
life among themselves, though little is known about it; no one even
knows, for instance, which boarding house or houses Margaret
inhabited. The women attended prayers together each day in the
college chapel, where a pew was set aside on the south wall for their
use.[20] The one protracted appearance that they make in the pages of
Acta shows them acting together in a sophisticated and humourous
manner. The seven women attending college during Margaret's
second year were holding a meeting. As they gathered to discuss
their role in connection with the Bob party (which they were not to
attend), all were dressed similarly in their high-necked blouses, tight-
sleeved jackets fitted at the waist, and long, heavy skirts. Margaret
Donly, as chairwoman, opened the debate in mild and mellow tones:

Gentlewomen, I suppose you are all aware of the object of this meeting. We
have assembled today, not to discuss politics, though we are quite capable of
doing that, but to discuss the latest and most scientific methods of combining
baking soda, flour and eggs, in such equivalence as to form a digestible com-
pound. The "Bob" in all its perennial glory is near at hand. Our custom has
hitherto been to furnish the Freshmen with a cookie each. We must not dis-
appoint them.

Louise Nelles moved the addition of a raisin to delight the freshmen,
"some of whom, as you are well aware, have never seen a raisin nor
tasted a cookie." Margaret rose with furrowed brow: "I think, ladies,
this is a matter in which we should move very cautiously. The
addition of even one raisin to the cookie may bring untold misery
upon the Freshmen. They are not accustomed to such delicacies. They
must be educated gradually. For these reasons I cannot support the
motion."[21] Giddiness nevertheless prevailed, and the motion was
passed. The women were really using their traditional nurturing role
to get a toe in the door: participating in some of the fun and excitement of the Bob even though they could not act in it. As a first step,
it was inspired.

By her fourth year, Addison was in a position to help consolidate
the presence of women at Victoria. In January of that year, when, as
Acta put it, "the honour men in moderns met at the house of Prof.
Horning to arrange for the organization of a Modern Language
Club,"[22] Addison was not only among them, but was elected president.
It was the first Victoria club in which men and women could interact
intellectually and socially. Addison helped to arrange the Friday
evening meetings, where the students read and discussed papers and

The class of 1889 at Victoria College.
Margaret Addison is second from left in the second row.

listened to music. She herself presented a paper on French literature, as did her colleagues Misses Highet and Delaney of second year.

Addison's essay, "French Literature in the Time of Louis xiv," was subsequently published in *Acta*, where it was the first contribution by a woman. It is a formidably learned discussion; at the beginning she regrets that she must pass over in silence "the scholarly influence of Budacaens," "the learning of Pasquier and De l'Hopital," "the literary genius of D'Aubigne, the eloquence of Duperron, and the oratory of De Sales,"[23] along with the achievements of a host of other little-known gentlemen not on the curriculum. One wonders how she found time to become acquainted with them, while keeping up with the blowpipe analysis and paleontology. But by this time her performance in modern languages was stellar. At graduation, she attained gold medal standing, and would have received the medal itself had W.H. Schofield not received even higher marks. Schofield – known as "Little Shoo-fly" among the boys – had arrived at Victoria at the age of fifteen, "the smallest, youngest, neatest, cleanest member of the class,"[24] but had overcome the handicaps of youth and minuteness to become literary editor of *Acta*. As he went on to get a Ph.D. at Harvard and became a full professor and head of the Harvard Department of Comparative Literature, he was hardly reasonable competition. Although not brilliant like him, Margaret was certainly intelligent; she had also been

Margaret Addison as a graduate

amazingly determined and perti-
nacious and by all means deserved
the silver medal in moderns with
which she graduated.

It is not easy at first glance to
pick out Margaret in her class-
graduation picture: her hair is
pulled severely back, close to her
head, and she wears the same
dark clothes and academic gown
as the men. The writer of her "senior biography" in *Acta* remarks
that "she is said to have strong
convictions on all the subjects to
which she has given attention."
He adds rather enigmatically that
she "has ever been ready to sympathize with the Professors in
their hour of tribulation."[25] Evidently this is a joke, alluding to
some incident now lost. But it
may also indicate a general trait: Margaret, like many an eldest child,
liked to see due authority respected. Not that she was obstinately
conservative – in her essay on literature under Louis xiv, she sym-
pathized with the abject misery of the people and saw the French
Revolution as a very necessary struggle for freedom – but she certainly preferred reform to come in a civilized manner and deplored
unnecessary hurt. Perhaps she had been distressed by even the mild
rebellion and vexing of authority that must have occurred. At any
rate, she left with a solid education, an abiding love of books and
learning, and a permanent interest in the well-being of Victoria.

With her silver medal in moderns, Addison could no doubt have
obtained a good position teaching languages in one of the province's
high schools. Instead, she chose to spend two years as an instructor
in mathematics and chemistry at the Ontario Ladies' College (olc)
in Whitby. Her reasons for doing so can only be surmised. Mathematics had been her first love, though the Victoria registrar had
advised her to go into moderns if she wanted to be a teacher.[26]
Possibly, too, she felt the need to earn money immediately: the school

did not demand of its teachers the four months of training in a designated collegiate institute that had recently been introduced as a requirement for first-class certificates in the public high schools. Possibly, as well, she was attracted by the school's situation near the shores of Lake Ontario, only twenty miles or so from friends at Newcastle. (Her family had moved to Aurora, Peter Addison's second-last posting.)

But of more weight to a serious nature like Addison's were the character and ethos of the school. It was one of the Methodist institutions that had grown up after the closing of Upper Canada Academy to women, and now provided a feminine education for the young women of the province. A boarding school, it saw itself as a "home away from home" that supervised every aspect of life, combining provisions for exercise, the arts, and the life of the mind with solicitude for the character and moral and religious development of the girls. For Addison, a daughter of the manse, its attempt to incorporate Christianity and morals into the fabric of education was like placing the cornerstone in a building, without which the structure could not stand; perhaps even then she had read Newman, later to be so congenial to her. As for its being a girls' school: she herself had just been through university, studying what had traditionally been men's subjects in a milieu overwhelmingly male. She could not have been entirely at ease. Perhaps she wanted to see whether a feminine institution might provide a more encouraging environment for learning.

The OLC certainly began with the premise that young women were not young men, and that they both would and should most often find fulfilment in the domestic sphere, as wives, mothers, and homemakers. In addition to weaknesses needing attention, women were considered to have positive virtues and strengths such as sympathy, purity, and love of beauty. Their education, then, should be different and separate, but not inferior.

At the OLC, the academic program was extensive, embracing history, English, classics, languages, mathematics, science, Christian evidences, and philosophy; Victoria professors travelled to the college to administer some of the exams. After the last year's work, students were given a diploma such as Mistress of English Literature and were accepted into the second year of Victoria College if they desired further education. This was no pared-down course designed to accommodate a weak female intellect: on paper, at least, it was more demanding than that in most collegiate institutes, which were themselves the cream of the province's high schools. There were even hopes that the school might develop into a women's university in conjunction with the federation scheme.[27]

The curriculum also included what were then known as "the accomplishments" – chiefly music, drawing, elocution, and modelling in wax. Even at the time these subjects were sometimes criticized as "ornamental";[28] modern commentators on nineteenth-century education have tended to stigmatize them as mere "frills," foisted on girls to enhance their attractiveness as potential wives. No doubt some parents did view their investment in their daughters' education in these terms, and the board of governors, with an eye to the market, would have been obliged to accommodate them. But to view this as their sole motivation is to take an unduly dismissive view of what was an enriching part of the curriculum on many levels. Looked at economically, the artistic subjects could lead to financial independence instead of to matrimony. Educational specialist Johanna Selles, who has made an extensive study of Methodist education for women, has pointed out that the school's diploma in the fine arts was often pursued more vigorously and consistently than the one in the academic course, since it offered the chance for paid employment.[29] Even more importantly, the arts enriched and completed an education that in the twentieth century had tended to be unduly scholastic. They provided a language that was just as valid as that of literature and science. They trained the ear, the eye, the hand, the emotions; at their best – and excepting perhaps the wax modelling – they touched the spirit. Such capacity for artistic expression was thought to be particularly necessary in the domestic sphere; it was a resource, though, that might be envied rather than scorned by male labourers in their daily grind.

If the arts (except for drawing) were slighted by many other schools, this was partly for financial reasons. The OLC was not for the impoverished. Not only was there a tuition fee of $8 per term (small fees were customary in public high schools too), but "extras" such as French and German were truly extra, to the tune of $5 per term each, as were piano and organ. There were fees, too, for some of the more elaborate physical activities, such as riding: one paid $5 a term for riding lessons, and $10 for the use of a horse and saddle. Basic gymnastics and walking exercises, however, were free to all. In return for their outlay, parents could be sure that the educational advantages were pursued in a setting both beautiful and ennobling – for, as the calendar expressed it, "handsome buildings indirectly and unconsciously tend to grace and culture."[30] The main building was an impressive mansion once known as Trafalgar Castle. It had been erected in the early 1860s by the sheriff of Ontario County, Nelson Gilbert Reynolds, who lavished $70,000 on it at a time when a substantial home could be built for $2000.[31] Though he could afford to live there for only a few years before selling it to the Methodists for about half its cost, legend had it that he would return at midnight and sit mournfully outside the gate, gazing for hours at what he had lost.

Given that Reynolds was a member of the board of directors, he probably indulged in no such erratic behaviour; nonetheless, it was the kind of romantic building that encouraged legends. Outside, it was a fantasy of battlements and turreted towers, with two stone lions flanking the entrance; inside, doors with hand-painted glass swung open to reveal an enormous hall, at the end of which a staircase swept up to a stained glass window and then parted to either side. It was designed for the descent of women in ball gowns, not for the demure tread of Methodist young ladies – nor for their sliding down the polished bannisters, as some of the livelier ones did at night, in defiance of the calendar's hopes for grace and culture. Outside were ten acres of grounds, stately trees, and a gymnasium.

The school accepted girls of all religions, but its Protestant tone was assured by the general supervision (though not the financial support) of the Toronto Conference of the Methodist Church, which appointed officers and "visitors" or inspectors. The church had chosen as principal the Rev. John James Hare, and a staff that was predominantly, though not exclusively, female. There was also a lady principal who was concerned with the development of the girls as individuals, with their characters and manners, and all that the calendar called the "home and social life" of the college. Johanna Selles has drawn attention to the family model inspiring this structure, which she calls patriarchal.[32] Indeed, the metaphor was made flesh in that the position of lady principal was originally held by Dr Hare's wife. But in 1880 she had been succeeded by Mary Electa Adams, the noted Methodist educator, who was by no means a traditional second-in-command.

Adams had had a distinguished career that included posts as lady principal of Picton Academy and as first principal of the Wesleyan Female College in Hamilton. More recently, she had been founder and principal of Brookhurst Academy in Cobourg, where female students were educated in close conjunction with Victoria College. Unfortunately, the school had just closed for financial reasons. Adams had developed her ideas on women's education earlier in the century, as chief preceptress at the female branch of the Wesleyan Academy at Mount Allison, Sackville, New Brunswick. The *Dictionary of Canadian Biography* portrays her as a pioneer in the advanced education of women: "Women, Adams believed, should be offered a rigorous academic education in a Christian setting, and Mount Allison became a testing-ground for these principles."[33] Not that she was for emancipation, careers, and total equality in the masculine world. Had she been so radical, she would never have risen to the prominent positions that allowed her ideas to be carried out. But she paid her dues to womanliness, even retiring for four years from her career to care for her widowed mother at home. She made sure that her pupils had the unselfish spirit and refined manners conducive to domestic harmony. Her distinction was that she believed the trained mind was equally valuable to both men and women. And in her genuine desire to follow the will of God for his people, she was able to enlist the support of the Methodist body as a whole for her educational endeavours, which gently nudged the patriarchy in the direction of equality.

Into this milieu – cautiously forward-looking, progressively traditional – the twenty-one-year-old Addison settled in the fall of 1889. She lived in the main building, in a bedroom on the second floor with a lovely view of trees. Beneath her floor, connecting the larger student rooms at either end of the hall, was a secret passage or crawl space along which the girls sometimes wiggled and where they could hide contraband food; she was quite literally surrounded by the life of the school. During her two years here Addison comes briefly into focus thanks to three surviving letters to her brother Arthur – one of them written on school exercise paper while she was supervising a study class. These letters provide a fascinating glimpse of her hard work, her interest in her pupils, and even something of her inner life.

As a teacher, Margaret was exacting; she remarks to Arthur that she nearly made one unfortunate girl cry yesterday, though this was not her intention. While drilling a class who were faulty in their recitation of the bays, islands, and points in the Great Lakes, she explained, she made them go over it repeatedly. "I think they will have their lesson thoroughly next time, and if they don't I shall make them come until they do – for thorough recitations I *shall* have at any cost." There was a good deal of this drill and memory work, and the repetition could be boring: "Really if I had not so long and so strongly held, that with sufficient patience and tact in teaching any common knowledge is possible to anyone not an idiot, I should sometimes despair. The patience is the worst, but I get dogged and could go on for any number of days and explain the same questions." In her advanced arithmetic classes, the girls laboured to find the cube root of 1,785,874,351,203,125, or to solve $(8^{3/4} + 4^{3/2}) \times 16^{-3/4}$. The chemistry lessons were interesting, especially when the experiments failed to work: once Addison provided a fine blaze when some phosphorous caught fire. The junior literature class she taught had fireworks of its own, in that they studied poems like Byron's "Prisoner of Chillon," which she told Arthur had some magnificent parts: "Isn't it full of power?"[34] With another teacher she was reading *Pickwick Papers* and finding it very funny.

Addison's duties were not confined to the classroom, but covered all aspects of the pupils' development. As the calendar put it, "Teachers and pupils constitute one family, eating at the same table, and sharing the same social life; thus securing, as far as convenient with the discipline of the school, the advantages of the home circle."[35] This was comforting to parents, and the administration took its duties *in loco parentis* very seriously. Girls were required, for instance, to have a letter from their parents specifying whom they might visit on the first Saturday of each month, and which friends might visit them or receive a letter. The school day followed an orderly pattern, from rising at 6:30 a.m. to lights out at 9:30 p.m., but with considerable free time in the afternoons. Evenings were free too, although meetings of the school societies occurred at this time. Addison supervised a dinner table and carved the meat – leaving, she confessed, a mangled heap of bones and scraps. (The school fell short of home in that the girls were often hungry, thought little of school meals, and begged their parents to send boxes even though fruit and biscuits were all they were allowed to contain.) As her contribution to extracurricular activities, Addison became secretary of the Christian Endeavour Society, part of an interdenominational, church-centred youth movement that had spread rapidly since its founding in the United States in 1881. The society's main feature was weekly prayer meetings for inspiration and fellowship; each member made an active contribution, ranging from a simple Bible verse to a confession of Christ, and a Lookout Committee rounded up those who had been unaccountably absent.[36] During Margaret's years, the membership rose from twenty-four to fifty.

Margaret took a personal interest in her girls, describing to Arthur those who sat before her in class as "just as different as twelve girls could be": one sensitive and wearing glasses, one sulky and shockingly rude, though "withal not so bad," another terribly tired.[37] She particularly remarked on a new family of girls, aged seven, eleven, and twelve, who arrived in the spring of 1890 after their mother died. There were probably a number of such pupils, coming and going in the middle of term as family circumstances dictated. These three sat at Margaret's table, the youngest in her high chair. Margaret told stories to them every other Sunday evening, particularly stressing Bible stories: to her horror, "the little one does not know Adam from Eve."[38] In a sense she was substituting for their lost mother.

In spite of the amusing vignettes of school life that Margaret relates, a melancholy underlies her three letters to Arthur. She seems lonely and reaches out to her brother as if feeling the need for love. She fears that they are becoming strangers: "Where I have been so selfish, brother mine, forgive me, but please don't punish me too severely, by never letting me know you any better." The absence of her family is painful. She suffers too from a spiritual unease: "This year has been a very hard one for me. There have been so many things within, that I never knew were there before, and it has seemed almost to take my whole strength to fight against them."[39] She does not give a name to these psychological demons, whether unwelcome emotions or troubling thoughts. Was she discovering flaws where others would see none; or were black imaginings threatening to overwhelm her? Whatever the nature of her troubles, they must have had their root in her religious experiences. Like many people whose faith is at the centre of their life, she may have gone through a period of drought and dryness. There is no particular evidence that she struggled with the intellectual doubts that were so widespread in the late nineteenth century. The essence of her religion was experiential rather than theological: actual communion with God, as both her father and Dr Burwash maintained, provided the necessary proof that he existed. But due to some flagging of the spirit, this experience was less available now. "What is there to compare with God's presence?" she wrote for Arthur's birthday in October 1890; "would it were mine; but to my shame be it said I have less than in other days."[40]

As she was to do throughout her life, Margaret found solace in nature. She seemed to echo Dr Burwash – who preached in the college chapel on the glories of the creation – when she told Arthur that "I've come to the conclusion, that the things which all should read and learn, are – history, botany, physiology, chemistry, physics, geology and astronomy." Through nature she was able to renew communion with its maker:

I have grown more and more to believe that one part of man's greatest safety is in living close to nature. There is so much speaking of God, peace, rest, and trust, in the little flowers, in the trees, in the stones – indeed in all that God has made around us. When the heart is oppressed with care and trouble, what is so soothing as a long walk alone – except of course intercourse with God; but even this seems to come when one stands alone by some little brook, or before the lake or under some tree.[41]

There is an almost oriental quietism in her seeking to follow the way of nature: "Nature is so comforting sometimes. When there is hurry and unrest in man's portion, she smiles serenely and goes through her various phases without a tinge of impatience. She seems as content where there is mud as where snow or grass. Why doesn't man follow her example and do just the thing which he has before him instead of fretting or worrying or anything of the sort?"[42] Humanity is a surging mass, she writes in another letter, "and in the rush onward, we become entangled, and lose our own balance unless we seek a rest outside ourselves."[43]

Music was another resource, again a lifelong one. Her family had long possessed both a piano and an organ, and at the OLC Margaret continued her lessons under Professor Harrison, director of the School of Music. She also thought of joining the choral class. Professor Harrison was exacting and the hours of practice long, but the music filled her soul. Beethoven's "Farewell to the Piano" she described as magnificent: "so full of pathos and music and strength and beauty."[44] There is a wealth of emotional life here scarcely guessed by those who saw only the formal figure of Miss Addison in later years.

The politics and social life of the school could be a source of anxiety. Addison did not always find it easy to work with the principal, Dr Hare. The problem was ostensibly not so much his masculine perspective as his weak and vacillating character; as she put it, he "talks like a spoiled little boy when he wants his own way."[45] Addison was particularly indignant when he berated her for marking too high, since she had tried in vain to get some guidance about the marking system before she began. Others found him difficult too; Miss Adams called him weak, self-indulgent, not very manly, and underhanded.[46]

With Miss Adams, Addison had a good relationship, and the older woman, who was now in her late sixties, was something of a heroine to her. Tall and stately, Miss Adams contrasted amusingly with her younger sister, "little Miss Augusta," who also taught at the school. Her portrait shows a gentle woman, with straight Roman nose, thin lips, and hair descending close to her head in undulating waves. There is no hint of rancour in her sweetly tentative expression.[47] Yet Miss Adams must have been rather a disappointed woman at this time, since she had had to close the female academy that she had hoped might grow into Ontario's first women's college and accept a subordinate position in the school that had been her major competition. Hare had rubbed salt into the wound by introducing a paragraph into the school's circular claiming that her duties would be performed under his supervision; she forced him, though, to withdraw the paragraph under threat of resignation and insisted that she had freedom to act independently in her own sphere. Clearly, she chafed under an effectual subordination.[48]

Addison must have conversed with Miss Adams, and, since she loved to broach serious topics and always preferred deep conversations to shallow, it is virtually certain that they talked about education and the possible directions of a woman's life. Not that we are to imagine them muttering like a pair of bolsheviks against the "lady-like" regime enforced, or resenting the fact that young women were being kept down – as in a sense they were – by an emphasis on manners and decorum. Addison would never rebel against these values, and she cultivated them in her young charges when she was dean of women. Nor were the two likely to complain that the Christian teaching of the school encouraged self-sacrifice, thereby, from a feminist point of view, buttressing an unequal social system. Self-sacrifice, or at any rate unselfishness, was something Addison admired immensely in both men and women – though what she thought of the social system at this time is not known. But surely she and Miss Adams discussed much, including some of the difficulties of functioning in a male-directed environment. They were earnest, responsible, and committed women, and one can hardly blame them if they had the odd uncharitable comment about Dr Hare.

Another particular friend of Addison's on the staff was Helena Coleman, then teaching piano at the School of Music. She was Miss Adams's niece, the child of Adams's older sister and her husband Lucius Coleman; her brother Arthur P. Coleman, later to be famous as a geologist, was a young professor at Victoria at the end of the Cobourg period. Eight years older than Margaret, Helena was a woman of five feet seven inches, with a high forehead and dark arched eyebrows, who used crutches as a result of having had polio at the age of eleven.[49] One of her young admirers described her as rather untidy in her dress and possessing "a determined and intellectual look" but, nevertheless, as being sensitive, retiring, and poetic.[50] Later in fact she was to become a published poet. She and Margaret shared an interest in music and letters throughout their lives and spent much time together.

Possibly Helena Coleman had something to do with Addison's leaving the OLC in June of 1891: she herself was taking the next academic year off to study music in Germany. Or perhaps Addison saw an attractive opportunity. At any rate, Addison decided to go back to school for teacher training, taking advantage of the new School of Pedagogy that the Department of Education had just opened within the Toronto Normal School in an effort to intensify its very lax provision for the training of high-school teachers.[51] This school offered a fourteen-week course: teachers could attend between September and December and obtain an interim certificate with which they could teach in a high school for the second half of the academic year. In June, if they passed a practical teaching exam, they were awarded full professional certification.

At the end of the nineteenth century, requirements for high-school teachers were in a state of flux.[52] There were two criteria – nonprofessional standing, or level of education reached; and professional standing, or teacher training – and three classes of certificate. Requirements for higher qualifications were from time to time introduced, but high schools were often staffed by teachers who had qualified under earlier regulations, and who might themselves not have finished high school or received any professional training. A distinction was made between high schools and collegiate institutes: the latter were required to have special equipment, such as a science laboratory and gymnasium, and their teachers were more highly educated. From 1887, a collegiate had to have specialists to teach all major subjects. Not until 1891, though, was a university degree in one's chosen field made a condition for specialist qualification; before this, the completion of the work of the first and second years was acceptable. By enroling in the new school and adding first-class professional qualifications to her degree in moderns, Addison could place herself on the cutting edge of her profession.

Attendance at the Toronto School of Pedagogy also gave Margaret the opportunity to live in Toronto and be with her brothers: Will, who was in fourth year chemistry at University College; and Arthur, who was just beginning university at Toronto. It was rather an unhappy time for Arthur, who had gone to university mainly because his parents thought he should. The long-awaited move of Victoria to Toronto was finally under way; the injunction had been lifted, and a fine structure was going up at the northeast corner of Queen's Park. Since the building was not yet finished, however, Arthur had enroled at University College, which he found an impersonal, unfriendly place: "Then there was no compulsory attendance, no essays were exacted, no track kept of how much a student did work; and the teachers made no effort to become acquainted with the students ... [professors] lectured on set subjects, never asked a question (except in Latin), came and went without greeting anyone."[53] The following year he transferred to Victoria, which he found much friendlier. Meanwhile, he found some solace in the presence of his family. The three Addisons boarded together with Mrs Hay, a minister's widow and schoolteacher, at 36 Brunswick Avenue. She had been a friend of the family in Newcastle.

The course at the School of Pedagogy had two divisions, theoretical and practical. Mandatory subjects included reading, writing, temperance and hygiene, drawing, stenography, drill, gymnastics, calisthenics, psychology, the history and criticism of educational systems, the science of education, lectures and practical illustrations of the best method of teaching various courses, lectures on school organization and management, and observation and practice of actual teaching.[54] Unfortunately, after the first year of the school there were no actual classes on which to practise, and "the students were reduced to practising on each other."[55] With all this to be covered in fourteen weeks, it is no wonder that the school day lasted a gruelling twelve to fourteen hours.

The school espoused an enlightened, child-friendly type of education. Among the prescribed texts was Herbert Spencer's *Education* (1862), which had been influential in spreading the ideas of Pestalozzi and in criticizing education by rote and by the book. Though Spencer's stress on sense experience and developing the powers of observation were particularly relevant to the earlier years, his notion that the child's own efforts should be utilized to draw inferences and make meaningful generalizations was very relevant to the high-school years: "[Children] should be *told* as little as possible, and induced to *discover* as much as possible."[56] For Spencer, such practices would make the acquisition of knowledge what it was supposed to be – a pleasure and delight. His ideas were given a more practical and school-centred application in *Lectures on Teaching* (1881) by Sir Joshua Fitch, also a prescribed text. Sir Joshua's praise for the cheerful and sympathetic teacher strikes a modern note, as does his belief in the right of girls to as high and demanding an education as boys.

Lessons were perhaps rather dull, as lessons on pedagogy are apt to be. And the teachers-in-training were kept in an absurd state of pupillage, with strictures that sound to a modern ear like a ban on the very ends of education: "Communication between the sexes is strictly prohibited, except by permission of the Principal or one of the Lecturers or Masters."[57] The prohibition extended to leisure hours (if there were any), since "ladies and gentlemen shall not board at the same house." Presumably an exception was made in the case of siblings. This may not have been the most dynamic period in Addison's life, but it was productive, and she could call up the stoical spirit that she urged on an exam-bound Arthur only a year later: "When you are such an old philosopher as your big sister you will be gladder for the hard places than for the easy ones, for even though one in heart rebels against putting aside what one loves – even music, and books, and pleasure – after all, it is the very putting aside of our own desires, for something higher, which makes noble men and women of us."[58] In this case she emerged with the certification that allowed her to spend the next ten years in the elite collegiate institutes of the province.

∽

In January 1892 Addison took up a position as teacher of French and German at Stratford Collegiate Institute, under the principalship of C.A. Mayberry. The school, built in 1879, was physically imposing, its three stories of white brick with red bands rising to gables and a cupola. This gracious aspect, combined with its situation on a woody slope, prompted Egerton Ryerson in a burst of enthusiasm at its opening to rank it second in combination of geography and architecture only to the great cathedral of Milan.[59] Though the school's proceedings never matched those of its exemplar, it did win a reputation for fine teaching, particularly under the tall, frosty, and distinguished Mayberry, a specialist in classics. There were over 250 pupils, with around sixty (nearly half of them girls) in the prestigious upper years.

Addison joined a staff of six men. Her salary of $800 a year was close to average for the province.[60] But it still reflects the ingrained sexism of the system, since a completely inexperienced male, hired at the same time, received $1000. She continued to be the low earner on the staff, making less than everyone else (including new appointees) until 1895, when a "technically unqualified" teacher of bookkeeping without a degree was taken on with a slightly lower salary than hers.[61] In 1896 her salary was raised to $900, and in 1898 she reached the benchmark $1000 offered to her male colleagues. These formed a bulky, impressive phalanx. When anticipating a visit from the inspector, Addison wrote that "the man Seath is daily expected to pounce down on us innocents, and throttle us – mentally if not physically, for our six teachers are pretty big men for even *Seath* to tackle."[62] Luckily, she was herself solid and substantial, unlikely to be trampled underfoot; a testimonial from the mathematics teacher, Wilson Taylor, calls her "a lady of good physique, and well able to perform the labours of her department." Her teaching frequently earned a first-class rating from the rigorous Seath, prompting Mr Mayberry in his testimonial to call her "one of the most successful teachers we have ever had – a hard worker, and a splendid disciplinarian."[63]

Towards the end of her time at Stratford, Addison published in *Acta* some reflections on being a teacher, "Education and our Relation to it as Graduates," that reveal a characteristic blend of moral earnestness and progressive faith. A certain humility is induced, she remarks, in a classroom where one must view oneself "as seen by sixty or more pairs of bright critical eyes."[64] She goes on to describe education as "the highest and fullest development of the will, mind and heart, for the sake of serving humanity – for the sake of 'making righteousness prevail in the earth,' as Matthew Arnold says."[65] In this definition the Hebraic side of Arnold's Hebraic-Hellenic dichotomy has been placed uppermost, as one might expect from one of Addison's background. The emphasis is not on knowing but on doing; the goal is not personal fulfilment, but service to others. Addison declares that the teacher can forward the development of character by encouraging the taste for reading wholesome and enlightening works: "The amount of trash devoured by a modern juvenile is something to be deplored."[66] Moral training, she notes, should also be worked into the curriculum, perhaps by non-denominational study of the Bible, but preeminently by the influence of the consecrated personalities of the teachers. Addison gives the high-school teachers a responsibility far beyond the teaching of their particular subject – for the care, virtually, of their pupils' souls.

Education, being a valuable tool in the shaping of good citizens, must give students a reason to stay in school. In her essay Addison argues strongly for manual training and domestic science (subjects just being introduced into the curriculum in Ontario thanks to the efforts of Lillian Massey Treble, Adelaide Hoodless, and Sir William Macdonald) in order to engage the interest of the non-bookish and to provide practical preparation for life for boys and girls, respectively. Typically, her focus is not on the elite she taught – the 5 percent of Ontarians who went on to high school – but on the wider society where the less advantaged and less clever called to her social conscience. Though her essay does not address the question, she was also concerned with the physical well-being of the students and committed to the rising movement for adequate physical education. Stratford C.I., for all its cathedral-like qualities, lacked facilities for a proper physical education program: the absence of a gymnasium is a complaint running through all the otherwise favourable inspectors' reports. In place of gymnastics the students engaged in simpler calisthenics (or exercises) and drill, weather permitting; Addison herself taught some of the calisthenics classes.

Addison boarded, for at least some of the seven and one-half years she spent at Stratford, with the Dent sisters: Lydia was a teacher, and Bessie kept house. Her sister Charlotte often joined the household as well, and the four became lifelong friends. It was a home away from home for one who still felt the pull of her own home and family, and who was liable to bouts of low spirits and discouragement. Perhaps the trouble was the familiar one: she gave out too much, and left herself too little time to replenish her energies in quietness or prayer. Her head frequently ached and her nerves were on edge. A letter from Arthur provoked a disproportionate reaction: "There are sometimes occasions when a letter is like a benediction to one. And such a time it was with me when your letter came. I was tired out and nervous, and just sat down and cried – not out of sadness, but gladness for the remembrance of my two noble true brothers."[67] Recognizing that she was overextended, she often tried thereafter to cut down on extracurricular activities, such as prayer meetings and the Sunday School class she taught, and to spend most evenings at home.

Addison's father, Peter, was superannuated in 1893, and the family moved to Toronto, where the boys could live at home while studying. At first they rented 666 Parliament Street. Then in 1896 they had a comfortable house built at 513 Markham Street, just north of Harbord. Margaret still hankered after the time she had boarded in Toronto with her brothers and, in one of her letters, treats Toronto as a veritable mecca: "But never mind, some of these days, I'll be in Toronto too, and have one of these [sic] good positions, and then things will be easier for you and Will, and I hope I'll see more of you."[68] Meanwhile, she loved to hear news of the university, to which she still felt attached. As Stratford was linked to the metropolis by railway, she came home whenever she could afford it: for school holidays, for meetings of the Modern Language Association, and later in connection with the Victoria alumnae.

One memorable visit occurred in June of 1895, for Will's graduation as a Bachelor of Medicine. Arthur had just won his B.A. and was off travelling in Europe, having delighted all the Addisons by committing himself at last to being a minister, and Charlotte too had passed some unspecified exams. "As the one sole remaining member of the younger generation," Margaret wrote to Arthur, "I am casting about in my mind what I can do to render myself distinguished and worthy of such clever people. Mother suggests I shoot myself to gain fame, but I tell her I want to share in the fame, and I couldn't then." She resigned herself to not disgracing the family: "We are in agonies over our appearance for this afternoon. Being the poor lorn country maiden, I must needs be furnished up for the occasion, and Charlotte is manufacturing a hat for me ... [I shall wear] my Sunday best new spring suit – the best and most fashionable so country a place as Stratford can produce."[69] It was, in truth, a time to rejoice. After a period of uncertainty and underachievement, Will had found his métier. Arthur, for a while an awkward gangling youth, had developed splendidly, being class president, president of the Athletic Union, and president of the Literary Society in his last year at Victoria. His meeting Elizabeth Scoley, his future wife, at Sherbourne Street Methodist Church contributed to his positive outlook. Charlotte's career had been in doubt: in fact her father had favoured her becoming a milliner, and perhaps Margaret's hat was a test case that contributed to the decision that she should become a piano teacher. As she loved music, she was happy with the decision and eager to begin studying music at the university.

That Margaret felt a responsibility for her younger siblings is obvious. She sent money to both boys and expressed distress at Arthur's severe economies, though also noting that economy, as a form of self-denial, allows one to become more Christlike. At the same time she worried that her gifts might seem patronizing: "I hope you do not think, that I am posing as the very generous older sister, who counts it her right to rule and exact, and who expects untold gratitude in return. I love you much too dearly to assume such an attitude, even were it my desire or nature to do so."[70] In addition to the money, she sent a steady stream of advice. In one letter she did declare that she was going out of the business of preaching, except for a mere occasional homily;[71] she might have known, however, that the decision was premature.

CHAPTER THREE

European Interlude

Addison spent eight years teaching in Stratford, followed, after a year's absence, by two and one-half years at Lindsay Collegiate Institute. There is little biographical information about this period, during which she changed from a young woman of twenty-three to a mature one of thirty-four. It is tempting to imagine her developing, through teaching, the skills and knowledge that would prepare her for her life's work as dean of residence and dean of women. Tempting, but perhaps overly teleological. At this time the position of dean of women did not exist. There was not even a women's residence to require a head, nor were there any women teachers on the university staff. Certainly, there was no reason to suppose that a woman was headed towards a position where she could directly influence the way in which university women were taught and housed. For the main, Addison probably thought of herself simply as a high-school teacher. She threw herself into the demands of the profession, attending meetings of the Ontario Teachers' Association (OTA), rejoicing when her pupils did well, and taking seriously her responsibility to shape the young minds of both boys and girls. If she could not realistically expect to become a principal, at least she could look forward to increased mastery and respect, and a higher salary.

There is nevertheless a sense in which Addison was unconsciously moving towards her future position. She was herself helping to create the conditions under which a dean of women would be needed, especially by furthering the erection of a residence that would require a head. As well, through studies in educational theory and in theology, she was obtaining a clearer conception of the way to nurture Christian women in a university setting. Perhaps above all, her eight-month trip to Europe and its educational establishments, to be discussed in detail later, proved to be pivotal in ripening her commitment to the cause of a women's residence.

A women's residence had perhaps been a gleam in the eye of Dr Burwash from the date of Victoria's move to Toronto in 1892. At any rate the chancellor envisaged, in their new setting, a dignified quadrangle defined by the main college building, a library, and "residences."[1] His plans were too extensive for the circumstances, which called for increasing the endowment and recouping the expenses of moving. But the hope for a women's residence was taken up by – or perhaps originated with – his wife, Margaret Proctor Burwash, who, having four sons, looked on the women of the college as might a mother in search of daughters.[2] She was herself a gifted teacher, having taught before her marriage in 1868 at the Wesleyan Female College in Hamilton and having served as preceptress of the Ladies' Academy in Sackville, New Brunswick. Now in her fifties, she was a mature and thoughtful woman. The earliest known reference to the women's residence occurs in a letter she wrote to Addison on 25 February 1895 – a letter which suggests she had been trying to drum up support for the scheme among graduates and others:

Your friendly earnest interest in the subject of a Woman's Residence for Victoria is specially grateful to me. But alas! I find none like minded with you. The need of it is great, and at times I feel as though every one must realize it as I do, if it were fairly put before them, but it seems impossible to strike an answering chord anywhere, except among the professors. Dr. Potts [College Treasurer] is not willing to discuss the question. His financial burdens are already too heavy ...[3]

This was the first of many letters of mutual encouragement and support Addison and Mrs Burwash were to exchange in the following eight years, before the residence came to fruition.

The pattern of the campaign was that of one initial success followed by protracted struggle and difficulties. The success occurred when Mrs Burwash, undeterred by her lukewarm reception, continued to air her idea among influential Methodist women and managed to enlist the interest of Lillian Massey. Miss Massey, soon to become Mrs John Treble, was the daughter of Hart Massey and a member of a family that was a solid financial backer of Victoria. She evidently convinced her father to support the cause, for, after his death on 20 February 1896, his will was found to contain a substantial bequest for Victoria, including $50,000 to build a women's residence (the remaining $150,000 went into the general endowment).

Hart Massey's money would cover the cost of erecting a building. First, however, it was necessary to buy or obtain land; later, more money – as much as $15,000 – would be needed for furnishings and equipment. The land question proved difficult, as Victoria's campus was already too small, and the men's sports facilities were crowded.[4]

The university was willing to consider selling to Victoria an additional plot of land on the southwest corner of the lot, known as the Drynan block, but this was not extensive. Victoria had its eye on a far larger parcel north of the present Charles Street, then a sandy lane known as Czar Street; extending to the backs of the houses on Bloor Street, this could accommodate both a women's residence and playing fields. But this parcel too was owned by the university, which rented it out as a cow pasture. As Burwash pointed out, the university "said plainly that [Victoria] did not need it and could not use it."[5] Negotiations dragged on for some years.

Meanwhile, to raise the needed funds, the Board of Regents in February 1897 sanctioned the establishment of a Barbara Heck Memorial Association. The woman so honoured was often referred to then as the "Mother of Methodism in North America," especially by Canadians, though this title is a somewhat inflated one.[6] An immigrant to New York from Ireland with a Methodist group in 1760, she had accosted some of her male relatives who were putting amusement before zeal in the New World, snatched the playing cards from their astonished hands, flung them into the fire, and asked their leader when he would be about his proper business of preaching the Word. Continuing to act as an efficient cause, she had him found the first Methodist congregation in New York. At the end of the American Revolution, she emigrated to Canada and eventually settled in Augusta township near the modern Prescott, where she encouraged other congregations and tended her large family. Dr Withrow, book steward of the Methodist Church Book Room, editor of the *Canadian Methodist Magazine*, and a member of the board of regents, had recently written a small book on Barbara Heck,[7] and he and Dr Burwash had the idea of perpetuating her fading memory by associating it with the proposed residence. Unfortunately, the suggestion proved to be a liability: Heck Hall would be an obvious invitation to wisecracks, and, as Professor Bain's daughter Gladys pointed out, the girls were sure to be called either Heckites or Barbarians.[8] In 1901, the fundraising and supervisory group was renamed the Victoria Women's Residence and Educational Association (VWREA) – an organization which exists to the present day.[9] It was a group composed of graduates, wives of professors, Methodist churchwomen, and others interested in the cause. The meeting to launch the association was held in the college chapel in March 1897, with Mrs Burwash taking the chair as a sign that women were up to the demands of transacting business.[10]

The $15,000 that the committee needed was raised painfully, dollar by dollar, through the network of Methodist women. Addison kept in touch by mail and, when not fully occupied in preparing lessons, marking exams, and helping with student presentations, wrote letters to· likely donors. She offered to address interested groups: "I'm afraid I'm very audacious, but really, I'm willing to do anything righteous to help the Residence on ... I think only personal effort will really do much work, and we shall need to find some one in each city, town, and village who will be able and willing to do personal work."[11] Women in Stratford, St. Thomas, Hamilton, Brantford and all over southern Ontario raised money by means of bake sales, bazaars, and entertainments. Mrs George A. Cox, VWREA treasurer, wife of the bursar and with her husband one of the most liberal benefactors of the college, held a bazaar and auction at her house on Sherbourne Street; Mrs Treble and Mrs Bain stirred themselves as well. Even school children were pressed into service, as recalled by Ethel Bennett, later married to lecturer John Bennett but at that time the young Ethel Patterson:

While I was still a schoolgirl I was asked to contribute a piece of fancywork (as it was called then) made by myself, to be sold at a bazaar in aid of the [renamed] Annesley Hall Fund. I presented my pink-ribboned contraption with some fears as to its usefulness in aiding such an important undertaking, but it was received so graciously by the late Miss May Skinner, that I was encouraged to hope that the pennies it might bring in would buy an Annesley Hall brick – perhaps even two, since bricks were not as expensive then as they are now.[12]

The work of fundraising proved extraordinarily difficult, and Mrs Burwash sometimes lost heart. "Our encouragement was not very great," she wrote in retrospect: "Indeed at the outset the coldness and indifference were so great that it was discussed whether we had not better let the whole matter drop. Our treasurer Mrs. Cox was indefatigable, although she confessed she had never undertaken anything that seemed so hopeless ... Everywhere we met with some success, but also with very positive opposition. Strange to say the fiercest opponents were women."[13] Of course part of the opposition was financial. Was it worth spending so much money on the women of the college, who in 1900 numbered fewer than sixty? But more potent, among conservative women who felt that the college woman was not a phenomenon to be encouraged, was a dislike of what the residence implied: the official recognition of a new field of activity for women. Was this not the thin edge of the wedge, part of a campaign for "equality" that would encourage women to forsake their traditional duties and try to become like men, to the destruction both of the social order and of their own peace of mind?

To Addison and to Mrs. Burwash the opposition seemed strange, because for them it was not really an equality issue at all. Indeed, the men themselves were no better treated: the only men's residence at the University of Toronto was a small one at University College, housing a mere thirty-six men, generally frowned upon as a hotbed of riotous living, and to be closed in a few years because it encouraged cliquishness.[14] No, it could rather be called a "difference" issue. Men might perch around the city in boarding houses if necessary, but this was an unsuitable mode of life for the young women at Victoria – even though the college kept a list of approved houses, and riotous living was not their characteristic. Mrs Burwash believed that women were capable of the same intellectual feats as men, but she also believed as strongly as her conservative friends in a distinctive feminine nature that needed to be accommodated. Women, she felt, would be the losers if they were introduced to the university scene like spice added to a stew, to be blended in smoothly. Rather the university should adapt to their presence, allowing them to carry on a feminine style of life within the confines of the larger university.

In their fundraising statements, then, Mrs Burwash and Addison stressed the traditional values that would be safeguarded by a well-supervised residence. When Addison invoked the notion of the residence as a home in a 1901 speech to the VWREA, for instance, she struck a chord that she knew would resonate with her Methodist audience: "If our girls spend the four years of their college life in a perfectly kept home, where the rooms are spotless, the linen immaculate, the furnishing simple but tasteful, the table dainty, the food suitable to student need, and prepared just as it ought to be, they will know the value of good housekeeping, and shall have learnt something at least to help them towards what always will be woman's work – home making." She was not trying to limit the career possibilities for women by implying that this was their *only* work, but undoubtedly she was addressing fears that college education might denature women and make them scorn the less glamorous part of their role. On the contrary, she argued, education enhanced their functioning: "We still hear in society, though less frequently than formerly, a moan over the uselessness of higher education for girls, if perchance, at the close of their college career, they marry, and enter homes of their own. As if educated, disciplined wives and mothers were not more needed than any other class of society."[15] Mrs Burwash struck the very same note when she argued: "The chief object of all training of women, is the perfecting of the home. Home is the heart of the nation, the heart of the church, and out of it are the issues of life. The higher education of women brings bane instead of blessing unless it gives them a higher ideal of the nobility and sacredness of their calling as homemakers."[16]

A residence with some of the qualities of a home would not only teach the girls homemaking skills, but would nurture and develop them in a continuation of their families' care. As Mrs Burwash said in her earliest published appeal for support, "Any one can understand that when four years of early womanhood are spent away from the direct influence of home, without definite social or church ties, when the whole energy is given to a mental training ... there is danger of falling into Bohemian habits of thought and life." A home or its substitute had as its aim "to secure the symmetrical development of the whole woman."[17] For Addison, too, intellectual training must proceed hand in hand with improvement in physical, social, and spiritual life. The rhetorical questions of her speech of 1901 are eloquent:

Have we any right to take our Canadian girls from their homes during their most impressionable years, and say we educate them, when we leave the training of their characters, morals, and manners to stray influences? Who is there whose business it is to teach them that the greatest thing in this world is charity, and the next greatest self-control? Who is there to point out that but few may be scholars, but that every girl may and must be a woman of worth, refinement, and tact; that one's life's work is not estimated by the greatness of the sphere, but by the spirit of the worker.[18]

This approach to university education might well be called paternalistic (if the word had not such inappropriate overtones of gender) in the sense that the students were assumed to be still in process of development and in need of guidance. Maternalism is a somewhat more apt term, however, in that another strongly held belief of the early supporters of the residence was that the women could best be supervised by a woman. Not that they needed a substitute mother – they were not considered quite so unfledged as that – but that other women knew their needs and could provide role models. Mrs Burwash's letter of 1895 supplies a text:

I believe in men and women standing together in intellectual work, but there is a side of our nature which is exclusively feminine, which cannot be developed or moulded by men. It is a great misfortune for any young woman to be dwarfed or warped in this 'quality' – I do not know how better to name it. In time I hope to see women instructors in university work. But if we could now have a cultured woman of strong personality, who had the gift or grace of keeping in touch with young people at the head of college home life it would be a great step in advance.[19]

The need for young women to be somewhat sheltered thus led to the call for older women to assume positions of authority and leadership.

One means of gaining support for the residence was to form an alumnae association that would keep women graduates in touch with each other and with their college, in imitation of the "old-boy network" of the Alumni Association. A circular to the graduates was sent out by Nettie Burkholder (B.A. 1891), the future lady principal of the Ontario Ladies' College, and Clara Horning (9T5), inviting them to attend a meeting on 12 April 1898. Eighteen graduates responded – not a particularly encouraging turnout, considering that ten were from the class of 1898. Adeline Shenick of the class of 1887 was the oldest graduate present. Next oldest was Margaret Addison, who had travelled down from Stratford for the purpose. She was elected president, with Nettie Burkholder her vice-president.

Addison did a great deal of work for the fledgling Alumnae Association. The paper already referred to, "Education and our Relation to it as Graduates," was given as her presidential address in April 1899. She helped to organize the alumnae's yearly course of readings, centred on such topics as "the condition of women wage earners." But she was overwhelmed at times with the familiar discouragement. To Mrs Burwash she wrote that "the year [1898–99] has been so hard by reason of depression, that I felt as if the heart and courage had gone out of things. You were the means of giving me the courage and help I needed to gather up again the threads and try to weave them into something of use."[20] Her phrases suggest that she judged herself a useless person, not contributing sufficiently to the good of those around her. The Alumnae Association, she told Mrs Burwash, had been the means of "heartening" her. But her work there was not easy: initially, the women resisted bonding. In April 1900 a circular was sent out "owing to the lack of interest in the Alumnae Association"; it asked graduates pointedly, "Are you a member of the Alumnae of Victoria College? If not, why not?"[21] When Addison was asked to continue as president in 1899–1900, she refused.

Through that year of 1899 she struggled and, though there is no direct testimony, one may posit a breakdown – not the last, and perhaps not the first. At any rate she resigned from her position at Stratford c.i., probably at Christmas 1899,[22] and the next year found her embarked on an extensive European tour with Charlotte. That its purpose was partly restorative is suggested by a paragraph in Charlotte's only extant letter of the tour: "Margaret is I think some better. She still has those spells of exhaustion, but I do not think them as frequent or as severe as they used to be. She eats a much better quantity of food, is a little fleshier, and carries herself with more straightness and less languor, but she is far from well yet. She knows a little better when to stop working now."[23] And if the trip was restorative for Margaret, it was also, Margaret thought, beneficial for Charlotte – the unfortunate sibling left at home to care for aging parents. In a letter to Arthur, Margaret had asked him to be good to Charlotte, as she had a good many crosses to bear. "Do all you can to broaden her character," she counselled, for Charlotte is growing old before her time.[24] It was a happy arrangement for both of them to set sail for Europe together.

The trip – which took place between May and December, 1900 – invites an amount of attention that may seem disproportionate simply because it is well-documented: during the holiday Addison kept a diary, two volumes of which are still extant.[25] But there are good reasons, apart from its simple existence, for lingering over this diary. The trip *was* a turning point in Addison's life – that was why she wrote an extensive journal and preserved it for so many years. Moreover, though it was a pleasure trip, her Methodist conscience ensured that it was also an occasion for mental profit. She had studied French and German literature: now she could see the cultures which gave them birth. She had thought much about the need for education in a modern democracy: now she could visit progressive institutions and read in educational libraries larger than any she had known. She had worked hard to organize support for a residence for Victoria women: now she could visit women's residences in Oxford and Cambridge and learn how they were managed. Like many travellers, she probably hoped that in obeying the urge to get away she would obtain a fresh perspective on her own life, and perhaps envisage a better one. Less expected was the light shed by other cultures on the nature and needs of Canada itself. In all these ways her perceptions were enlarged, and the way was prepared for a change of career.

The diary, the only extensive one of Addison's known to exist, also provides an unusual glimpse into her mind and personality. Although she has left many letters that are personal, letters give a different perspective, being written for the eyes of a particular recipient. Not all diaries, of course, are undertaken with the object of self-analysis or with the teenager's insistence that no one may glance therein, and Addison's is not a private diary that lingers over matters of the soul or emotional reactions. It may even have been written to share with her friends and family, and much of it is taken up with description. Nonetheless, opinions and thoughts abound, and a character that had been shadowy begins to take shape. Even her syntax and her manner of expression are characteristic.

Margaret and Charlotte left Toronto on 21 May 1900, took the train to Montreal, and embarked on the *Tunisian*, reaching Liverpool on 4 June. Unfortunately, the first volume of her diary, describing their progress south through England to Southampton and on to London, is now lost. Apparently both she and Charlotte were sick and unable to enjoy much. The only extended passage on this period, written later at the back of the next volume, describes a parade that escorted the aging Queen Victoria through London; the queen had come up from Windsor for a garden party at Buckingham Palace. The highlighting of this event is significant, for it defines Margaret's loyalties. After waiting with Charlotte in Hyde Park to see Victoria pass, Margaret writes: "What a crowd to see her! And how they love the dear little woman who is so wise and kind, whose life has been spotless and blameless, and given up to good works, who has tended her family well, and been a model woman as well as Queen."[26] Having obtained only a glimpse of Her Majesty – "a sweet but sad little lady, so wee one could see but little of her" – they determined to sit on a curb near Constitution Hill for three or four hours to see her again on her way home. Such devotion was typical. Addison adored the queen – her queen – and was emotionally devastated when she died the next January after a sixty-three-year reign. Through her father, she identified herself as English, a normal identification at a time when "country of racial origin" on the Canadian census form did not include Canada as an option.

Addison's attitude to England was very much that of a colonial who claimed the works of Englishmen as her heritage. She looked on England as a parent, more sophisticated and cosmopolitan than its offspring and still able to show how things are done. As she said in the rough draft of "Glimpses of Education in Europe," the essay she wrote for *Acta* on her trip, the prevalence of English-born teachers in Canadian universities was not to be deplored, since they disseminated England's learning and culture. Nevertheless, she continued:

The very fact of the necessity of English instructors should show us some of our own crudeness, and it is high time we took stock of ourselves, so as to consider what we need for the new century. We cannot, of course, in a few years reach the heights which our forefathers in the old land have taken centuries to climb. But certainly it is time for us to climb a little faster towards them and to make sure we are climbing in the right direction, and with the best aids for sure and steady climbing that are to be had.[27]

Her loyalty and sense of national identification explain why she learned more from Britain than from the United States, and why she looked naturally to English models for a Canadian women's residence.

Margaret planned to return to London after Charlotte went home, for more serious study. Meanwhile, the two joined a group of Canadians led by the Methodist editor, Dr Withrow, for a European tour that started with a ten-day visit to the *exposition universelle internationale de 1900* in Paris. This was no ordinary world's fair. Taking place at century's end, it was intended to be a grand culminating gesture, summing up past achievements and previewing wonders to come.[28] It was also a milestone in the development of mass tourism: thousands were transported from all nations. Many travel companies offered package tours, so that even labourers, by using layaway plans, could take their families across the Channel for a few days.[29] Paris was the tourist destination *par excellence* that summer.

The Withrow group was travelling with the enterprising Thomas Cook and Son, which had built several large hotels in Paris to accommodate its clients, and which offered its usual services of ground transportation, interpreters, and prepaid tickets to be exchanged for meals, accommodation, and railway travel as required. Cook's arranged for the party of seventy-one to be taken in reserved train compartments to Newhaven, ferried them across to Dieppe "with six hundred passengers on a boat meant for half that number," and then put them on a train to Paris. Not all went smoothly, however, for just short of their destination the train stopped. As Margaret was later to write: "Really we thought never to go again, as we sat in the stifling car, supperless and weary, after an insufficient lunch at noon, while the hours seven, eight, nine, ten, eleven, and finally twelve struck, before the débris of a wreck which blocked our way could be removed."[30]

After this trying journey, Cook's Exhibition Hotel on the Boulevard de Grenelle at 1:30 in the morning appeared less than alluring. It crammed in accommodation for 1500 "on the principle of most rooms out of smallest space, and on smallest expense," by means of a system of entries labelled *A* to *F*, leading to a warren of rooms on eight floors. Dinner was served each day by waiters in grimy linen in "an immense building put up in cheap style, finished with cotton overhead to conceal the beams." On either side of the main entrance passage crowds of people gathered: "French, German, American, Canadian, and Russian – and such a gabble and chatter and noise, and confusion! Some demanding information, some letters etc., and peddlars selling wares, and buses arriving cracking the whip to get passage, porters calling, etc."[31] Though the Addisons' room on the seventh floor was comfortable, they never got used to the hotel's unseemly tumult.

In Paris the Addisons were not part of an organized "Cook's tour," but were free to come and go individually or with companions from the group. They did, however, take advantage of group tours of Paris, during which they saw all the principal sights: Napoleon's tomb, Notre Dame Cathedral, the Panthéon, and so on. Margaret was particularly interested in the tombs and memorials of the writers she had discussed in "French Literature in the Time of Louis xiv" as well as in the buildings they frequented and in the sites of the revolution that brought to an end the courtly and corrupt era. At the Bon Marché department store she and Charlotte bought a silk dress for their mother. Two days were spent at the Louvre, where Margaret conscientiously noted the pictures seen. She was somewhat alarmed at the more Gothic manifestations of Catholic taste, finding Giotto's *Saint Francis of Assisi Receiving the Stigmata*, for instance, "horrible," and other "subjects and their execution peculiar." The impressionist paintings now principally associated with the Paris of the time were not readily seen: even in the Luxembourg, which housed modern paintings, the works were generally of a more academic school. Margaret tried to use her French, not always successfully. She was doubtless not the first tourist to ask if there was an elevator in the hotel and to be politely shown the wc – there was no alternative to the six flights of stairs she climbed daily to their room.[32]

Paris, as the city of exhibitions, had hosted most of the world's fairs of the nineteenth century. That summer the Eiffel Tower, which had been erected for the exhibition of 1889, looked down on a sea of pavilions in the Champ de Mars (technology); the Esplanade des Invalides (decorative arts); the area of the Trocadéro; and the banks of the Seine, which itself had become a main thoroughfare for the exhibition. Civic improvements included the new Pont Alexandre iii, which opened up an imposing panorama across the river to the Invalides; the Grand and Petit Palais with their sculptured groups; and the new Métro from Vincennes to Maillot, its entrances decorated with wrought iron in *art nouveau* style. For those who preferred not to travel underground there was a moving sidewalk, offering three different speeds, which was the subject of much cartooning and merriment.

In her diary, Addison wrote mainly about the national pavilions in the Quai des Nations on the right bank of the Seine. These buildings, like most of those at the exhibition, were finished with thick plaster that could be sculpted to resemble any national style and period, giving rise to an eclectic collection of turrets, crenellations, Gothic cathedrals, allegorical sculpture, and heraldic devices. The British pavilion, however, was made of real stone in the form of an English manor house. Decorated with tapestry and stained glass from Burne-Jones and Morris, Wedgwood china, and antique furniture, it called forth Addison's enthusiastic praise: "Altogether, it was very evident John Bull likes good, substantial, solid, fine things, not made for show, but real, and comfortable. I was proud of being English." She also admired the United States pavilion (a miniature Capitol), not only for its provision of comforts for visiting American businessmen, but also, and especially, for the presence of a lavatory: "Actual water, running from an actual tap into an actual basin, is a luxury we've seen but rarely since leaving home." It must have been a luxury, indeed, for the traveller accustomed to making do with a washstand and a jug of hot water in her room. The Canadian display received only qualified approval: "Canada's tea room under a chestnut tree and awning was cool and enticing. Canada exhibits gold, minerals, fruits, cold storage, furs, birds and animals peculiar to the country, granite-ware, stoves, agricultural implements, pianos, bicycles, leather, paper, pictures of the mountains, exhibits of the c.p.r. even to a sleeping car made up. There was quantity, also quality, but very little skill or taste in arrangement."[33] Addison wrote little about the technological marvels on display – dynamos, X-ray machines and so on – and does not seem to have visited any of the cosmoramas, mareoramas, and stéréoramas that transported the visitor to outer space or the seabed in an early attempt at virtual reality. Although the electricity that was widely used was not new to her – electric light had been installed in the Ontario Ladies' College in 1890 – she did find the ornate Palace of Electricity "beautiful beyond expression – a very fairy-land of light and beauty."[34]

Paris was packed that summer, reputed to be the hottest in a hundred years. There were over 50 million visitors, consuming 1.8 million kilos of potatoes, 243,200 kilos of apples, and mountains of other foods.[35] The Addisons found it exhausting, what with the market that had sprung up in the Boulevard de Grenelle beneath their window, the crowds on the boulevards and in the lighted cafés through the small hours of the morning, and the chatter and clatter and "gabble." Addison's summary in a letter to Mrs. Burwash was not completely favourable:

Of course it is unfair to judge a city during Exposition time, especially in such hot weather as prevailed during our stay. But, we were disappointed in Paris, and the Parisians. We concluded that the Parisians we had heard of and read about were in the country for the summer, for certainly we saw none of them. And as for the character of those we did see, far from being surprised at the number of Revolutions they have had, I am surprised they have not had more, and shall never wonder at their doing anything of a revolutionary kind. They are so excitable, illogical, and emotional. But, as I said, I am sure we saw the worst, not the best of Paris. The public buildings are very grand, but I couldn't forget that so many of them were wrought at the expense of the people's welfare, and that much of the grandeur had its foundation in bloodshed.[36]

Perhaps she had been unfavourably predisposed by the advice of a friend: "Never look a man in the eyes on a street in Paris. Take no notice of people – especially Frenchmen – and you will be fairly safe."[37] On the whole they were not sorry to pack their bags, have done with the pesky Frenchmen, and rejoin Dr Withrow's group for the train ride to Switzerland.

Addison was delighted with Switzerland. She gloried in its mountain scenery; admired its cleanliness; and, in its Protestant parts, felt more at home than in Catholic Europe, welcoming the sterner and more bracing moral climate and, in particular, the quieter Sundays. In Lausanne they stayed in the Hotel Gibbon, a "heaven" compared with Paris: "With what a feeling of luxury we swept through the wide, well-carpeted halls, and how delicious the most ordinary things tasted in the immaculate, large, airy dining-room, looking out on the beautiful garden where Gibbon wrote his history."[38] After a week's delightful travel, visiting Berne, Thun, Interlaken, Grindelwald, and finally Lucerne, Charlotte and Margaret left the group (most of whom were travelling on to Italy) and retired for a complete rest. The week they spent in a converted Swiss farmhouse near Weggis was the most idyllic of the whole trip. Ideally situated about a mile from the village, the farm was set in the midst of an orchard and surrounded by gardens; in the background rose peak over peak of mountains, the distant ones capped with snow. Margaret found the people "simple, and delightful."[39]

They regretfully left this sequestered spot for Zurich, where they spent over a week. Here Margaret sought out the historical traces of two of her heroes: Zwingli, a major figure in the Reformation; and Pestalozzi, the educational reformer. The latter was honoured in the Pestalozzianum, a small house filled with mementoes of his life and examples of the specimens, models, pictures, maps, and charts by which he hoped to make learning sensuous and meaningful. There was also a fine library: "I couldn't help wondering to myself, where in Toronto which is fully 60,000 more in number of inhabitants, we could find such a library, so well maintained, and who would go to it to read if it were there?"[40] In short, wrote Addison later, it was "a very paradise for a teacher wanting new ideas and fresh incentive."[41]

On the morning of 14 August, Addison awoke to find the streets beneath her window in Zurich converted into a lively market for flowers, fruit, and vegetables. "When we returned at noon along these streets not a vestige of the market was to be seen. The streets were empty, swept and garnished, though I did see a square inch of a cabbage leaf which had missed the broom."[42] In Paris it had been the dirt and flies of the market that were noticeable; the image that had stuck in her mind was that of a child in a brown paper bonnet, asleep in a cart full of vegetable rubbish. Clean, orderly Zurich was the city, next to Oxford, where she would most have liked to spend a year. She could not get over the evident contentment of its citizens. Her delight in the gaiety of an outdoor concert (like her more ambivalent amazement at Parisian nightlife) is an indirect comment on Ontario stolidity:

Germans, French, English by the score come in, papas, mamas, grandmamas even, sons and daughters, seat themselves at table and order beer, coffee, cakes, wine, or other drinks, and the men puff their cigars, roll out the smoke luxuriously, sip beer, and joke, while the ladies, too, sip their beer and coffee, put in a few words, and laugh with their spouses. I can't but admire the pleasure continental couples take in each other. So many men and their wives go about together, and seem to enjoy each other's company so thoroughly.[43]

But it was time to leave this agreeable city. Dr Withrow and his party returned from Italy, and on 18 August they all departed for a journey north by way of the Rhine.

During their journey up the Rhine, they stopped to view several universities. In Heidelberg they encountered what they thought an unwarranted piece of male chauvinism. Three of them – Margaret, Charlotte, and a woman doctor from Denver – stopped in the Chancellor's office, where Margaret asked in German for a prospectus of lectures. As she wrote later to Mrs Burwash, "The learned gentleman glowered at us over his glasses, and with much disdain flung down three on the table and without a word turned his back on us. I've no doubt in his heart he wondered why three American females should trouble themselves about the University of Heidelberg – or more probably cursed the interruption."[44] Or perhaps he was merely showing scorn for a foreign accent. Margaret's German made her an interpreter for the party, but, as her sister pointed out in her letter home, she made some funny mistakes. In that letter Charlotte reflects humorously on the group:

It has been a great deal of fun being with the party. Some of them afford us much amusement. One meek quiet little woman with a troubled face looked up at us one day after she had been in the place about 36 hours and inquired what the name of the place was. One day just after Dr. Withrow had got through a long discourse on some weighty subject of interest, one lady piped up a shrill voice, "What's the name of our hotel, Dr., I've forgotten?"[45]

Margaret and Charlotte were sorry to watch these English-speaking companions depart at Cologne for Brussels and home. Canada was particularly on their minds because their brother Arthur was marrying Elizabeth Scoley on 11 September, and they would miss the wedding. Somewhat downcast, they travelled through Weimar (home of Schiller, Goethe, and Herder) to Leipzig and then on to Berlin.

Margaret and Charlotte stayed a month in Berlin, capital of Prussia and of the recently formed German Empire. Unfortunately, the diary is blank for this period, except for a long description of their hunt for a furnished lodging where they could have a piano. Charlotte planned to study music and German. Margaret too had a serious purpose: to visit some of the Prussian schools that were setting the pace for European education. Prussia had been one of the first states to provide free, universal education and to adopt some of the reforms of Pestalozzi; in 1900 it was also admired for its *polyteknikums*, which offered university-level training in engineering and chemistry. In the best schools, education included music, physical education, and manual training, just as Margaret had advocated in "Education and Our Relation to it as Graduates." She applied to the authorities for permission to visit several schools and, after long waits and fruitless encounters with Prussian bureaucrats, was finally allowed to observe the Charlottenschule, a school for daughters of the higher classes. In the essay "Glimpses of Education in Europe," she particularly praised the progress made in modern languages with quite young pupils, as well as the physical education program:

A marked feature of the school is its perfect attention, and prompt obedience. There is an entire absence of the indifference so often found in a Canadian school-room. The enthusiasm with which the German girls enter into their studies is delightful. As for gymnastics, one could not but covet for our Canadian girls the thorough training these girls have. Perhaps this is part of the secret of their power of attention. The gymnasium is large and excellently furnished. Half the hour is taken in formal drill and marching, the remainder spent somewhat informally. In the absence of a piano, the girls sing, and keep time to the words of the song. From the quaint little maidens of seven, in their odd dresses and black lustre pinafores, up to the young ladies, there is an elasticity and spontaneity of enjoyment of both work and play, with a thoroughness and calmness of character in which Canadian schools might well take lessons.[46]

More and more she was coming to believe in the interdependence of mind and body.

After a month in Berlin, a seventeen-hour train ride took them to Antwerp, where there were three days of sightseeing. Then Charlotte boarded the S.S. *Kensington* for Canada, leaving Margaret rather lonely and homesick. Soon she was to become seasick as well – her inevitable fate – as she recrossed the Channel to England by boat. She settled in the Germania Hotel near the British Museum with the intention of being a student as well as a tourist. Some of her days were to be spent in libraries; in the evenings she planned to make notes, as well as to write up her journal and dispatch postcards and voluminous letters (all but one now lost).

Imperial London in 1900 was really, as Addison described it years later to her niece Louise, "the hub of the universe."[47] There was so much to see:

Every inch seems to be historic, and one could write volumes on almost every street, and church. Verily, there are some virtues in living in a new country – one has a so much easier task to see everything and understand it. I felt as if I knew something of Berlin, but though I've been nearly three weeks in London, I feel as if I knew nothing of it yet. Oh London – big, dirty, and ugly, but for all, so interesting and liebenswürdig.[48]

Fortunately, Margaret had some acquaintances in London, and her fellow lodgers were compatible . A German actress, Elli Ramberg, took the place of Charlotte to a degree. Together they visited museums, churches, and theatres. Addison developed a great fondness for Westminster Abbey and dropped in from time to time for quiet contemplation. She viewed the colonial exhibits at the Imperial Institute and was disappointed in Ontario's display of pictures, raw materials, and undistinguished products: "A lady came in while I was there, put up her eyeglass, and remarked, 'oh seeds and things.' I felt like saying something to her, and yet she was quite justified from the exhibit in her conclusion. Do we do no manufacturing? Is all our wood crude, and our minerals too? Do we make nothing of them?"[49] Her Canadian pride was affronted in another way when she went to visit Wesley's house: the custodian, a melancholy individual, took her for an American and, on being corrected, averred that it was "all the same to us." Although Addison indignantly pointed out that "I should think it would make a great difference whether we stood fast for the old flag or went against it, and were rebels,"[50] her protestations left the man unmoved.

Addison pursued her studies mainly in the science library of the Victoria and Albert Museum and in the educational section housed separately at 52 Cannon Row, where "you may read ... from ten to five, your back to a cosy grate fire, no sound but that of the librarians and an occasional cart rumbling by."[51] Here she had access to many educational periodicals, particularly to the *Special Reports on Educational Subjects, 1896–97*, put out by the Education Department.[52] Her copious notes from this blue book reveal that her chief interest lay in the growing movement for technical education and, especially, the teaching of domestic economy to girls. Cookery was a well-established subject in the British system, the lessons suited to the needs and habits of the working people of the surrounding neighbourhood. Addison particularly noted practical methods of obtaining space and equipment; she praised the Belgian practice of having children bring mending and leftovers from home.

Adding domestic economy to the school curriculum was only one method of increasing the skills and raising the living standards of the poor. The visitor to London could hardly help noting that much needed to be done – that side by side with the imperial splendour of the capital was a depth of poverty, drunkenness, and degradation surpassing anything in the colonies. Addison was exposed to it on an occasion that should have been a happy one, the return of the City Imperial Volunteers from their service in the Boer War. A triumphal welcome had been planned for this corps (the city's contribution to the war effort), but the crowd got out of hand and surged across the parade route. The soldiers had to fight their way to their destination – something they no doubt thought they had done with – and over a thousand people were treated by the St. John Ambulance Brigade. Addison, who was caught in the East End crowd, lost her bag of refreshments and very nearly her arm. She wrote in her diary: "I couldn't but have a new reverence for a Christ who could and did *live among such creatures*, before he died for them. If they were only clean – but they were dirty, slovenly, rude, vulgar, though on the whole good-natured. The smoking was horrid, and ah me – how many men and women there would be drunk that night! Oh London, you are the greatest city of the world, but the saddest, so full of sin and degradation."[53]

Addison believed primarily in amelioration through the strengthening of individual character – by education, and especially by religious experience and devotion to the person of Christ. She was nevertheless not immune to the rising tide of sociology, which sought improvement through the correction of social conditions. Methodism had always had a strong undercurrent of social activism, particularly in temperance work: seeking holiness for themselves and others, Methodists naturally wished to remove all occasions for sin. Thus Ontario Methodism proved hospitable to the "social gospel" movement that grew up in the closing decades of the nineteenth century. This movement emphasized and reinterpreted Christianity's promise of a Kingdom of God that was to be realized on earth – not at some remote millennium, but as the working out of God's will through human history. The regime was to be characterized by justice, brotherhood, and peace, and so necessarily by harmonious social relations among different groups. Indeed, it seemed a logical extension of John Wesley's belief that individual perfection, in the sense of sinlessness, could be achieved in this world. To Methodist eyes, the Christian churches, co-operating to bring about this new social order, should logically be in the forefront of the fight for social justice; Christian values such as love and unselfishness should be incorporated into the institutional fabric of the nation.

One of the most influential proponents of this view for Canadian Methodists was Hugh Price Hughes, the British evangelical preacher who edited the *Methodist Times* and ran a mission among the poor in west London. In his *Social Christianity* he made an impassioned plea for the church's mission to eradicate slavery, drunkenness, lust, gambling, ignorance, poverty, and war.[54] Addison too could see the reasonableness of curbing drunkenness, discouraging prostitution, and working for a more equitable relationship between capital and labour. One Sunday she went to St. James's Hall, the mission Hughes ran with the help of his partner Mark Guy Pearse. She stayed for two services and heard both men preach, but, though she praised their dedication, she was ultimately repulsed by the message of class hatred she found in their condemnation of landowners and the aristocracy. "People are much to blame that London is as it is," she wrote in her diary. She added:

But is there any sense in blaming the landowners to the working men? The latter are ready now, to be censorious towards those richer than themselves, and yet, let them change places, and the poor who become rich are no better than the rich they blamed ... The ignorant are always touched personally first, and I doubt if some of those who wagged their heads in great assent do any more in proportion to their power than some of those they censure.[55]

Her reaction shows a characteristic focus on the quality of individuals rather than on systemic solutions. It also shows a dislike for violent and disruptive change, as she decried the church's descent into the political arena, where problems of partisanship were bound to arise.

Addison spent much time in London investigating other responses to poverty, such as the People's Palace, which sought to enliven and enlighten the lives of East Enders along the lines suggested in Walter Besant's *All Sorts and Conditions of Men* (1882). In this novel, an heiress in disguise erects a "Palace of Delight," educational and recreational, for the workers in Whitechapel. Among the amenities provided by the real-life counterpart of this fantasy (funded by charitable donations and opened by Queen Victoria in 1887) were free concerts and dinners, a swimming pool, a gymnasium, a library, a reading room, classes, and a children's playground.[56] Addison was also interested in the university settlement movement, an outgrowth of the social conscience of T.H. Green and his circle in Oxford. The scheme sent university students to live temporarily among the poor in settlement houses, where they led classes and offered counselling and practical help. Thus monetary charity was replaced by personal service, and the educated person used his knowledge in what Green called the gospel of active citizenship.[57] It was another example of the religious impulse expressing itself in work of a social nature. As well, Addison visited both Toynbee Hall (the Oxford and Cambridge settlement) and the Women's University Settlement at Nelson Square; her visits would bear fruit later.

By the end of October Addison was ready to go on to Oxford and Cambridge, where she would absorb the most lasting impressions of her European tour. She stayed for only a week in Cambridge – though it was one of the most memorable weeks in her life – before spending nearly five weeks in Oxford, in a family-type lodging with fellow boarders who would become her friends. She visited the most famous

men's colleges and libraries and attended public lectures and cere-
monies. The bulk of her time, though, was spent in the women's
colleges, thanks to a network of introductions and letters of reference,
and it was on these colleges that she was to base her own ideals for
women's education. Even years later, when she retired after a long
career as dean, she saw advantages in a continuing British influence.
In a private letter, she noted that those responsible for choosing her
successor might look for a Canadian dean of residence, "and a Dean
of Women about forty – *an Englishwoman*, or a Scotch or Irish graduate. I have such profound admiration for the ideals and quality of
English education, and for our women of to-morrow, I want to see
far more intellectuality."[58] In one of her dean's reports she recalled
the great impression made on her by the heads of the Oxford and
Cambridge women's colleges in 1900; she called herself "the humble
disciple of these great leaders."[59]

Ironically, Oxford and Cambridge were far from hospitable to
women scholars: unlike North American and more progressive British institutions, they did not award degrees to women. Women had
arrived there uninvited to write the local (matriculation) examinations, had stayed to study the men's curriculum independently, and
had gradually been admitted to the examinations and some of the
college lectures. Although by 1900 they were taking the same final
exams as the men, they received a certificate rather than a degree on
passing. The separate women's colleges were born of historical necessity, not of conscious preference for single-sex education: they provided lodging, and sometimes tutoring, for women who would
otherwise be completely unsupported. But they also provided,
Addison found, an atmosphere in which women thrived. A female
community with female tutors and administrators had much to offer.

Addison toured six colleges during her stay in Oxford and Cambridge: Newnham and Girton in Cambridge; and Lady Margaret Hall,
St. Hugh's, St. Hilda's, and Somerville in Oxford. Thinking constantly
about the proposed residence for women at Victoria, and half envious,
half excited about the fact that similar institutions had really been
brought to fruition here, she learned all she could. She made notes,
for instance, on the ideal design for a residence building, and on such
practical details as the best size of tables in dining halls and the provision of linen. She admired the expensive two-room suites of the
Girton girls, but saw the necessity too for the more economical rooms
at St. Hugh's College, where some of the bedrooms were double and
others too small to hold a desk. From the history of Newnham, she
learned that it would be feasible to begin in rented quarters, and she
fell to calculating a possible fee-structure in her diary.

But more important than all these housekeeping questions was the ethos of the colleges. Addison enjoyed herself immensely because she felt accepted in a society of educated women, whose kindness and courtesy almost overwhelmed her. Her reception at Newnham left her "ecstatic" and gave her a headache. "I wish I enjoyed things more moderately, for I am worn out with the intensity of my pleasure," she lamented.[60] What she responded to was a sense of dedication – consequent, no doubt, on the "garrison mentality" of the pioneering colleges. When she discussed this question with Miss Miller, a fellow lodger who had been at both the University of Chicago and Newnham, Miss Miller remarked that at Chicago not one of the dons influenced her character. "None of the women at Chicago," she explained, "seemed in earnest; they were technical and learned. At Newnham every don was in earnest." Addison agreed, writing that here, "everybody is in earnest about something, and there is a college spirit, an *esprit de corps*, which is delightful. As I look at these, I am forced to the opinion, that if there is a falling off of girls in our universities at home it is partly due to the absence of the college spirit."[61]

These colleges gave Addison an idea of the extent to which a women's residence could develop character. If in one sense it functioned as a home, providing care and quasi-parental guidance, in another it could be a cultural force, enlarging the residents' horizons and training them in social responsibility. When she returned to Canada, she described the potential of a residence in terms that echo the diary and leave no doubt that she had the English colleges in mind:

College residences for women should be centres of culture and social influence, and form a nucleus of intellectual and literary forces. They should be ideals religiously, morally, socially, intellectually, physically, and practically, of all that we would see prevail in our great and beloved Canada. We must give them the highest prestige, we must gather in them from time to time the choicest minds that are in our country. The best our country or any other can offer will be none too good. Then it will be an increasing honor to be a member of such a residence, and the resultant "esprit de corps" will be one of the strongest factors in spreading throughout our country high ideals of character, life, and education.[62]

Implicit also in these words is a suggestion that the traditional view of women's abilities needs to be enlarged. The officers of the English women's colleges seemed almost a new breed of capable, active women, and in her diary Addison tried to capture the effect of some of their strong personalities. Helen Gladstone, William Gladstone's daughter and the former vice-president of Newnham, sat next to her

Blanche Athena Clough of
Newnham College

at a dinner and "rather awed me, with her strong personality." She had, said Addison, "thought, decision of character, energy, and possibly sometimes a little intolerance, arising from the force of her opinions or prejudices."[63] Bertha Johnson, wife of a history professor, was head of the Association of Home Students in Oxford, coordinating the studies of those women not enroled in a college. "She is a tall, slight woman," noted Addison, "I should fancy a little aggressive, but good in intent. Her name and works are well known in Oxford, and she is a woman of power."[64] Another woman of power was Agnes Maitland of Somerville, who Vera Brittain felt would have made an ideal hospital matron.[65] To Addison, Maitland was "strong in her opinions, and a woman of much originality in carrying out what she desires. I would not think her particularly philosophical, or medi-tative, and not in the least given to sentiment."[66] As for Elizabeth Welsh, mistress of Girton, Addison characterized her as an older and more traditional woman, one who reminded her of her late friend Mary Electa Adams.

The women who impressed her most were Blanche Clough at Cambridge and Annie Rogers at Oxford. The former was the head of Newnham and the daughter of the poet Clough; she brought forth a rare rapture:

She says little, but that is to the point. There is a strong vein of humor, and when she smiles, it is as if one were suddenly enveloped in sunshine. There is such sweetness, such tenderness, such reserve in her face and manner – a most sensitive nature, indeed my ideal of what her father must have been. There's an inimitable charm, an indescribable attraction, a subtle bewitchery, a personal magnetism, that no pen can describe. I fell to hero worship at once, and henceforth Newnham College shines to me in rosy light because Miss Clough is there.[67]

To her amazement, Miss Clough offered to be her guide round some of the colleges and, in fact, took her sightseeing on her last day in

Cambridge: "Really, the courtesy which has been extended me makes me feel like dust and ashes."[68] Annie Rogers was the strong-minded head of the Association for the Education of Women in Oxford, and the daughter of the political economist Thorold Rogers. As the winner of an entrance scholarship as "A. Rogers," and the loser of it when she was revealed to be "Miss Rogers," she had stayed in Oxford to head the fight for women's degrees and to co-ordinate the arrangements for their tutoring. Initially rather brusque, she warmed to Addison when she discovered that the latter was not wasting her time, invited her to tea at her home, and showed her many kindnesses.

Annie Rogers of the AEW in Oxford

Reflecting on the achievements of Miss Rogers and other women, Addison questioned the received wisdom about women's characteristics. Many of the university women, she noted, had so-called masculine traits of decisiveness and executive ability; indeed, they could hardly have succeeded in their uphill task without them. Miss Rogers was called "masculine," Addison mused, but what did that really mean? – "Is it because she is so clear-headed and business-like?" She possessed unusual brain power, and keen insight, yet she was "strong, practical, common-sense, individual, business-like, and yet womanly."[69] As for Miss Clough, her face "might be almost a man's, so decided are the lines, and so strong."[70] Although Addison did not conclude that women were denatured by entering the university sphere, neither did she argue that there were no real gender differences. Her position seemed to be that those differences could not be equated with specific character traits and abilities: women could take on new roles and still remain essentially women.

Addison decided, too, that the organization of colleges such as Somerville or Girton, communities where women studied as well as lived, could not be precisely duplicated at Victoria College, where lectures were all coeducational. But perhaps some of the "atmosphere" of these colleges could be recreated by adopting their practice of appointing a strong, educated woman as head, rather than a mere chaperone. Addison was becoming more than ever convinced that residence was a necessity, and that solitary life in a boarding house while attending university provided only half an education. Her convictions were strengthened by the reading she did in the Radcliffe Camera and elsewhere among theorists of English education. Writers such as Benjamin Jowett, the reforming Master of Balliol, and Michael Sadler, one of the founders of the University Extension movement, stressed the social side of university life and the advantages to be gained from living in a society of one's peers. Sadler even argued that the real benefit of a university education for students consisted not so much in study as in "the effect on his mind of the traditions, the habits, the spirit of the place, in the undefinable influence of its history, its society, its point of view."[71] His observation was perhaps more applicable to Oxford than to Toronto, which was not steeped in a great deal of ancient tradition. Sometimes Addison despaired of emulating the spirit of Oxford, with its venerable architecture, magnificent libraries, and cultured discourse. Still, one could but make a start, and even in Toronto one might plant an intellectual community whose traditions would develop over time.

As Addison wrote the final pages of her Oxford journal, she reflected on her tendency to pursue too seriously, and exclusively, whatever occupied her mind. "I must find some sort of relaxation," she wrote all too prophetically, "– something that will occupy my thoughts and help me forget, for a few hours each day, the seriousness of living. I think I must try to find recreation in something out of doors, and something gymnastic."[72] And how did she address that serious part? "How I should like to do something for the education of my own country," she writes after ordering Alice Zimmern's history of the English colleges, *The Renaissance of Girls' Education in England;* "but when I look around, and see the advantages others have had, which I have not, my hopes grow rather small."[73] This is the closest she comes to suggesting, in a backhanded way, that she might have certain hopes – ambitions would be too strong a word. It is hard to believe that the thought of becoming dean of the planned Victoria residence had never crossed her mind. Yet she is typically restrained and decorous in not admitting it, perhaps even to herself. As will be apparent when the offer finally came, she was not one to depart radically from the religious and social norms of her society, which frowned on self-seeking in women. Not for her the boldness of her contemporary H. Carey Thomas, president of Bryn Mawr, who declared frankly in a letter to her mother that "I should love to have the presidentship of Bryn Mawr" and that she was the best possible choice for the position.[74] It is quite likely that Addison had set out on her tour with the submerged consciousness that, were she called upon to play some role, she would at least have garnered the necessary background and experience. But the rest, she left in the hands of God.

CHAPTER FOUR

Towards a New Career

The telegram received in Oxford read simply, "Will you accept Lindsay?" After a split second of wondering who Lindsay was, Addison realized that she had been offered an appointment teaching modern languages at Lindsay Collegiate Institute (some one hundred kilometres northeast of Toronto), beginning in January 1901.[1] It was more than ever necessary to leave Oxford before Christmas – which she did with some reluctance, so enlightening had been her stay. "Oh that every woman I know might visit Oxford, might travel, might have money and leisure to drink in a little of the wealth of learning, scholarship, and character to be found in classic Oxford," she wrote in her diary. "What delights me most is the fact that learning and character go hand in hand."[2] Travel enlarged the horizons, she was convinced; she even toyed with the dream of establishing scholarships to send deserving people abroad, or, in the regrettable absence of money, leading foreign tours herself, like a well-paid female Dr Withrow. Meanwhile, cramming into her trunk and a supplementary satchel all her belongings and purchases, including forty-two gifts for her friends, she set off for Liverpool and the ship home.

The first days of Addison's voyage were spent – as she had dreaded – being seasick. But when she was able to get up and look around, she cast a sharp eye on the company aboard. The *Lake Champlain* had been given a tremendous send-off in Liverpool because it was carrying 260 homebound Canadian soldiers, the remainder of the First Contingent of volunteers that Canada had sent to the Boer War. Although Addison was not markedly political, like the majority of English-speaking Canadians she supported the British in their struggle against the Boers; like many, she saw the growth of the British Empire as a means of introducing justice and the rule of law into backward areas. She had watched two war-related parades in London and gone to see Lord Valentia honoured with the freedom of Oxford for his contribution to the war. Now she enjoyed the company of the officers – a jolly group, except for the morose commander, Col. Otter, who "minds his own business, and says nothing to anyone."[3] Addison had no way of knowing that the probable cause of his discontent lay in the insubordination, looting, and general unprofessionalism among his volunteer troops, whose conduct had been far less valiant than their image suggested.[4] She did, however, exercise her satiric perception on the polite but relentless jockeying for status among the few women saloon passengers.[5] On 23 December the ship reached Halifax, and on Christmas morning her father and Charlotte met her at the station in Toronto.

Her mother was able to accompany her to Lindsay on 3 January 1901 and, after a brief stay with friends, to see her settled in comfortable lodgings at the house of a Mr Bones. Lindsay was a pleasant small town – praised, indeed, by the biographer of Lindsay Collegiate Institute (c.i.)'s next principal as a town with a warm and friendly communal life, where "men and women whose intellectual capacity and judgment, kept stable by a leisurely and healthy life, were in vital contact with contemporary thought and slowly mediated that thought to the community at large."[6] Addison did find much friendliness, though at first she had trouble locating the thought. Her social life, she characterized as lacking in wide views. "How shall one talk to people who are nice, pleasant, and refined, but whose conversation is entirely personal?" she wondered in her diary. But she recognized that her own peculiarities were partly to blame; that her earnest avoidance of the personal – by which she meant both gossip and egotistical absorption in one's own affairs – made her somewhat daunting to talk to and deprived her of the normal small change of social intercourse. As she wrote in the diary,

I have little social instinct, and no social gifts, hence I have been trying to school myself into being a good listener, and taking my proper share of conversation. But the way is a hard one. Most people are not interested in what interests me, and I don't seem to have the tact to find out what interests them. They all ask how I like Lindsay, and the school. I enlarge on these, and then usually I am wildly hunting about in my mind for something to talk about next. The atmosphere of the town, the district, the weather come in next, and then I am floored. Well! I daresay the practice is good, and perhaps I ought to go to the places, and do the things that interest others, so as to know what to say.[7]

Besides trying to improve her social manner, Margaret resolved to provide her own intellectual food and strengthen her mind. She was too emotional, she wrote in her diary, and should temporarily read fewer devotional books: "I want to train my head now, for a time, and my will – both need training sadly." She decided to write fewer letters, to read a little solid history every day, and to become better acquainted with British and Canadian literature. Unfortunately, her diary breaks off on 27 April, just after she had declared that the rest of it was to be devoted to her thoughts on life and education. But it would not be fair to conclude that her mind was barren; rather, as so often happened, she became caught up in schemes and projects that left her no time to elaborate on her theories in writing. Most of her energy went into teaching, of course, but the documentary evidence that survives concerns two extracurricular activities: the physi-

Margaret Addison
in the Lindsay period

cal education movement, and the Victoria women's residence. Both provided her with what she loved, a combination of idealism and practical action.

The Lindsay Ladies' Physical Culture Association was the creation of a group of Lindsay women, including Addison, who wanted to improve the health and well-being of women and girls. "We believe the question of Physical Culture as much as that of Domestic Science is the question of this century," wrote Addison in late 1901 to Mrs Burwash, who shared her views.[8] Physical education for college women was well established in other institutions as a counterpoise to the Victorian superstition that brain work weakened the female frame and drew vital energy away from the reproductive organs. In the American colleges, for instance, gyms and programs had accompanied the admission of women, while, at Oxford, Addison had been assured that there was "little difficulty in inducing the girls to take exercise as public opinion is so strong on that point."[9] At Victoria, the VWREA had been providing gymnastics in an informal way to Victoria women since the spring of 1900. In the fall of 1900, they had hired as a regular instructress Mrs Scott Raff, an enterprising young widow with a varied training in the dramatic and expressive arts – including painting, drama, elocution, and movement – who was then teaching a number of pupils in Toronto.[10] By the fall of 1901, a

Margaret with her mother and
her sister Charlotte around 1900

basement room at Victoria had been turned into a gym, with apparatus provided by Mrs Cox. At this time, or shortly after, Mrs Scott
Raff with Dr Burwash's help established a School of Physical Culture
and Expression near Yonge and Bloor Streets. It was sometimes
referred to as the Victoria School of Expression, although its relation
to the college is somewhat problematical: in the same classes were
Victoria women, independent students, and professional students of
expression. There Victoria women could take classes in voice culture
and English literature as well as in gymnastics.[11]

Happy with the progress of the college women, Mrs Burwash on
behalf of the VWREA "lent" Mrs Scott Raff to Lindsay several times
a week to set up the fledgling enterprise. The association arranged a
fee structure that included an honourary $1 membership for men
who wanted to help with expenses, hired a room over the YWCA (then
a religious, not an athletic organization), and by February of 1902
had eighty townspeople enroled in classes.

Mrs Scott Raff seemed an ideal teacher, believing as she did in a
"Greek" fusion of physical, moral, and mental development and in
the freeing of bodily energies for artistic expression. The Martha
Graham of Ontario, she flitted amongst her tweedy contemporaries
in flowing robes, long ropes of wooden beads, and sandals. It is
unclear to what extent she was able, in Lindsay, to deploy her full
Delsartian program, but certainly her physical education classes had
an aesthetic and spiritual component. "Surely God has sent us Mrs.
Raff!" wrote Addison to Mrs Burwash in the first flush of enthusiasm.
(Later in their long association she may not have been so grateful to
God.) Mrs Raff, she continued, has shown the Lindsay women the

Margaret with her mother and her brother Will

idealistic side of what had started out as a practical endeavour, and left behind her "the sweet aroma of a pure, lovely, Christlike woman-hood."[12] Later, Addison remarked that "her sympathy and sweet personality, her idealism, and her self-sacrificing spirit have done for us here, what could not have been touched but for her."[13] By 1903, when Mrs Scott Raff was busy with her other enterprises, her assistant Florence E. Walton went to Lindsay three days a week and did very satisfactory work.[14]

At the same time as she was addressing groups to organize support for the physical education movement, Addison was busy with the Victoria residence project, which, since her trip to Europe, had taken on a more tangible reality. Some members of the VWREA favoured the idea of renting a building, as the founders of Newnham and Girton had done; or of renting a men's playing field and building a residence in the space now occupied by the alley- (or hand-ball-) board. But rents were high, and the board of regents favoured purchasing more land. Fortunately, by April 1901, the University of Toronto's President Loudon had a change of heart and agreed to sell the coveted four acres north of Czar Street. In a tremendous boost to the VWREA's fund-raising efforts, Mrs Cox agreed to give $20,000 to the church's Twen-tieth Century Fund, provided that half be used for the purchase of this property; Victoria then secured the property for what seems today like a modest $55,000.[15] The women's residence was to occupy the western portion of this land, and the men's campus the eastern. The name of Barbara Heck having been respectfully shelved, it was eventually decided to call the new residence "Annesley Hall," in honour of Susanna Annesley Wesley, mother of John and Charles Wesley. The Methodist community revered her as an exemplar of pious and productive womanhood, apparently unaware that she was a tartar, who practically crucified her unfortunate daughter in an effort to subdue her will – at least if radicals such as W.J. Fox and John Stuart Mill are to be believed.[16]

There is little documentation of the building of Annesley Hall, although the few notes that survived suggest that the VWREA was not much involved in the planning process. In fact, Addison seems to have had no occasion to discuss what she had learned in England about the best form of a residence, such as the advice of Miss Maitland of Somerville who felt that to ensure airiness, one should build in small quadrangles – with passages running alongside the quad and the windows of students' rooms opening to the outside. A small committee of the board of regents, understandably including Hart Massey's sons Chester Daniel Massey and Walter Edward Hart Massey along with Dr. Burwash, undertook the whole matter. They chose as architect George Martell Miller, a Canadian who had been in practice for some fifteen years and who was later to design the very different Lillian Massey Building next door, as well as other distinguished buildings. In consultation with the committee he drew up his plans by the fall of 1901, and tenders were called for. On 29 April 1902, Chester Massey laid the cornerstone of the new building.

Annesley Hall was built during the years 1902–03 for an opening in the fall of 1903. Miller had chosen the architectural style known as Queen Anne Revival, which was especially favoured for domestic architecture, and which had been used in many of the large houses on the east side of Queen's Park. Based loosely on British domestic architecture of the Tudor and Stuart periods, it has been characterized as "colourful, cheerful, comfortable, undogmatic, dedicated to charm and homely pleasures."[17] Among the features adopted by Miller were an asymmetrical front with one wing projecting more than the other, bay windows, prominent gables reminiscent of Flemish architecture and echoed in the smaller gables above the dormer windows, freestone trimmings ornamenting rich red brick, a steep roof line, prominent ribbed chimney stacks, and the fanciful round turret that was a hallmark of the style. At the back were shady verandahs; at the front a semicircular carriage drive swept over a tree-dotted lawn. The facade was surely pleasing to Addison, as it united graciousness with a welcoming aspect (thus suggesting the ideal of home), while at the same time its banks of Tudor windows provided the light and air so important in an institution. Most important, it had a vaguely English

Annesley Hall on the occasion of a royal visit, 1905

appearance and, in fact, rather recalled the beloved and exemplary Newnham College, erected starting in 1872 during the early phases of the Queen Anne Revival in England.[18]

Inside, the design of the residence was equally pleasing. Like a stately house, it had an imposing entrance hall surrounded by a sitting room, library, music room, assembly hall, and dining room, while a double staircase curved up to the first floor. There were about fifty rooms for students opening on to the wide halls of the first and second floors. Contemporary descriptions pass over the bathrooms in silence, but certainly they existed. In the basement, besides utilities and laundry, was a gym with showers and dressing rooms. A wing on the north housed kitchens designed with help from the new Lillian Massey Normal Training School of Household Science, with servants' quarters above it, and above that an infirmary that could be isolated from the main building. There were also quarters and offices for the dean and the director of the household. All modern comforts were laid on: electric light, steam heating by radiators, fan-driven ventilating flues, and even an elevator in the service wing.

Although passed over when it came to structural questions, the women were nevertheless deeply involved with the plans for decorating, furnishing, and managing, which began long before the residence was completed. In the summer of 1901, Mrs Burwash went to England to tour the women's residential colleges, as Addison had done. The VWREA formed a furnishing committee and redoubled their fundraising efforts; fortunately, Margaret Eaton agreed to furnish and equip the dining room at her own expense, Mrs Hart Massey did the lower hall, and Mrs Chester Massey did the reception room. The Alumnae Association too had a furnishing committee, on which Addison served, writing letters asking past graduates for donations. A favourite device was the "dime treasury" in which modest contributions from schoolchildren could be slotted. Eventually the alumnae agreed to be responsible for the furnishing of the library. Margaret's brother Will helped with the tenders for this and made a handsome contribution, promising a further $25 if the shelves were of the best quality.[19] The Alumnae Association was quite active at this time: in September 1901, at Addison's suggestion, they also embarked on collecting the materials for a history of the education of women in the Methodist Church. The project, which eventually resulted in a 1905 essay by Addison in *Acta*,[20] further developed her stamina as a letter writer, as she appealed to alumnae for their recollections of college life.

In September 1902, the Victoria University Board of Regents authorized the creation of a women's committee of management to supervise the residence. Under its constitution, members were to be nominated by the VWREA (subject to the board's confirmation) and to serve for three years, one-third retiring annually. Retiring members could be re-elected, and generally were, so that the committee's composition varied little from year to year. They were given the power to nominate the dean or head of residence, the housekeeper, and other officers (subject again to the board's approval); to hire the domestic staff; and to fix their duties and salaries. Thus, at the outset the personnel of the residence were responsible to the committee, not to the dean – an arrangement which led to difficulties and struggles for power until resolved in 1912. The committee was to make regulations for the government of the students in the residence, subject this time to the approval of the senate and president. It was to be in charge of the finances and responsible for the equipment and upkeep of the grounds and buildings. Theoretically, these women had a good deal of power over the dean.

Was it a signal of things to come that Addison herself was not made a member of this body? It was not a specifically academic group, being composed, like the VWREA itself, of women who had a special interest in the education of Victoria women: seventeen in all, to be chosen from among graduates, wives of professors, women of means, representatives of churches, and miscellaneous others. Addison through her activism had earned a place in the group, had she not been a possible candidate for dean in the minds of the VWREA. It was true, however, that in practice its composition understandably favoured wealth. It drew on prosperous middle-class Methodists, particularly on that group of interlocking entrepreneurial families who were leaders equally in the church, the college, business, and social life in Toronto. The surviving children of Hart Massey were all represented, Mrs Lillian Massey Treble serving along with her two brothers' wives, Mrs W.E.H. Massey and Mrs C.D. Massey. The wives of prominent businessmen included Margaret Eaton, wife of Timothy; Mrs Kemp, wife of sheet-metal manufacturer and politician Sir Albert Kemp; Clara Flavelle, married to Joseph Flavelle of William Davies meat packers; Hannah Fudger, wife of businessman H.H. Fudger; and Mrs G.A. Cox, whose husband Senator Cox was president of, among others, the Bank of Commerce and Canada Life Assurance Company. Fudger, Flavelle, and Cox formed a veritable Methodist mafia, if such an oxymoron can be imagined, meeting on the Victoria Board of Regents; on the Methodist Board of Missions; on financial boards where they provided various underwriting, loan, and insurance services to each other; and at Sherbourne Street Methodist Church. No doubt they dined together at Simpsons, which Flavelle and Fudger owned.[21] Links between Cox and the Masseys included their participation in the forming of the Canadian Cycle Manufacturing Company in 1899 at the height of the cycling craze. In March 1904, when Mrs C.D. Massey died, she was replaced on the committee by Mrs E.R. Wood, wife of the financier and investment dealer who was another key player in the Flavelle and Massey enterprises.

These women – who were no mean workers on the VWREA themselves, being tireless speakers, letter writers, and fundraisers – through their connections ensured that the women's side of Victoria was linked to the corridors of wealth and power. Unfortunately, the natural corollary was that the establishment, with its conservative notions of decorum, gained a preponderant influence, a situation which would give trouble later. In a continuing tradition among those well-to-do families who cared about Victoria, the husband would serve on the board of regents, the wife on the committee of management; thus were Mrs D.E. Sutherland and Mrs J.R.L. Starr (the former Louise Nelles, Vic 9T7) appointed. Other members of the committee included representatives of prominent church families (Mrs Carman, wife of the general superintendent, and Mrs Courtice, wife of the editor of the *Christian Guardian*); representatives of the college (Mrs Burwash, and Mrs Bain, wife of Professor Abraham Bain); and Annie Le Rossignol, an active graduate of 1896, who was the sole unmarried woman. Mrs Burwash served as president.

While Annesley Hall was rising, this committee and the VWREA laid plans for the manner of life within. Most notable perhaps was the mandatory program of physical culture, for which Mrs Scott Raff

The sitting room at Annesley Hall

had been made supervisor (though not formally appointed by the board of regents until November 1903). The committee hired a female physician, Dr Lelia Davis, to oversee all matters of health and physical education. She was a lecturer in histology at the Ontario Medical College for Women and the first of several distinguished female practitioners to be associated with the residence: the next doctor, Helen MacMurchy, was one of the founders of Women's College Hospital, and her successor in 1920, Dr Edna Guest, was to become Chief of Surgery at Women's College, 1926–31. Every resident was required to have a complete examination by Dr Davis and to take appropriate exercise either in the gym or via activities such as basketball, tennis, and skating.

The gymnastic program was perhaps less ambitious than its director would have liked, owing to a disagreement the previous year. The program sponsored at the college by the VWREA involved a Swedish type of rhythmic gymnastics, which expanded very naturally into more artistic forms of expression such as movement to poetry, elocution, and music. At the time it had seemed an enrichment of the narrow bounds of college life. But even at its introduction, some members of the VWREA had opposed the program, especially the Chown family. In a letter to Mrs Burwash, Alice Chown of the Canadian Household Economics Association argued that the course suggested training for a particular profession (presumably for the diploma that the university offered to prospective teachers of gymnastics and physical drill). Besides, she continued, it was hopelessly superficial because of the nature of Mrs Scott Raff herself; her niece Mabel, a recent graduate, had complained to her about Mrs Scott Raff's "constant desire to train for poses and effects."[22] This was an unfair criticism of the woman who tried to expose her students to the symbolist drama of Yeats, Strindberg, and Ibsen and who later put on some of the earliest Toronto productions of Irish Abbey Theatre works, though it was true that she believed that "all culture should carry with it a bread-winning power."[23] But the Chowns' criticism was based not just on disapproval of Mrs Scott Raff but on a belief (albeit a minority one on the committee) that the organized training of college women should be restricted to the intellectual sphere.

In November 1902, Victoria women themselves had embraced this view, sending a petition to the board of regents protesting against the Department of Expression. It was, they contended, not a true university-level enterprise, as students of no academic standing could enter, the instructress herself had no degree though she had faculty rank, and the course of studies was not approved by the senate. Consequently, they argued, the Department of Expression could be "a serious menace to the academic standing of Victoria University" as it became more widely identified with the college.[24] By arguing in this way, they set themselves against the views of the majority of the committee, who believed that education should involve all the faculties. Perhaps they objected less to physical education as such than to Scott Raff's poetical slant on it, which seemed to them, perhaps mistakenly, reminiscent of the "accomplishments" curriculum foisted upon women in lieu of more solid fare.

The VWREA, naturally hurt at the students' rejection of their efforts, thought they should have been consulted before the complaint was taken to the board. The upshot of joint discussions was a decree by the board of regents that no study other than physical culture be approved for the new residence.[25] Thus the possibility of introducing innovative programs was severely curtailed at the outset. The committee nevertheless did what it could to provide for a well-rounded education: besides sponsoring physical education, it collected books and magazine subscriptions for the library and art to hang on the walls.

The building of Annesley Hall aroused intense interest among the Victoria students, both male and female. The women looked forward to abandoning the "almost unavailing search for comfortable quarters within reasonable distance of the College,"[26] and the isolation of boarding-house life. As Dr Withrow put it, college days seem less rosy in memory "when part of your college career was lived in the back-room over some one's kitchen, with the gray cat on the back fence for a companion to your thoughts, and the washerwoman's voice talking to the curly dog on the steps below."[27] The men greeted the new structure with a characteristic blend of reverence and jocularity. "Some have hinted that the police, who were formerly guarding the safety of His Excellency and Lady Minto at the Flavelle residence, will be distributed about the various corridors during next October," intimated *Acta*. "The Local Editor would suggest that this is not necessary; it would involve needless expense. We have College men who are large of stature ... who would probably undertake the job."[28]

On 19 May 1903, Mrs Burwash took the culminating step in organizing the residence: she phoned Addison on behalf of the committee of management asking her to let her name stand as their choice for dean of residence. As suggested, the offer was probably not a complete surprise. Yet prevailing mores, as well as Addison's own predisposition, had militated against her actively seeking the post, or even admitting to herself that it might be offered. She was only too aware of her shortcomings. Her experiences in Lindsay had convinced her, whether or not she had known it before, that she was not strong in the social graces – an important consideration at a time when women's education had to be seen to keep women womanly. However, the lack of such graces was not an insuperable obstacle. "A knowledge of the small points of etiquette" could be acquired, as Mrs Bain had pointed out some years ago, when Addison was apparently considering becoming principal of a girls' school. "My dear Miss Addison," she had written reassuringly, "if there should be any lack in the latter – from lack of opportunity – I am sure you have all [the] necessary foundation to build on and only need to observe in order to be fully equipped."[29]

Less easy to achieve were inner and spiritual gifts – strength of character, and depth of religious faith – without which, Addison was convinced, the residence could never rise to its full potential. Addison's ideals for a dean were extraordinarily high. The English women's colleges were impressive, she noted, because their heads were no mere matrons or housekeepers, but women of character and intellectual attainments. In her speech of 1901 to the VWREA, she had sketched some of the qualities a Canadian residence should seek in its principal. A principal should be a woman of culture, she declared, accustomed to society, acquainted with educational theory, and in contact with the best minds of our universities and society. Of course, she must also be capable of running a large household. A principal, she continued, should be at the same time masterful, charismatic, and sympathetic: "She should have that rare gift of personal magnetism, should be of strong, decided character, yet loving and tender-hearted." Above all, she must be a Christian, one who enjoys "an actual and dominating sense of the constant presence of God."[30] Even in her private notebook she did not venture to think that she herself filled this bill:

Between working spaces, I have thought and thought over our Women's Residence, and many leisure moments have been devoted to putting on paper my ideal of what it should be and do, and what the Principal ought to be. Miss Stover recurs frequently to me as the nearest to my ideal of any I can think of. Miss Kenny is extremely clever, self-possessed, would think things out well, and would give social prestige. I question however, whether she has the warmth of nature, the sympathy and self-sacrifice which would make the institution reach its best. That, Miss Stover has in a marked degree.[31]

No doubt it would have seemed presumptuous to consider herself close to the ideal, or to have made practical plans for a response should an offer arrive.

All sorts of doubts had still to be overcome, then, practical as well as psychological. Addison hesitated to give up teaching, which she loved, in exchange for duties that were somewhat nebulous. She also had to balance the pain of leaving Lindsay, where she had been so happy, against the advantages of living in Toronto, close to her parents in their declining years. And then there was the money. When Mrs Burwash phoned, she said that the salary was $500 a year plus residence. Addison, who had been receiving $1000 a year at Lindsay, wrote in her diary that it was hardly reasonable to ask her to take such a drastic reduction in pay; she thought that $800 plus residence might be an acceptable offer. After much prayer, she concluded that she might do it for $700 and residence.[32] Mrs Burwash went back to the committee of management, and on 6 June she wrote that they had agreed to guarantee this sum, at least for the next year, if Addison would accept their offer of the deanship.[33]

When Addison finally did accept, it was with humble conscious-ness of her "imperfections and limitations": "my tendency to hasty judgment when all the data for decision is not yet given or carefully thought out, my tendency to irritability, my impatience, and the lack of the foresight which makes a good statesman."[34] Carolyn Heilbrun has pointed out how women until recently have felt constrained to label ambition or a high self-estimate as unfeminine; they could justify their assuming a prominent place only by believing that God had insisted on it. For women such as Joan of Arc and Florence Nightingale, then, the voice of God was a physical call.[35] One can certainly see this mechanism at work in Addison's case. "If I had in any way sought the position," she wrote in her notebook, "or done anything to procure it, I might enter on the duties with a different attitude. I am sure I should be overcome with fear and trembling. As it is, God graciously removes all fear, I feel *so* sure it is He is sending me, and that I have nothing to do but to say yes to His bidding."[36]

In truth the committee had chosen well. She *was* the person for the job, with her strong ties to the church and her belief in progress, her intelligence and sympathy, her idealistic vision and (as would appear later) a certain toughness in fighting for her rights. Certainly, she would give her all to it over the next twenty-eight years. Through her faith she was able to overcome her hesitations and to enter her new sphere serenely: "So I assume the new and increased responsibilities with perfect faith in God, knowing He will keep me, and give me wisdom in all I have to do."[37]

Toronto had changed considerably since 1891, when Addison had boarded for some months with Mrs Hay on Brunswick Avenue while attending the School of Pedagogy. For instance, the very next year the streetcars had been electrified, greatly increasing the mobility of an expanding population. Then in 1897 – despite fierce opposition from the Protestant churches – a plebiscite allowed these streetcars to run on Sundays in the first breach of Toronto's funereally quiet and godly "Lord's Day."[38] Immigrants and native Canadians had continued to pour into the city, filling up vacant lots east of the Don Valley and west around the Humber River. Along with streets of modest dwellings were prestigious avenues that housed the mansions of the rich: Sherbourne Street, Jarvis Street, Queen's Park Crescent, and St. George Street. An imposing new city hall, built in 1899, proclaimed the importance of a metropolis whose population in 1900 topped 200,000 and which was rapidly consolidating its position as a manufacturing, financial, and governmental hub for the province. Contemporary pictures suggest that it was an unlovely city strewn with dumps, yards, and building lots; festooned with hydro wires and hoardings, its streets were at times ankle-deep in mud. It was an alien environment for a young woman who had spent her thirty-four years in peaceful small towns. That first year in Toronto, Addison had a great deal of difficulty coming to terms with the uncongenial atmosphere of the city. As she wrote to a friend, "The commercial spirit, the suspiciousness, the tendency to believe in nothing that has not its root in self-interest – these things, not perhaps so much in individuals as in the collection of them, have filled me with doubt and dismay."[39]

Annesley Hall, her new home, was on the northern extension of Queen's Park Crescent, at that time called North Park Drive. On the east side of the park, East Park Drive traced a gentle curve of gracious homes inhabited by some of Toronto's wealthiest citizens; west of the park, southbound travellers turned at Hoskin Avenue and only narrow paths led down to University College. North Park Drive, broad and sandy and flanked by a grass boulevard and sidewalk, was still used more by horse-drawn carriages than by that new phenomenon, the motor car. Across the drive from Annesley were the imposing mansions of A.H. Campbell, E.R. Wood, and Joseph Flavelle; behind them, gardens and terraces sloped down to a wooded ravine where until recently the Taddle Creek had flowed.[40]

Potentially, Annesley Hall was a gracious and efficient residence. In practice, it presented a chaotic appearance all that summer of 1903, given the builders' and carpenters' strike in late July that halted all work on the interior, after completion of the basic shell. Addison had moved in – to a room on the third floor, which she found airy – as had the residence's housekeeper, Helen Scott of Ottawa, appointed in late 1902. In the midst of a litter of abandoned sawhorses, shavings, and half-empty paintpots, Addison set herself to her main preliminary task of letting the rooms, the endless difficulties of which preoccupied her during the whole of the summer. A committee that included the housekeeper and the head of the Lillian Massey School had set a schedule of fees that took into consideration the size of the rooms, as well as their aspect, light, and so on, to produce eleven price categories ranging from $120 to $200 a year. Fifteen rooms were in the mid-range of $165; only four rooms were to be doubles.

When news of these prices reached the Victoria women, consternation reigned. An average of about $5 a week for room and board! Did not most Vic women – and some of them the daughters of hardworking and underpaid ministers, at that – usually pay $3.50 a week, and did not the YWCA manage while charging a mere $2.50 for its lowest-priced rooms? Indignant letter writers sometimes leaned heavily on the moral argument in their missives to the dean. "Even if the parents of some of us would, by sacrificing their own comforts, pay that for us, do you think we would be justified in letting them do so? I think we would be unworthy of an education if we were so selfish," wrote Greta Peterson in August 1903. Others noted that the most deserving would be barred, and the long-awaited residence would fail in its purpose. Edith Weekes, who was in her last year, wrote quite bitterly and outspokenly about the "utter folly" of the high prices that would keep out all but the wealthy. She then took the moral argument even further: "And even if I had the money myself, I could not spend it thus, when there are so many needy in the world – when the missionary cause is constantly hampered for lack of funds. An extra $1.50 per week would mean nearly $50 and that would support a Bible woman. Ten of us by saving that amount could support a missionary in China." Addison answered this letter pacifically, in effect thanking Edith for sharing her thoughts, pointing out the need for a spirit of helpfulness and thoughtfulness, and offering her one of the scholarships that had been earmarked for cases of need. Edith, heaped with coals of fire, wrote back to apologize for a letter that was written in bitter disappointment, and "which you were considerate enough to designate merely as 'frank.'"[41]

Addison wrote letter after letter, thus gaining a foretaste of her future life. She explained that the YWCA was open all year instead of a mere thirty-three weeks and, besides, could draw on revenue from transients, who paid a higher price. She pointed out that the Annesley rate included physical culture, a medical examination, and the use of the library and all furnishings except for bath towels and napkin rings. She reiterated that physical culture was part of the regime and that the girls could not save money by dropping it. She wrote to girls who wanted to bring their own pianos, assuring them that there would be practice rooms with pianos, and that practice time could be booked at reasonable rates. She answered numerous queries from girls or their parents or guardians worried about the size of the offered room, its orientation, the view from the windows, and even – a consideration unlikely to arise in a men's residence – the colour of the walls. In painstaking longhand, she sent each applicant a description of the rooms available, outlining their advantages and drawbacks.

The meagre result of all this correspondence was that, by 1 September, only five rooms had been let. Disaster loomed. Fortunately, the month of September brought families from all over southern Ontario to Toronto for the Exhibition, at which time they also toured the residence and registered their daughters. By the end of September, thanks partly to making a few more rooms into doubles – they were the cheapest and most in demand – all but six rooms were spoken for. The carpenters had taken up their tools, though belatedly, and managed to get at least the dining room into usable shape. The last of the beds were delivered on 30 September, the day before their occupants were due to arrive. There was enough in place to sustain life, though for the next six weeks the residence would be filled with the sound of workmen's hammers and the smell of turpentine and paint as the ground floor rooms were finished. Under the students' eyes these rooms were transformed: wood was stained and polished, flowery curtains were hung, and furniture and finishing touches were added according to the designs of the committee of management. During October the last six rooms were let, resulting in a complement of forty Victoria undergraduates and fifteen others (who paid an extra $10 a year) from University College or the Conservatory of Music. Construction was finished, the occupants were stowed inside, and the ark was ready to set forth.

CHAPTER FIVE

Early Days of the Residence

The first few years at Annesley Hall were not plain sailing. The residence was a pioneering venture; there was nothing else of its size and scope in Canada to provide a model. It is true that both the Royal Victoria College in Montreal and St. Hilda's in Toronto predate Annesley Hall, but these were different in nature: they were small residential colleges for women that originally incorporated teaching functions, on the English pattern.[1] The tradition of the "college girl" and her "dorm" was American, stemming mainly from the private universities and exercising only an indirect influence across the border.[2] Addison knew that the task of shaping a community out of fifty-five young women – let alone moulding their characters and touching their spirits, her ultimate goal – would involve a series of adjustments, trials, and inevitable errors. She thought originally that it would take three years to establish a system of administration, and she was not far wrong; it was actually four years before the residence was on what she considered a sound footing, with its inner life beginning to develop.[3]

Addison had drawn up a daily schedule for residence life, with a rising bell at 6:45, breakfast at 7:20, lunch at 12:45, and dinner at 6:15. There were two ten-minute prayer sessions, one after breakfast and one after lunch. The house lights were put out at 10:00 p.m., and all student lights were to be extinguished by 11:00. The one telephone was considered to be private, but seniors were allowed to use it for an hour in the evening between 7:00 and 8:00; at other times, the maids would send and receive phone messages on behalf of the students. On Saturdays, the residents could use the laundry for washing by hand.

Two periods of the day – 8:10 to 8:40, and 11:00 to 11:30 – were set aside for physical culture in the gymnasium, where Mrs Scott Raff, with her limited mandate, did her best to develop grace and mind-body coordination as well as strength. Perhaps she tended to overestimate the power of gymnastics: "The short girls have been given special work in extension, and are working for greater height," she wrote in her 1905–6 report, "while the tall girls are working for corresponding breadth."[4] But she was ahead of her time in introducing exercises in relaxation and scientific breathing. Addison joined the forward movement – after a sharp tussle with Dr Burwash – by allowing the girls to discard their long skirts in the gym in favour of simple gym tunics, later described as *Ladies' Home Journal* pattern #1690, view "Bathing Costume."[5] Other exercise was available on the skating rink that was set up in winter on the new campus area to the east of Annesley Hall. Here on Friday nights a band played, and young men would ask young women to skate – the closest the Methodists came to dancing, and as such an exhilarating occupation. Dancing itself was somewhat tamely imitated by "promenades" on official occasions, when couples walked about arm in arm while the band played a number.

Of course, there were rules and regulations. Every institution needs them, but particularly a women's residence at a time when boarding houses locked their front doors at 11 o'clock, and even more particularly a residence erected by subscriptions from the Methodist church. Addison tried to explain to the students the underlying purpose of these rules. "If rules and regulations stand by themselves," she argued in one of her typical speeches, "without any relationship to a larger world, they are meaningless, and every wholesome minded student must be in revolt against them, and every right-minded Dean bored to death by them."[6] But by encouraging courtesy and consideration, reducing the friction apt to occur in unregulated conglomerations of individuals, and developing a community spirit, continued Addison, rules could function to prepare girls for life in the community. Her belief was that in a regular and orderly environment, the soul could blossom. Addison hoped that the daily life of the hall would be gracious and dignified, as in a well-run home. She would have responded warmly to Yeats's wish, in "A Prayer for My Daughter," for a home

Where all's accustomed, ceremonious ...
How but in custom and in ceremony
Are innocence and beauty born?[7]

Thus dinner – the chief communal event – was a formal meal for which the girls were expected to change. They gathered in the assembly room, until the dean and officers arrived, and followed them into the dining room – waiting at the door for the dean's nod if they arrived late. Grace was said before they sat down. They sat till all had finished, theoretically enjoying a leisurely meal with courteous conversation. Each year the dean explained to the incoming girls that it was bad form during the meal to discuss the food, the servants, or personalities. After dinner all took coffee together in the common room. For the sake of harmonious community living, absolute quiet was required in the halls after 10:00 p.m. and the students were to wear slippers; for the sake of graciousness, no kimonos or nightwear were to be seen in the public area downstairs.

Some rules were really moral safeguards, designed to guard propriety and discourage nascent Bohemianism. Unfortunately, the rules curtailing freedom of movement – with their underlying purpose of controlling sexuality – became identified with the residence in the eyes of many, both then and now. They were the focus of endless skirmishes between conservatives, progressives, and rebels, as new standards for the behaviour of women took shape. The dean was at the centre of these controversies, with conflicting loyalties, to both students and college authorities. For many years, the rules were a tiresome drain on her energies.

It is not clear who actually drew up the initial rules, though the committee of management had the ultimate authority to do so. Mrs Burwash had remarked as early as April 1901, when talk of possible "restrictions" had first surfaced, that the supervisory group of women (at that time the VWREA) were not experts in college life; she feared "crude ideals being dogmatically enforced" if they tried to make the rules themselves. Their role was rather to "work to provide the residence with the necessary furnishing(s), and whatever is necessary for carrying it on, and then unitedly support the principal in her methods and ideals."[8] Later, in answer to a request for a copy of the rules, Addison told a student that she was unable to formulate them until the students arrived and she saw what was needed.[9] It seems likely, then, that she drew up the rules herself and submitted them for approval or changes to the committee of management.

According to these regulations, a student's room was a private space. Lady student friends were free to enter it, and certain other visitors were admitted between the hours of 3:00 and 6:00 p.m., but "no visitor not a member of the student's family may go to her room without being personally escorted there by the student." Gentlemen were severely restricted, being permitted to make formal calls in the downstairs area on the second and fourth Fridays of the month between 7:00 and 10:00 p.m., and on Sunday evenings after church if the occasion was not too overtly social. Women friends, on the other hand, were welcome to stay to any meal on payment of a small fee. After dinner, the Hall's doors were closed and no student was allowed to leave without the knowledge of the dean or the director of the household. These are the stated restrictions on evening leave in 1903, as far as is known;[10] judging from the more formal rules elaborated in 1906, however, the dean had her own criteria for allowing egress, which involved considerations as to chaperones, destination, time of return, and the probability of being alone with young men.

Addison believed that these restrictions were such as to win the assent of any well-brought-up young woman. She had expressed the hope to one inquiring student before residence opened "that every young lady will conduct herself with such perfect dignity and propriety, and show herself so courteous and ladylike to all around her, as to make 'restrictions' unnecessary." To another student she explained "my earnest desire, that we be as far as possible one family in Annesley Hall, and that our regulations be as simple as will meet requirements."[11] If students kept the good of the whole in mind, and valued their own reputations, why need there be conflicts? It was, after all, a Christian college. At first Addison could not reconcile herself to the fact that the young had a different agenda. Her familiar moralizing note is apparent in an early speech to the girls, in which after chiding them for some trifles of misconduct ("but in the formation of your character there are no trifles") she laid upon them the burden of her own perfectionism:

You think that we stand somewhat alone – that people do not know what we are doing. Let me tell you the eyes of the city are upon you ... What shall I say to these people? Shall I be obliged to say that we have had only a common – a cheap success, for our young ladies, who should govern themselves, have broken every rule of the house? – just a success that outsiders may call success, but that which lacks the highest ideals, one of which is, the giving up of one's own rights and pleasures for the sake of a nobler whole? There are no little things in life – every trifle is the making of perfection, and it is to the full stature of Christian character we must grow. "Be ye therefore perfect, even as your father which is in heaven is perfect." So to your rooms young ladies, and think on these things.[12]

Unfortunately, to judge by the letters of protest against the fees written by Victoria women before the opening, they were a feisty group, not likely to surrender their point of view without an argument. And as Florence Kenny had remarked prophetically in a speech before the Barbara Heck Memorial Association on the need for a residence, boarding house life tends to make one self-centred: "Afterwards, you have to fight strenuously the desire to have no one interfere with you, to do exactly as you think fit without a thought of how it affects others. For years that was your moral training, nobody did interfere with your plans and purposes; it was your business to see that no one did."[13] Ebullient students, usually in a hurry, could not be counted on to appreciate leisurely, courteous meals. And girls of college age, more accustomed to independence than the high-school students Addison was used to, were unlikely to warm to the concept of an extended family of fifty-five, let alone of an angel factory.

There was a spirit of silliness abroad that Addison could not comprehend, as witness the following vignette in *Acta*:

SOPHOMORE: The Freshettes behaved just like spoiled babies the night Miss Addison entertained us at dinner. They made *bibs* of their table napkins and generally misbehaved. One of them got off a nursery rhyme in a stage whisper and it shocked the Dean. I believe they all had to walk the carpet.[14]

In spite of the loyal support of the fourth-year students, Addison found herself in the disagreeable position of playing the disciplinarian to those whose confidence had yet to be won. Though she gave no details, she confessed that at the end of the year "there was general rebellion against all control, and this was naturally enough directed against the one who stood in the way of doing as they pleased."[15]

The year had not been a total failure, of course. The Hall had almost paid its way, ending with only a small overdraft at the bank. There were expressions of appreciation for Addison's efforts from some of the girls. Bessie Lingham wrote from home after her fourth-year finals, "Miss Addison, I don't know how I could have endured that last trying week if it had not been for your mothering love and sympathy." A letter from Ethel Wallace suggests a tutelary relationship resisted by some: "It is harder for us to say what is in our hearts – about what you have meant in our lives – but you will not think me presumptuous if I tell you that some of us whom you have helped are longing for the time to come when others will let you help them as you have us."[16] Such tributes were heartwarming; nevertheless, by late June Addison was exhausted and glad to retreat for a while to her father's cottage at Orchard Beach, Lake Simcoe, where she could enjoy the more congenial companionship of her family. Writing to thank Mrs Burwash for her and her husband's help and sympathy during the past trying year, she hoped "that next year we shall not be so much of an anxiety to you, and that with added experience we shall not have to call you to our assistance so often."[17]

Addison was convinced that the wayward and insubordinate nature of undergraduates was only encouraged by their hectic social life. Time was frittered away in committee meetings, clubs, and gatherings, and all real work was crammed into the last frantic weeks before final exams. At a meeting of the University Women's Club, Addison "created a sensation among her audience by simply reading a partial list of the college and university 'events,' which apparently must be attended by all undergraduates."[18] The Annual Report of 1903–4 had concluded that "there is something wrong about university or student life which brings our young women to their final year, and sends them out as nearly physical wrecks as they are." The social life itself was not of a high order, the report continued, because the young people socialized too much among themselves, without the benefit of their elders' company. Addison thought the words of St. Paul described their shortcomings perfectly: "they measuring themselves by themselves and comparing themselves among themselves, are not wise."[19] As for the Bob, in which the women now fully participated, the 1904–5 Annual Report maintained that it was a source of strain, excitement, and idleness: "Each year the young women of the second year have lost some of their womanliness and a great deal of their courtesy, have come out ruder, more boisterous, more lawless, less studious, less considerate, less amenable to the recognized conventions of society, and this we must surely deplore."[20] The result was a dissipation of spiritual power. Addison's report on the first year of operation came down ultimately to the moral argument: "It is with sorrow I confess there has been a great lack of deep spiritual power, and the working out of the highest principles of Christianity. The spirit of self forgetfulness and self sacrifice has dwelt little among us. We hope and pray for better things next year."[21]

Addison prayed for a change of heart in her students, but she would not have lasted long as an administrator had this been her only recourse. In fact, she was well aware of what might be called behaviour modification techniques, and of the possibility of changing the environment in order to influence conduct. Her first effort, it is true, was not successful. This was at the college level, where she recommended to the senate of Victoria that social events should largely be removed from the college, and that the young women's participation in the Bob should be restricted to a small role in the event itself. More emphasis should be placed on term work, she suggested, and less on the final exam. The senate members expressed themselves in sympathy with her views, saying that they hoped to do whatever lay within their power;[22] unsurprisingly, this proved to be little.

In a second initiative, Addison took action at the university level, together with several other women colleagues. For some time, a friendship had been developing between herself and Mabel Cartwright, the dean at St. Hilda's (still on Trinity College's Queen Street campus, though Trinity had now become a federated college of the university). The two women shared many interests besides their role as dean, such as love of England (where Cartwright had attended Cheltenham Ladies' College and Lady Margaret Hall) and a deeply religious outlook. Both in their ardent way considered friendship a meeting of mind and spirit. As Mabel remarked, expressing the high expectations they both brought to personal relations, "I suppose half the basis of any friendship is that one sees a sort of 'imprisoned angel' in the person – a glimpse of what he might become if the good possibilities came to fruition."[23] They had another ally in Mrs Campbell, the dean of Queen's Hall, a house converted into a residence for forty-eight women of University College which opened in January 1905. On 10 April 1905, Addison and Miss Cartwright, together with Mrs Campbell and Miss Salter (the superintendent of women students at University College), sent a petition to the university council, requesting that the university limit the number of social functions for undergraduates.[24] They suggested restricting the events to Friday evenings, and ending them promptly at midnight. They maintained that the proliferation of events was harder on the women of the university than on the men, because the women were fewer and thus in greater demand. Although the petition was referred to a committee on social functions, nothing seems to have come of it.

Addison's third effort occurred in her own domain of Annesley Hall, where she perceived that a change of governance was necessary. The model of a home had not proved workable among so large a group, with some strangers to each other and few acquainted with the mother figure. She decided, instead, to think in more political terms, using the model of a community. In community life, some inducements were required to make it worth the individual's while to observe the necessary constraints. Experience suggested that self-government was the form that most effectively engaged the co-operation of the governed and identified their interests with that of the group. The students had asked for a measure of self-government at the end of the first year; during the school years of 1904–5 and 1905–6 this was duly granted them, though the responsibility they shouldered was probably minor. Perhaps it was the lack of senior students – first three and then four were in residence during those years – that rendered the scheme only partially successful. Whatever the reasons, in the 1906–7 school year, Addison introduced a constitution setting out a more elaborate form of student government. It proved to be one of her most valuable and lasting contributions to the evolution of student life.

For the time, the government put in place was almost revolutionary, though it seems mild today. Modelled loosely on the student government of Wellesley College in Massachusetts,[25] it represented a new departure in Canada. An Annesley Student Government Association (ASGA) was constituted, to which all residents belonged and paid 25 cents a year. An executive consisting of a fourth-year president, third-year secretary and treasurer, and various year representatives was to meet every two weeks to transact business. The student association was empowered to frame new rules of conduct for the students, provided that these did not encroach on the academic domain or on matters of health, safety, residence property, or the management of the household. Rules framed by ASGA were to be communicated to the dean and would come into force two weeks later, provided that they were not judged to be beyond ASGA's competence. Disputes over ASGA's powers were to be referred to a joint committee composed of the president, dean, and representatives of the committee of management, the senate, and ASGA. The rules were to be enforced by proctors on each floor, who were to report infractions to the executive. The latter body was allowed to levy small fines, as one of the difficulties of the previous regime had been its lack of sanctions. Second offenses would be reported to the dean and, as a last resort, the faculty would judge offenses that merited expulsion. Changes to this constitution needed the agreement of the dean, ASGA, the committee of management, and the senate.[26]

These arrangements, thought Addison, would go a long way to alleviating the disaffection of the early years. Since the students set their own rules, they should be more kindly disposed to them. A public opinion would grow up favouring compliance; it was a question of adherence to group standards, rather than of deferring to an external authority. Addison also believed that the system encouraged a friendly co-operation between dean and students. She liked to compare the relation between the two to the division of powers between Lords and Commons in the British government. And finally, she was convinced that by assuming responsibility for their own conduct, the students developed character, and that by governing, they learned skills of management.

It was not easy for Addison to loosen the strings, to give up some of her own authority, and to allow the students to run their own operation. Her upbringing had tended to inculcate the view that there was one right way of doing things – the way of Christ – and that the Methodists were pretty sure what this entailed. She found it difficult to stand back when obvious mistakes were being made. But she schooled herself to do so for the sake of a greater good, and, in so doing, she introduced a considerable shift of paradigm into the Methodist church. Instead of being treated as fragile young saplings, to be shielded against the blasts of the world and their own less worthy impulses, the young women were considered adults in training. The patriarchal model favoured in Ontario Methodist colleges suggested that young women were destined primarily for a maternal and familial role;[27] now the implication was that they needed skills that would allow them to function in the public sphere. The inauguration of ASGA was a small but highly significant step in the general movement that would see women become voters, legislators, and professionals. Thus it aligned Addison with what was most progressive in the twentieth century.

Of course, the reality of student government was somewhat more modest in practice than this analysis suggests. Some years later, when the arrangements were being re-evaluated, a few former students suggested that it was student government in name only, conveying the obligations but not the privileges of real self-rule. True, the students were responsible for policing their contemporaries. But they could not frame the rules they really wanted; the power of outside veto was too strong. Muriel Hockey (1T0), picking up the simile she must have heard from Addison, suggested that the students needed to struggle for more power just as, historically, the British Commons had done.[28] But this was a minority view, and other students testified to the improvement of residence life when ASGA was introduced. Its educative value is suggested in an anecdote by Gertrude Rutherford (2T1), which dates from about 1919 but which could have happened at any time:

Well do I recall an occasion when officers of the Student Government, including myself, went to the Dean to say we wanted to resign, but before doing so we wished to tell her that we thought it would be better to do away with Student Government and turn over the total responsibility for the life of the residence to her and other college authorities. A benevolent dictatorship seemed to us less time-consuming, less irritating and much more efficient. It was a long session that followed and we went away with a sounder idea of the meaning and the difficulties of democratic government. Needless to say, our resignations were never submitted.[29]

The form of government had by this time proved its worth and been copied by many other institutions. Over the years, many college administrators wrote to Addison for her advice and used ASGA as a model in setting up their own student government schemes.[30]

Improvements came less from changes in its fabric than from a gradual relaxation of the rules themselves.

❦

The rules initially drawn up by ASGA were of a stern and quaint character; in later years, when Addison read them out to students, she was greeted with roars of laughter.[31] More elaborate than the rules Addison herself had enforced, they perhaps reflect a kind of self-censorship and consciousness of authority; they may equally represent a desire to spell out precisely the permissible limits. After dinner, the Hall's doors were still closed except to those who had the dean's permission to leave; such wanderers left a note as to their destination and had to be back by 10:30 p.m., when they reported their return to the dean. First- and second-year students could stay out until 12:30 only on Friday night, and then only to attend Victoria College events. Third- and fourth-year students, however, could be late on other nights for legitimate reasons, and groups of three or more could let themselves in with a latch key – a sign of trust much appreciated by older students. To go to public evening events such as theatres and concerts, the young women needed a chaperone approved by the dean or by a letter from their parents. The hours for gentlemen callers were restricted as before, and first- and second-year students were not to go to evening church with a man not a member of their immediate family. Nor were any students to go walking or driving in the evening with a man of any description.[32]

Although Addison welcomed what she considered the sensible nature of these rules, she did not feel that they relieved her of much of her responsibility. On the contrary, her life was one of constant vigilance. *Acta* slyly insinuated that the term "gimlet eye" was much used around Annesley Hall,[33] and there is little doubt to whose eye they were alluding. Further light is provided by the diary of Kathleen Cowan, who lived in Annesley Hall from 1907 to 1911 while attending Victoria. This diary, now published with useful annotations, provides a student's-eye view of Addison as well as a revealing picture of residence life. Kathleen records that Miss Addison made a gracious impression when she greeted the new students, wearing a red skirt and red-striped silk waist, but that her after-dinner "getting acquainted" chat "turned out to be a lecture on musts and must-nots." During Kathleen's first year she appears periodically in a Gorgon-like role, waiting at the door or skulking about the halls to see who is or is not in on time, glaring at malefactors with a basilisk

Officers and women residents sitting on the steps of Annesley Hall, c. 1908.
Miss Richardson, Mrs Sheffield, and Miss Addison are second, third,
and fourth in the second row

eye, and lecturing the girls on the error of their ways. She kept a
dignified distance between herself and her charges, so that when she
entertained the freshies in her room after dinner "we nearly 'busted'
it was so proper," and at breakfast at the dean's table "you could feel
ice bergs floating all around." But as Kathleen's university career
went on, she began to realize the complex and interesting character
beneath the dean's forbidding exterior and came to "like her better
and better." She spent more time talking in Miss Addison's room,
and declared her at times "charming," "very nice," "a dear," and
(after a public speech) "splendid."[34] Her diary also reveals that the
young women were still of a girlish nature, and those with a talent
for mimicry kept their friends in stitches by sending up the dean and
her earnest ways.

The young women residents probably did not realize the strain of
Addison's position. She wanted so much for all to behave and was
fearfully let down by thoughtless behaviour – by rules broken, taps
dripping, lights left on, and in later years even sanitary napkins
stuffed into toilets. Burdened with the self-imposed dimensions of
her task, she felt she had not only to run the residence smoothly but
to come to love the girls – not easy for one who was shy in approaching others and naturally a bit censorious. There is a mantra-like
quality, as if she was trying to convince herself, in what she wrote
after visiting a new crop of residents: "They are all interesting, they

are all good, and although some are going to be trying, still they are good, and lovable."[35] Kathleen Cowan refers rather scathingly to "the dean and her smirk," and although one person's smirk may well be another's smile, the phrase does suggest that Addison, in attempting to moderate her exasperation, was producing that odd look that comes of smiling through gritted teeth.

Physically, too, she was stretched to the limit by her duties. The Annual Report of 1903–4 lists, in addition to her responsibilities for student development and her position as final arbiter and repository of blame, such time-consuming tasks as personally nursing the sick, making reports and announcements, allotting rooms, assigning practice hours for piano students, obtaining tickets for entertainments and railway tickets at vacation time, and attending official functions. She reported to the committee of management in November 1906 that in the past month she had written thirty letters; attended seven Annesley Hall committees; hosted four afternoon receptions and seven teas; given a Sunday afternoon talk; received thirty-two visitors in her room; chaperoned students to one afternoon and five evening events; talked to students by class, en masse, and individually; paid bills; received fees; and taken care of the banking. Every night she stayed up till past twelve until the last stray sheep was safely penned. And this went on relentlessly for seven days a week. No wonder she begged the committee in the report for a few days off every month to relieve the constant drain on sympathy and attention. And no wonder she sometimes appeared preoccupied, suspicious, and far from relaxed.

Perhaps it was overwork that led to her illness in the spring of 1906, though the fragmentary allusions to this illness allow no conclusions to be drawn. Her personal life had suffered a blow: in August of 1905 her beloved mother had died. However, in the summer of 1906 she took complete break, travelling to England and Scotland with her father and Charlotte. Centred mostly in the north of England, they took advantage of the opportunity to visit the residences at St. Andrew's University in Scotland; they also made a grand tour of the Lake District by horse-drawn coach, motor, and on foot. As this area was already famous for its beauty and its association with Wordsworth, it was not surprising that they bumped into other Canadians doing the same thing, such as Dr and Mrs. George Blewett from Victoria College, Miss Thomas of Jarvis Collegiate, and Caroline Macdonald of the YWCA. Nor was it surprising that, succumbing to the current craze, they bought over three hundred postcards. For several weeks, however, they removed themselves from the main circuit and put up at the Hare and Hounds Inn in the village of Levens or Beathwaite Green, home of their English ancestors. Here they met several "cousins" from the scattered family.[36]

When Addison returned in the fall, it was to an expanded domain. The residence was by now such a success that there were forty-two additional applications for rooms and only fifteen vacancies. So the women took over "Drynan House," a handsome property just south-west of the main college building that had recently been acquired by the board of regents. For some months the board had been trying unsuccessfully to let it at a high rent. Now they gave up and – much to the annoyance of the college men, who still had no residence – agreed to allow the committee of management to use it as an extension of Annesley for five years, provided the committee would assume responsibility for the running expenses. Renamed South Hall, it had room for twenty-three students plus a directress and two maids. The girls were to take their meals at Annesley Hall but have their own residence association. Mrs Mary Sheffield, who had previously worked at the YWCA in London, Ontario, was hired as superintendent, and the draft agreement regarding student government was amended to include South Hall and to read "the Dean and the Superintendent of South Hall" where previously it had read "the Dean." South Hall opened in the fall of 1906 with fifteen paying occupants.

In her Annual Report to the committee of management for 1906–7, Addison drew attention to the immense improvement in residence life since the difficult days of 1903: "The spirit of self-satisfaction so prominent a feature of the first year has given way to something approaching humility. The lawlessness and license of that time have been superseded by popular opinion in favour of the recognized conventions of society. The ideals of conduct in both morals and manners are higher and the amount of study done each year has been more than in the preceding one." She also broached the idea that her labours were insufficiently recognized:

There is no position which Canadian Methodism may confer upon a woman in the church, which opens larger opportunity, occasioning at the same time greater responsibilities of a kind unapparent to the ordinary observer, than the Deanship of Annesley Hall ... If the officer of the Hall to whom its most delicate and important work is entrusted is to do that work in the best way, her position should be recognized by this Committee in the greatness of its scope and the dignity of its calling.[37]

In other words, Addison felt her status should be higher. She attacked this problem in several ways. In the first place, she asked for a raise, pointing out to the committee (with apologies for descending to a personal level) not only that she had sustained a loss of from two to three hundred dollars a year since she had left her teaching post, but that her present salary was inadequate to the demands of her position. Secondly, she noted that in most institutions, whether educational or financial, the chief executive was a member of the governing board; she therefore asked to be made a member *ex officio* of the committee of management.

These questions were involved with the politics of a third, and more problematical, drive for prestige. Believing that her influence would be much greater with the women if she were a member of the faculty, Addison had taken steps to be appointed as a lecturer. Actually it is unclear whether the initiative came from Addison herself (as Dr Burwash later maintained), or, as she herself believed, from the Burwashes. The first reference to the question, a letter from Addison to her friend Dr Helen MacMurchy, implies that Helen had urged her to broach the subject with Dr Burwash as early as July 1904.[38] When she did so, according to this letter, he mused that she was best prepared in German, but that she might gain more influence over the young women by teaching in the growing field of religious knowledge. He suggested that she start a Ph.D. course in philosophy. Addison bought a history of philosophy and began to study systematic theology, "so deeply moved was she by the dear Chancellor's fatherliness and good opinion." Her later recollection was that she would never have asked to be put on the staff – "I could not have been so presumptuous" – but that the original impetus came from Mrs Burwash.[39] At all events, the notion of the philosophy course died away. But in November 1905, Burwash reported to a committee of the board of regents that Miss Addison was prepared to assume some work in German at no extra expense to the board, provided that an arrangement could be made with the present lecturer.[40] In January 1906, she was formally made a lecturer in German.

Her difficulties in this position were exacerbated by the character of the incumbent professor, Lewis Emerson Horning. He had joined the faculty of Victoria as a temporary replacement for Dr Bell while Addison was a student there. Perhaps his modest qualifications at the time had made him unduly sensitive to status: he had only a masters degree and, as someone complained in *Acta*, he had not specialized in moderns or won a medal therein; instead, he had been plucked from a position teaching high-school mathematics in Peterborough.[41] Since then he had been sent to a German university, where he earned a Ph.D. in Teutonic languages; possibly he picked up too the German disdain for women scholars. In any case, during the spring of 1906, he allowed Addison to do some teaching for him.

Unfortunately Addison's faculty career was interrupted by her illness, but she nevertheless spoke in her Annual Report of 1905–6 of "the aid it has already been in the position of dean to hold a lectureship in the College, and to have been an examiner in the University examinations."[42] In the next school year (1906–7), she took over the first- and second-year pass German course from Dr Horning.

In April of 1907, having received her report and recognized the justice of her pleas, the committee of management saw fit to ask the board of regents to remunerate the dean for five hours of teaching per week, as well as to make both Addison and Mrs Sheffield *ex officio* members of the committee of management. But the board of regents, while eventually agreeing to make Addison alone a member of the committee of management, dismissed the question of her teaching salary after hearing Chancellor Burwash's explanation that it was a private arrangement between herself and Dr Horning. A few days later, the Rev. A.J. Irwin, a minister on the board who had been an undergraduate with Addison, wrote to her implicitly apologizing for the board's cavalier treatment. He explained that Dr Burwash had led them to believe that she had been acting as a supply teacher during Dr Horning's absence and should be paid by him.[43] Apart from teaching, he added, it was the responsibility of the committee of management to augment her admittedly inadequate salary as dean of residence. Addison was understandably indignant; she asked counsel from friends such as Helen MacMurchy and Nellie Rowell, a new appointee to the committee of management (and sister of Margaret's classmate Fred Langford); she also covered many pages of a little notebook of 1907–8 with explanations concerning her side of the question.

This notebook reveals a further humiliation: in the fall of 1907, a few days before the start of classes, Dr Horning had come to Addison to say that he had mistakenly believed she was receiving a lecturer's salary from the college and, realizing his error, he felt he could hardly ask her to teach this year. Addison writes: "He said he was much annoyed about it – it misrepresented him, but he would live it down – he even felt like resigning for a year, but was unable to afford it." There were no thanks among these egocentric lamentations for the work Addison had done, nor any offers to pay for it. Nevertheless, about 1 November Dr Horning did find himself in need of assistance and asked Addison if she could teach pass German twice a week. He may have been discommoded because Addison was booked to go to the Ontario Ladies' College for a few days in late November and he had to take a few classes for her. At any rate, though he sent her a cheque for $20 before Christmas, he then made other arrangements.

The upshot was that when Addison arrived to teach her class in January 1908, he turned her back at the door, saying that he was about to give the class an examination as a basis for a division into groups. Then, the following Thursday, Chancellor Burwash explained to Addison that more assistance was required than she was able to give, and that a Mr Owen has been hired to give it. Although she would continue to be listed as a lecturer in German in the calendar, this was to be an honorary position only. As Addison reported to the committee of management, Dr Horning "has made no explanation to me about it, has not even spoken of it to me, and the new man was installed before I knew that my services were no longer required."[44]

It was the greatest defeat of her career. And it continued to rankle. While wanting so much to contribute to the intellectual life of the college, and to be seen to do so, she was relegated to what was more like a housekeeping position. She was probably right in her estimate of the importance of the appointment: Mabel Cartwright had also publicly suggested that her position as dean of residence would be more tenable if she met the students as a teacher,[45] and Addison's successor, Jessie Macpherson, insisted that she receive a teaching appointment as a professor of ethics before consenting to become dean.[46] Self-respect and status among both women and the community at large were not the only considerations; the position would also have been a step in the expansion of available roles for women and the assumption of the kind of responsibility envisaged by ASGA.

The problem was not Addison's lack of a Ph.D., as such scholarly credentials were not a requisite at the time. Her replacement Francis Owen had a B.A. and the junior rank of instructor, while the popular Charles Earl Auger joined the English faculty in 1907 with a B.A. Nor is it likely, given Addison's excellent performance in undergraduate German and her experience as a teacher, that she proved inadequate to her task. It is hard to escape the conclusion that her sex was the decisive problem. For example, Victoria had no other women lecturers, while the only high-ranking women teachers in the rest of the university were two newly appointed associate professors in the Faculty of Household Science. Addison's brief stint was, in fact, a little-known first for a humanities subject, one not to be repeated until 1919. The English ideal of cultivated women educators was still in the future.

The dearth of women faculty may well have been one of the attractions of establishing a separate college for women at the University of Toronto, a scheme which was a preoccupation of the university government during 1908–9. But in order to set this proposal in context, a survey is needed of the progress made by women in Toronto since the days of Addison's B.A. studies. No longer excluded from the mainstream of student life, women took part in *Acta*, the *Varsity*, the Bob, and class meetings. Academically they achieved high rank. What is surprising to modern observers, however, is the degree of segregation maintained between the sexes. At Victoria, for instance, the women did not join "the Lit.," the main student organization; instead, they had their own Women's Literary Society where they discussed cultural matters and practised debating. Women's debating teams competed against teams from the other Toronto colleges, and there were also women's hockey, basketball, and fencing teams. The women of Victoria joined the YWCA or studied in Bible and missionary groups with other women.

Addison, welcoming these developments, spoke in her Annual Report of 1906–7 to the senate of the beginning of a separate social life for women similar to that at Oxford. In the spring of 1907, she had been corresponding about the problems of coeducation with Hilda Oakeley, an Oxford graduate and former warden of Royal Victoria College in Montreal, who was now working in England as tutor and warden of the women's residence at Victoria University, Manchester. "I gather from your words," wrote Oakeley, "that you would probably be glad of a return to separation in University Education, and that you even feel that the character of the education best fitted for women may not be identical with that appropriate to men."[47] Oakeley praised the Oxford and Cambridge women's colleges as well, where women now attended many lectures with men, while leading social lives centred in their own colleges.

Addison herself found her life more and more woman-centred. At Annesley Hall, she worked mainly with the female committee of management and female staff, especially with Mrs Sheffield, the head of South Hall, and Miss Richardson, who had replaced Miss Scott as head of the household (or housekeeper) in 1904. Richardson proved invaluable; she was popular among the girls, being somewhat more indulgent and understanding than Addison, if Kathleen Cowan's diary is to be believed. The only male officer was the janitor, James Mullin. Miss Addison tried to keep him on the straight and narrow path; a letter after his retirement and the death of his wife exhorts him to resist temptation – "you *know* you have not always done so" – and to "be a man – be strong and be *good* in every way."[48] James nevertheless thought highly of Addison and declared that "it is never no trouble to me to do anything for you for you have allways [sic] been very nice with us."[49]

When not at work at Annesley Hall, Addison was often busy with other women in the Victoria Alumnae Association.[50] She was also involved, with Helen MacMurchy, Mabel Cartwright, Mabel Chown, and others, in the University Women's Club. This club, founded in 1903 and open to all women university graduates living in Toronto, promoted relaxation and friendship and sought to further women's educational and social positions. After 1908 the club met once a month during the school year, often at Annesley Hall.[51]

In view of this active female social life, the idea of a separate college for women was not outrageous. The growth of the under-graduate body, which made another college an attractive proposition, was probably the main factor inducing the university authorities to consider the idea. Besides, the authorities saw that women were concentrated in modern languages. Was that because men predomi-nated in the other courses? Would a separate college give women more freedom to study what they wished, or in other ways cater to their special educational needs? In the spring of 1908, the university senate appointed a committee under the chairmanship of Professor George Wrong of the history department to study the question.

Arguments both for and against this college were made, many of them familiar from similar debates today. Assuming that the college would offer separate classes for women, many women argued that its chief advantage would be to allow women faculty and officers to act as role models, thereby ensuring that women's intellectual devel-opment would not be totally dictated by men. Some people consid-ered that an all-female class, free of the distractions of sex, would encourage intellectual effort; others believed that competing directly with men made women unfeminine and strident. Some men saw the departure of women from classrooms as the removal of an annoying and invidious source of competition. For others, a separate women's college might lessen the emphasis on the coed social life, considered by many besides Addison to be a hectic, time-wasting, and even soul-destroying distraction.[52]

On the other hand, many women cherished the coeducation that had been won with some difficulty, and that constituted a theoretical guarantee for the equality of the sexes. Though few at this time would argue that the sexes should be brought up entirely in a non-gendered manner, support was still considerable for the idea that higher edu-cation was purely cerebral and sexless. If women were admitted to have special needs, could it not be said that this was because they were not up to the intellectual demands of men's education? Men were perhaps less likely to have detailed objections to a separation, aside from the general desire not to lose feminine companionship. Many women, on the other hand, including most undergraduates, feared that forming a separate college would ghettoize women, and that the facilities of a such a college might be inferior to those for men. Others stressed the fact that women must learn to co-operate and compete with men. As for Addison of Victoria and Cartwright of Trinity, although they were sympathetic to a degree of separation, they were particularly concerned with the religious orientation of this proposed non-denominational college, and with its relation to the existing residences. As Cartwright mused in a letter to Addison, "Can such a college have a religious basis? and can you and I support it if it has not? It seems to me that the Holy Scripture and Christian Evidences should form part of its curriculum ... I was thinking of the appointment of a woman warden, and then wondering whether you for instance, would feel able to accept the appointment, suppose it were open to you, if the college had no religious basis."[53]

The University Women's Club was the first to take the matter into consideration. As members of the executive, Cartwright and Addison were discussing it as early as February 1908, before the formation of the senate committee. Initially, the club agreed to meet with Wrong's committee and to support whatever policy was decided upon by the university. They were not opposed to a women's college as long as it was treated with complete equality.[54] But another movement had emerged among university women that dealt with some of the difficulties of coeducation in a less drastic manner; that is, by the appointment of a dean of women to serve the needs of all university women, in residence or outside. At that point, no Canadian university had such an officer. Discussion of these two proposals gathered momentum in the alumnae associations of the individual colleges. In December 1908, Addison urged the Victoria alumnae to support the appointment of a dean of women at Victoria. In April 1909, she served on a committee formed by the alumnae to examine the post of dean of women at American universities.[55] As well, earlier that year she had begun her own interviews with the eighteen girls who lived neither at home nor in residence, whom she discussed in her February report under the pseudonyms of Misses A to R.[56] In her year-end report to the senate, she argued forcibly for a dean of women at Victoria, pointing out that non-resident students desperately needed counsel on their academic, as well as social, affairs.[57]

In April of 1909, the Wrong committee presented its report, recommending at the least a women's college for University College women; Victoria and Trinity could join the scheme if they wished.[58] Unfortunately – taking into consideration the elaboration and explanation that Wrong published in the *University of Toronto Monthly* in November 1909[59] – the college they envisaged was somewhat of a hybrid, unlikely to satisfy the proponents of single-sex education, while alienating the supporters of coeducation. Moreover, in his November article, Wrong struck a slightly patronizing note that no doubt irritated some of the women. Men and women have common interests, he wrote, "but it is wise to see too – the modern man knows this truth well, if the modern woman does not – that the chief charm and strength of woman is in her being unlike man." The initial proposal recommended that the college be staffed by lecturers from the university, though by November Wrong had decided that the college should probably have its own staff. Many men would be included, however, on the grounds that women often preferred to be taught by men. In a foretaste of the reorganization of the late 1960s, students would be allowed to attend lectures at different colleges, so that men might attend classes at the women's college and vice versa. "University" subjects such as the sciences would continue to be given in common. Unfortunately, this arrangement appears to defeat one of the initial aims, that of removing the distractions of inter-sex competition and flirtation from the classroom. There was, moreover, no compulsion for women to enrol in this college, though Wrong guessed most would choose to do so. And the relation with the federated colleges was left somewhat vague. In November Wrong suggested that if Victoria came into the plan, it might use Annesley Hall to house men and build a new hall for women close to the women's college. But since these women would presumably no longer be Victoria students, this costly proposition was unlikely to gain favour.

The women's reaction was largely negative. It is perhaps best summed up in the phrase of Mabel Cartwright's which was to suggest the title for Jennifer Brown's pamphlet on the subject: that women had a disposition to bear the ills of the present system, rather than to fly to unknown ones.[60] According to the Toronto *Star*, 230 of the 238 undergraduates it surveyed had signed a petition against the proposal.[61] But the report did have one positive result for the university women: it brought them together. After the publication of the report, representatives of the alumnae associations of Victoria, University College, St. Hilda's, and medicine, momentarily joined by the University Women's Club, got together to prepare a joint response. In May of 1909, they sent the senate a printed declaration in which suspicion is a dominant note.[62] The arts faculty is not the place to provide for the "special needs of women's education," they argued; women need the same liberal education as men before professional training can be considered. The sequestering of women would surely lead to a curtailment of library and laboratory privileges "such as prevails at Radcliffe." Moreover, the university could probably not afford to have senior professors duplicate their lectures at the women's college; more likely, the women would have to make do with junior lecturers or go to male-dominated classes as before. Even the religious education of Victoria and Trinity women would suffer if they joined a non-denominational college. The alumnae declared that the university women were not dissatisfied with the measure of coeducation that existed at the University of Toronto, if only more women could be appointed to the arts faculty.

The joint alumnae also pursued their alternative solution, the appointment of a dean of women at the University of Toronto. In July 1909, a committee convened by Addison sent a list of twenty-seven questions on coeducation and deans of women to leading universities in North America and abroad. Their report, based on the sixty-four replies received, concluded that the position of dean of women is "essential to the best interests of women students," and that it is most useful when the dean has some teaching duties – a point no doubt heartily endorsed by the chair.[63] By this time, deans of women in the United States had in fact become a recognized subgroup of the American Association of Collegiate Alumni; in 1913 that organization would similarly urge the importance of a dean of women's being a faculty member.[64] Fifteen hundred copies of Addison's committee's report were printed. When a delegation met with the Wrong committee and President Falconer in December 1909, Addison spoke particularly on the need for such a position.

Having acted and perhaps prayed together, the alumnae associations stayed together, drawing up a formal constitution for the United Alumnae Association in the spring of 1910. Women active in the association included Cartwright, MacMurchy, Maud Edgar (sister of Professor Pelham Edgar at Victoria, and herself later the co-founder of a private school for girls in Montreal), Clara Benson, Susie Chown,[65] and Marjory Curlette. Predictably, Addison was of their number, attending committee meetings (often held at Annesley Hall), moving and seconding motions, and participating in delegations and subcommittees. In 1911 her position as the Victoria representative on the United Alumnae was made permanent.[66]

Ultimately, the senate decided not to act on the Wrong Report, realizing that they had misjudged the sentiments of university women. Agitation for a dean of women continued sporadically but with little success; at Victoria, Addison found that the college simply could not fund this position at present. Instead, the alumnae associations decided to promote the candidature of women for the university senate. The Victoria alumnae chose Winnifred Leisenring (9T8) as their candidate and urged members to vote for her in the elections of 1910. Although she was not successful, Gertrude Lawlor and Charlotte Ross were elected to the senate in 1911 – the first women to sit on this body.[67] This was a rather meagre political outcome after three years of animated discussion. However, the United Alumnae remained a useful watchdog for women's concerns across the campus.

CHAPTER SIX

Residence Life

With the establishment of student government in 1906, Addison had solved her most pressing administrative problem. The framework she had put in place left her freer to concentrate on what she considered her proper work: moulding the communal life of the Hall, and helping individual girls to grow in understanding and grace. Between 1906 and the First World War – or more precisely between 1906 and 1912, when another administrative change took place – she supervised the evolution of a distinctive pattern of residence life, initiating or encouraging activities that she considered beneficial and imposing standards of behaviour through the rules and the force of her considerable personality. These years may fittingly be surveyed as a unit, in order to determine the character of the place she called home.

The young women under Addison's care were of an average age of $19\frac{1}{4}$ when they entered, with an overall average of $20\frac{1}{2}$.[1] Although the majority were Methodists or Presbyterians, a sprinkling of Anglicans, Baptists, and "others" leavened the mix; all professed some sort of religious belief and, for many, it was a cornerstone of their lives. Most came from the middle-class world of ministers, teachers, lawyers, merchants, industrialists, and farmers.[2] They were drawn largely from the small towns of Ontario, where, thought Addison, they had imbibed considerable freedom of manner. Not only had they enjoyed easy familiarity with boys through coeducational high schools, but also, partly because their parents had had fewer advantages than they, home discipline had often been weak. As a result they were "not at all the type of young woman found in the great English universities, young women who have had the advantages of cultured homes, intellectual companionship, whose social position is assured, for whom society plays no part until after college days are ended."[3] The dean had to work far harder than her English counterparts to ensure the required degree of seriousness and socialization.

Annesley girls did not necessarily enter college for the sake of preparing for a job; in general, they hoped eventually to marry and raise a family. But many intended to work for wages for a few years first, chiefly as school teachers and modern language specialists. Career possibilities were slowly expanding, though still in areas of traditional female activity such as nursing or meal supervision. As President Hutton of the University of Toronto said of the Faculty of Household Science, which opened in 1907, "Does not this new faculty open a way for reconciling the old and the new conditions of women? the old mission as home makers and the new mission as graduates of a university?"[4] Addison herself occupied a middle position, encouraging the girls to look at careers, yet emphasizing too the importance of educated mothers. Upon the mother, she told the alumnae, largely depended the child's ideas of right and wrong, "whether he will think that unselfishness, self-sacrifice and self-control are the things worth striving for, or whether pleasure, happiness and self-gratification are the first things on earth."[5] From Annesley Hall she hoped to send out dedicated and right-thinking young mothers who would form the nucleus of a stronger and more mature nation.

The young women were generally serious in their studies, adhering to the evening "quiet hours" when silence was required. But they could be frivolous in their free time. They emulated to some extent the highjinks of the men, particularly their odious initiation practices. Resident Ethel Kirk later recalled "'tapping' [or soaking with water] bidding fair to outrival the Deluge," and "excited Freshmen huddled together behind locked doors, and groups of Sophomores keeping an exasperating watch in the corridors without – onions, castor oil – and Limberger cheese!"[6] The dean tried to discourage grosser manifestations and overexcitement, while smiling on the "pure and kindly fun"[7] of which youthful inventiveness was capable: marshmallow roasts, skits, masquerades, ghost parades, Valentine luncheons, and "baby parties," at which apparently a little infantile regression was tolerated.

Food was a constant preoccupation. Photographs suggest that college girls at the turn of the century were heavier than those of today. This is not surprising considering the fudge, popcorn, cocoa, cake, and goodies from home they devoured. Undergraduate Kathleen Cowan's diary is partly a chronicle of feeds and teas, with interleaved recipe cards for such delicacies as "Coffee Cream – Annesley," "Boston Date Cakes – Annesley," and even "Fish Balls (Annesley Hall)." A typical luncheon banquet consisted of half oranges; soup; fish with egg sauce and cucumber; lamb chop, potatoes, and peas; tomato with egg, salad dressing, olives, and salted biscuits; salted almonds and sweets; ice cream; and lemonade for toasts. The glasses and plates borrowed from the Annesley dining hall for private snacks and the unwashed dishes and saucepans left beside the gas stoves that had

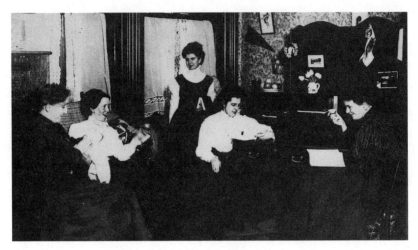

Students in a room at Annesley Hall, 1910

been installed for the girls' use constantly raised the dean's ire. Eventually she declared that all private utensils left in the bathrooms and sinkrooms after 9:00 a.m. would be impounded, only to be released on payment of 10 cents per item.[8] In one serious talk of 1909, she spoke to her charges of the dangers of wastefulness and conspicuous consumption, "of so much eating and drinking and of the vulgarity of display – that the money their parents gave them represented their parents' flesh and blood – of the need there was for all to be mindful of the feelings of others – to make it easy, for those whose incomes are small."[9] Although the girls saw her point, they munched on.

The dean hoped to encourage extracurricular activity of a more altruistic sort, involving service to others. One suitable vehicle was the settlement movement, which had so impressed her in London in 1900 for its bringing together of town and gown. Toronto had two main settlements. Evangelia House, a settlement for young women, had been founded by the Presbyterian Church in a store near Queen and River Streets in 1902. There was also a university settlement, founded in 1910 at 467 Adelaide Street, in a manufacturing district where 70 percent of the population were immigrants. Though Toronto did not experience the grinding poverty of East London, much still needed to be done by way of encouraging the bonding of mother and child, teaching self-help skills, and enlarging mental horizons. As Evangelia's founder Sara Libby Carson put it in a talk to the alumnae, "[We] work against, not poverty of money, but poverty of inner life and environment."[10]

At the settlement houses, Annesley girls served as teachers – of physical culture, music, and what is now known as English as a Second Language. Addison herself acted as first chair of the Delta Chapter of the Victoria Alumnae Association, formed in 1904 to work at Evangelia House.[11] She strongly approved of the attempt to break down class barriers. As in the English movement, the aim was fellowship, not patronage; in the words of Miss Elwood of Evangelia House, "It is a working *with* and not *for*; – a helping, and not a stooping down to."[12] Of course, this sentiment was not always observed to the letter, and social distinctions *would* intrude. Addison was keenly alive to these awkward moments of class consciousness, though she was not in a position to do much about them. When the University Women's Club went to the university settlement to put on an entertainment, for instance, she was quite mortified that after the show the settlement women were left downstairs to eat coffee and cake, while the club members were whisked upstairs for their refreshments. As she complained in a family letter,

I suppose one owes a certain amount of gratitude to busy uptown people who give a programme in a downtown settlement, but I cannot quite see why the uptown people, who have so much that is rich and beautiful in their lives, should not count it as a privilege to share everything they have with their less fortunate sisters ... I am a thorough-going democrat in these matters. I cannot see on what grounds any of us assume superiority, nor quite why we are entitled to sandwiches and cake and coffee in a nice library, when our sisters below had no sandwiches, and were not in so pretty a room. May I be forgiven for offering criticisms when I was a guest.[13]

Nevertheless, settlement work exposed the young women to a working-class lifestyle that was quite eye-opening to those who had lived sheltered lives.

Many of the residents were active in the Victoria branch of the collegiate YWCA, at that time a Protestant organization devoted to the study of Christianity and training in Christian leadership. Addison was an enthusiastic leader, becoming increasingly involved in planning and committee work as time went on. From November 1904 she served on the executive committee of the Dominion Council, where she helped to plan the annual conventions and to reorganize the council's activities.[14] Each year she was in frequent consultation with the current head of the Victoria YWCA, seeing her as one of her lieutenants and natural allies. The "Y" held prayer and inspirational meetings, and an annual conference at Elgin House, Muskoka, but it was also a democratic organization that involved social work of a quite daring kind. Besides teaching sewing at Evangelia House and cooking at the Central Neighbourhood Settlement,[15] the young women of the "Y" brought food and comfort to slums where normally they would never have set foot. As Ethel Granger Bennett recalled, "some people were kind of horrified that the girls could go down into such regions as we visited."[16]

There were usually several Bible study groups at Annesley Hall, led by older women. The young women were also deeply involved in foreign missions, as were many of their generation. Long ago at Addison's graduation Chancellor Burwash had sent the graduates forth as virtual Christian missionaries: "The infinite satisfaction of beholding the millennial glory must go hand in hand with the privileged toil of carrying it to its completion. This is the task which I would commit to your brave young hearts and to your strong and skilful young hands."[17] At that time, in 1889, the Student Volunteer Movement (SVM) for Foreign Missions was only just beginning. Put in motion by the evangelistic team of Moody and Sankey in the United States in 1886, the SVM aimed to induce young people to go out as Christian missionaries and thus to fulfil Jesus' last command, "Go ye into all the world, and preach the gospel to every creature" (Mark 16:15). The volunteers' watchword was "the evangelization of the world in this generation." Of course, they were not so unrealistic as to suppose that they could convert the whole of mankind in such a short time, but they believed it was possible at least to offer the Gospel message to every living person on earth – provided they could enrol 20,000 missionaries.[18] Like the social gospel of which it was a natural extension, the movement envisaged the establishment of a Kingdom of God on earth on a worldwide scale.

In the early years of the century, the SVM spread rapidly among young people. It served as a vehicle for their intense idealism, though exhibiting too the culture-bound myopia of those who believe that others need conversion. In the Protestant churches it was often led by women,[19] whose energies and organizational skills, under-utilized elsewhere, blossomed and were honed in overseas service and leadership in prayer and support groups. In Annesley Hall, when evening came and classes were over, the young women could often be found gathered in small groups, engaged in mission study. Each summer a delegation of Annesley girls would travel by train to the summer conferences of the YWCA and other organizations. In the rustic surroundings of Silver Bay, New York state, they met with delegates from Protestant churches all over North America to hear inspirational speakers such as Dr. John Mott and Robert E. Speer, leaders in the SVM.

At this time there was a heightened interest in the Orient as a missionary field. Though mysterious and still largely unknown, this area had already impinged on Addison's life: her undergraduate class had included Juzo Kono, the first Japanese man to attend Victoria.[20] Her brother Arthur, who as a minister was much involved with missionary work, had become an authority on Japan. His book on the mission field there, *The Heart of Japan* (1905), was widely used in church study circles. In 1911 Annesley Hall had a four-day visit from Caroline Macdonald, the Presbyterian missionary from Wingham, Ontario, who was home on furlough from her work with the YWCA in Japan.[21] Addison described her as "a woman of rare insight, of quick understanding," who "speedily found her way into the hearts of our young women."[22]

China also exercised a special fascination. In 1904 the residence had welcomed Ah Mae Wong, proudly (and perhaps with some exaggeration) identified by Addison as "[the] first Chinese woman student in U of T. [The] First Chinese woman in *Toronto*."[23] In early 1912 came Marjorie Hung, a young woman from Foochow, who hoped to become a science teacher in a university for the women of south China, to be established by the Methodist Episcopal Church of the United States. Many of the VWREA contributed to the fund that paid for her fees, board, personal expenses, books, and passage money. Addison took a motherly interest in Marjorie's welfare; during part of the holidays, she stayed at the Addisons' cottage. Oriental features were such a novelty in Toronto that Marjorie was rather isolated at first; Bertha Herington, for instance (head of the Victoria YWCA in 1913), confessed that she hesitated to talk to her "for fear she might think it was merely curiosity."[24] But sharing of class notes and explanations gradually led to familiarity, and the girls benefited from learning about a completely different culture. After Marjorie's return to China in 1915, she served in the same district as Ethel Wallace, a 1906 graduate and former Annesley resident, now a missionary. Ethel, who kept in regular touch with Addison via letters, wrote that "Marjorie and I often talk of you. You *surely* took her heart by storm – she has a very real love and reverence for you."[25]

To encourage a wider awareness, Addison brought into the Hall guests and noted speakers, some of whom stayed for an extended visit. Many of these speakers were connected with Christian outreach: for instance, Miss Paxson, the travelling secretary of the YWCA; Ethel Stevenson, its corresponding secretary; Miss Melcher and later Ruth Rouse, travelling secretaries of the World's Student Christian Federation; and Mrs Ross and Mrs Strachan, president and foreign secretary of the Women's Missionary Society. Others were professors at the college and university. But more daring choices of guests occurred as well. Perhaps the most unusual was Mrs Emmeline Pankhurst, the militant leader of the suffragette movement in England, who had already been incarcerated in Holloway Jail twice for breaches of the peace. A turbulent prisoner, she had refused to obey prison rules and was kept in solitary confinement; a few years later, she was to be charged with arson and window breaking. Unfortunately, nothing is known of her reception at Annesley Hall in November 1909. A later visit in 1916, however, caused Addison to remark that Mrs Pankhurst was "by far the best woman speaker I have heard."[26] The dean procured for the Annesley library subscriptions to two suffrage journals, one apparently the *Women's Journal* of the National American Woman Suffrage Association.[27]

Another guest was J.S. Woodsworth, then working as a "social gospel" minister at All People's Mission among the poor and immigrant population of Winnipeg; he visited in November 1912 to talk about his characteristic brand of Christian social activism. Though Addison's political affiliations, if any, are not known, it is obvious that she had left-leaning sympathies; family tradition has it that she supported the striking women operators in the Bell Telephone strike of 1907, even to the point of marching with them outside Annesley Hall, though this is hard to credit. At the time, though, public sympathy for overworked and underpaid women, especially among members of the evangelical churches, was considerable.[28]

In early 1914 Addison declined an offer of lectures from the Correspondence School of Gospel and Scientific Eugenics (Race Improvement), to be given by Mary E. Teats. In her diplomatic reply, Addison noted that, although eugenics was an interesting subject, the time was not yet ripe to introduce it to Toronto: "We are conservative, and we cannot move too quickly."[29] She was not squeamish about sexual and reproductive questions, however, recognizing that false delicacy and ignorance were far more dangerous than discussion. When a new doctor was needed for the residence in 1911, she argued successfully for the appointment of her friend Helen MacMurchy, who was making a name for herself as an authority on questions of women's and children's health, obstetrics, and later birth control. She also invited Dr Marie Stopes to address the girls in the 1910–11 session. Stopes had not yet achieved notoriety for advocating contraception and sexual knowledge; a prominent paleobiologist and distinguished as the first woman to join the scientific staff of Manchester University in 1904, she had been the youngest doctor of science in Britain when she received her D.Sc. in 1905. But she was famous even then for her "extremely unorthodox views"; according to one Annesley resident,

"She used to come down to dinner dressed in Oriental splendour, looking like the Begum of Oude, and after dinner went dancing down the hall with a staid and bewildered Miss Addison and then regaled us over coffee with her hair-raising adventures in the Black Forest, scaling mountains in Japan, and searching for fossils all over the world."[30] She was doubtless asked on the suggestion of Helen Mac-Murchy, who attended her wedding in Montreal in March 1911.[31]

In 1906–7, Addison began the practice of addressing the girls herself after Sunday dinner; in essence she gave what amounted to little sermons. "From the beginning," she explained to the committee of management, "I had hoped to have something which would fill the place in our Residence, which the college chapel services have done in Rugby, Eton, and other English residential schools"[32] – thus aligning herself with educators such as the revered Thomas Arnold, for whom an idealistic ethos was as important as book learning. Although Victoria University already had such services, presumably she wanted a gathering in which her own little community could define and affirm itself. In her talks she stressed the primacy of the spiritual life and the importance of service, and the occasion was generally concluded with the singing of a hymn.

She also took the opportunity to talk to the girls individually and in small groups, liking nothing better than to feel that they valued her insights and that she could be of help. Their concerns ranged from academic anxieties and questions about jobs to family worries and ethical dilemmas. To the committee of management, Addison described counselling such students as the young woman who felt guilty about leaving home when her mother was sick, the one whose increasing learning seemed to cut her off from her family, and the one who wondered how to break with the man she loved because his family was "fast" and non-Christian. She instituted an annual house party for the women of the graduating class, resident and non-resident, at some scenic spot such as a farm at Jackson's Point. These gatherings offered fellowship and a final opportunity to view the results of four years of college study. "There is nothing which fills one's heart so full of gladness," she wrote in her report of 9 February 1911, "as to see human flowers come into bud, and blossom into beauty."[33]

The pre-war years, here surveyed as a whole, were not devoid of crises and special events that stood out from the surrounding flow. These were years of constant growth. Despite the opening of South

Hall, the demand for residence rooms continued to exceed the supply. Indeed, the fifty-seven girls in residence in 1906–7 grew to eighty-four by 1914. As Robert Beare the janitor said when asked if Annesley Hall was full, "Yes, siree! If it had been twice as big it would have been full. It's just like the bicycle craze of some time ago."[34] The very popularity of the residence taxed Addison's ingenuity throughout her tenure, calling forth a variety of expedients. One was to make several more of the none-too-large Annesley single rooms into doubles. The dean adhered rigorously to her policy of giving Victoria students precedence and, in later years, they completely crowded out students from the Conservatory of Music, the School of Expression, and University College. However, Faculty of Education and Faculty of Household Science students continued to be accepted.

In 1910 Addison served as a member of the boarding-house committee of the VWREA. This committee scoured the neighbourhood, like Diogenes with his lantern, seeking rooms in clean, comfortable, and reasonably priced establishments (they also had to be willing to take in women only) to put on an "approved" list for the use of those not accepted in the residence; while many houses were visited, few were chosen. In September 1912, Victoria rented all five rooms in Miss Pattison's boarding house on Bloor Street; known as "Bloor Hall," it proved to be the precursor to a whole series of "Bloor Street houses" for Victoria. The nine young women residing there took their meals at Annesley Hall and used its facilities. In the same year, the committee of management acceded to Miss Addison's request that they install a second phone for outgoing calls only; with eighty-two people sharing the single phone, the lineups were long.[35]

An important milestone was celebrated on 28 March 1910, when a banquet was held in the Hall in recognition of the thirtieth anniversary of the admission of women to Victoria College. One hundred and fifty women were present, including Mrs Andrews, the former Nellie Greenwood, one of the earliest graduates. By November of that year, however, storm clouds were gathering. The dean had given the committee a rather rosy report in early November, praising the "ability and earnestness" of the ASGA executive, the public spirit of the senior class, and the good judgment and fine principles of Miss Richardson. "It came, then, like a thunderbolt out of a blue sky," she wrote to them in December, "to find the house rent on the question of the sorority."[36] Feelings ran high, and for the first time hostility divided students into factions; to Addison it was a critical period in the life of the residence.

The Sigma Chapter of the Kappa Alpha Theta Society had been established at the University of Toronto in 1905, and although no Victoria girls joined at the time, several of the University College girls resident in Annesley in 1904–05 attended the convention in Philadelphia. Two, Lee Edward and Maud Menten, were subsequently inducted. Mrs Burwash worried about the social implications in a letter to Addison: "I judge that in this particular chapter there is a tendency to extravagant and exhausting social life. Who will show us the way to the simple life? It is part of your high calling, and mine. I wonder if we can help each other to be faithful in the steadfast practice of it?"[37] The chapter was not large – involving eleven girls in the whole university – but its presence was ominous.

By 1908 Victoria, too, had a sorority, Xi Zeta Gamma, which consorted uneasily with the prevailing Methodist ethos of universal Christian fellowship. *Acta* spoke out about its adverse influence, not in terms of the simple life but in terms of its divisiveness. If no residence existed, the editor argued, there might be some call for the social amenities provided by a sorority or fraternity; no such need, though, existed for Victoria women, who had Annesley Hall.

Under such conditions a sorority can only be anti-social; it becomes a mere clique, with narrow outlook and selfish interests. The instinct of self-preservation and the desire for perpetuation engender jealousy, suspicion, and often alienation of the affections of dear friends. Loyalty to the class, the college, and the university becomes dwarfed to a mean, petty, self-aggrandizing loyalty to the sorority, while avowed or implied assumptions of superiority lead to attempts to manage affairs generally.[38]

Many Annesley women agreed and tried to prevent new students from joining. It is not clear by what course of discussion and negotiation a solution – a temporary one, as it turned out – was reached. But in December 1910, the sorority agreed that no girl was to be solicited until the end of her first year, when she knew what college and residence life had to offer. Peace then returned to the college.

Peace was disturbed again, however, by another crisis – one of the most serious of Addison's career. It began in early 1911 with Dr Burwash's criticism of irregularities in the residence; over the course of two years it led the Victoria senate, the board of regents, and the committee of management to question Addison's leadership and her wisdom in instituting student government. Apparently rumblings of discontent sufaced in the fall of 1910, for a note of Addison's offering to resign, dated 16 October 1910, exists in the archives.[39] Then on 30 January 1911, Addison received a letter from Burwash that formally set out his complaints:

I am told that many students have the habit of sitting up and visiting in their rooms until 12 o'clock at night, that students are allowed the privilege of going out on visits every night in the week, and that students have gone to dances without a chaperone and to dances probably the character of which we know nothing, and have come in as late as 2 o'clock in the morning. These are matters which, if mooted abroad, would destroy the value of our residence for young women in the eyes of our Methodist people, and, apart altogether from public opinion, they are things which should not be allowed in a well regulated college.[40]

He served notice that he had asked the senate to investigate these complaints.

Burwash's criticism implicitly involved several issues: inadequate rules (such as the absence of a prohibition against going to dances at all); rules that existed but were not strictly enforced (such as the requirement for a chaperone or the regulations on late leave); and the underlying question of whether the student government that allowed such a state of affairs was acceptable. The students policed themselves, though the dean had ultimate responsibility. Were they then sufficiently supervised, or was any degree of supervision, short of outright control, sufficient? A defence could have taken several approaches. One could deny the need for rules on some aspects of conduct, deny that the rules had been broken to any degree, or suggest that minor infractions did not endanger the morals of the young women. The benefits of student government on character, its supporters could argue, outweighed the occasional irregularities it let slip by. All these arguments and counter-arguments were put forth, though in a muted and implicit manner that was probably the result of not wishing to accuse the dean directly of incompetence. In broad terms, it was a struggle between Burwash's older Methodism – the desire to perpetuate a way of life that had been found good in the past – and the more flexible attitude of those like Addison, who were willing to adapt, albeit cautiously, to changing mores.

Ranged with Addison during this battle for her ideals and her reputation were many friends and supporters, not all of them of the younger generation. Mrs A.E. Lang, wife of Professor Lang of the German department and a member of the committee of management since 1905, urged in a note, "I know it must be just terrible for you, but *please* don't lose heart, and I think it will come right somehow … I really do, now."[41] "How brave you have been through it all," wrote Nettie Burkholder from the Ontario Ladies' College, "and I am sure right-minded people will see the injustice you have been called upon to endure."[42] Martha Bain of the committee was also a supporter. The well-disposed Rev. A.J. Irwin wrote, fearing that storms might delay his arrival at a senate meeting and prevent him from

Chancellor and Mrs Burwash

casting his vote. "I hope you will not let any outcome induce you to relinquish your task," he urged, hinting at Burwash's age of seventy-two in saying that "such changes must come shortly as will very materially alter many things around the college."[43] The Alumnae Association met and affirmed its support at special meetings on 8 and 14 March 1912 under the leadership of Nellie Rowell.[44] In the committee of management, Mrs Lang and Mrs J.R.L. Starr introduced a motion resolving that committee members "wish to send to the Senate an expression of our unreserved confidence in Miss Addison and in the general working of student government." Since a bare quorum was present and the president declined to vote, the motion could not pass. But nine members of the committee – Mrs Starr, Lang, Kerr, Carman, Gurney, Sutherland, Rowell, Fudger, and Miss Carty – sent a communication to the senate putting themselves on record as supporting the resolution.[45]

It was deeply painful that Mrs Burwash, so long a strong supporter and close friend, was now an adversary. For all her earlier policy of leaving discipline to the dean and backing up her decisions, she had a puritan streak that made it hard for her to countenance such activities as dancing and theatres. In the recollection of Ethel Bennett, it was she and not the dean who was strict: "Some people thought Miss Addison was too stern and rigid, but I don't think so at all, looking back. I think she did her best to moderate the rules. But Mrs. Burwash – wife of Chancellor Burwash – now she was a stickler for the rules. She used to invite students over for tea ... to check out our manners, we thought."[46]

Mrs Burwash represented an influential strain of thinking; she had many friends on the committee of management and at VWREA who shared her views. In the course of the dispute, Margaret Eaton wrote to her in a surprisingly uncultured style: "Take the First the Students going out to dances without a Chaperone and to *Public Halls* anyway, its a disgrace, and if write thinking Parent knew of it, I think it would be a bad thing for the Hall, for I assure you, if it were in my Case, none of my Children or Friends if I could help it would not be allowed to go to Annesley Hall." In Mrs Eaton's opinion, "its time Miss Addison were out of the Hall [for] nothing but trouble will be in the Hall while She is there."[47] Even more outspoken was Mrs Burwash's niece Margaret Proctor (later her daughter-in-law), a graduate of Household Science who had been at Annesley Hall from 1903 to 1906 and evidently nursed a grudge against the dean, as well as a tremendous chip on her shoulder. She fired off sarcastic diatribes from her dugout as housekeeper at Bryn Mawr: "... forget our FRIEND over the fence, and her queer ideas of what a Young Lady Ought To Be ... And I hope again that the Powers that be use their brains, and are not upset by a little bit of gossip, and show the Lady META that there are other people who have every bit as much right to live Comfortably, and sanely as she. She wont believe it but that['s] a trifle."[48]

Miss Addison's first action in the affair was to address the students on Wednesday, 1 February 1911, recalling the chancellor's accusations, asking whether these rumours were true, and reminding the girls that their conduct during this year would be taken into account in assessing next year's applications for residence. Her notes for the occasion include the headings "liberty turned into license" and "lax in our regulations, and the enforcement of them," but it is not known how the students reacted.[49] On Friday, 3 February, the senate (of which Margaret's brother Dr Will Addison was now a member by virtue of his place on the board of regents) took up Dr Burwash's concerns. The senators were particularly interested in the governance of the residence because plans for a men's residence had at long last materialized and it, too, would need rules and a constitution. They asked senate representatives on the standing joint committee for Annesley Hall to review the arrangements and suggest any necessary changes.[50]

The matter was also brought up in the committee of management by Mrs Burwash, who left the chair in order to voice her concerns. She read out the agreement on student government and said it had not been kept. The residents, she avowed, had interfered with the household management ("control of South Hall largely taken out of

Mrs. Sheffield's hands," read her notes).[51] She objected, furthermore, to changes in the rules of conduct that allowed students to substitute another night for Friday as their late night, and she drew attention to the absurdity of letting young women go three times a week to the theatre and to dances unchaperoned, while forbidding them to go to church with young men. Her conclusion was that "student government as administered in Annesley Hall was a failure."[52]

Contentious special meetings of the committee of management were held on 18 April and 15 May 1911 to consider the agreement and rules. Throughout the spring, drafts were sent back and forth between the committee, the senate, ASGA, and the standing joint committee on Annesley Hall. After a basic agreement had been reached, a last-minute hitch occurred when the senate held out for a clause stating that the minute-book of the ASGA executive recording its dealings with cases of discipline "shall at all times be open to the inspection of the Dean."[53] Addison objected to the clause, pointing out that there had been no disposition on the part of the executive to conceal its judgments. A deleted sentence in her draft letter to Professor Robertson, dean of arts and the most active representative of the senate on the joint committee, suggests her philosophy: "My experience leads me to believe that a large degree of liberty without espionage, develops a sense of honour and of responsibility, by which the student body is more effectively protected than it is by stricter rules and closer supervision."[54] The clause was eventually dropped.

The agreements that were reached did not differ greatly from the original documents; it would be tedious to detail all the changes. On the whole, they tightened up the rules of conduct, for instance, by specifying that leave after 12:30 a.m. should generally be granted only on the written request of a parent or guardian, or by adding "or boating and motoring" to the prohibited activities of "walking or driving" with gentlemen in the evening – unless accompanied by a chaperone approved by the dean. The changes to the agreement on student government were also minor, stressing the authority of the committee of management; as the senate committee explained, their amendments and additions "have been intended chiefly to remove ambiguities, to make more explicit the procedure to be followed at various stages, to give more definitely to the Ladies' Committee of Management that place in the government of the students which the Constitution prescribed by the Board of Regents had assigned to them, and to provide for certain contingencies on which the former regulations had been silent."[55] They did not enforce the strict prohibitions sought by the Burwashes; nor did they condemn or abolish student government. The senate accepted these revisions on 26 May 1911.

With this draft agreement, the matter might have been concluded. But it was not to be so simple. The community had been polarized and the issues went deep into the Methodist conscience; both sides felt themselves to be adhering to principle. Apparently in response to Dr Burwash's unwillingness to sign the documents, the senate agreement of 26 May stipulated that the new rules were to come into force immediately, but that the agreement on student government was not valid until further notice. In the committee of management, Mrs Burwash argued that the committee could not sign until the agreement had been approved by the board of regents, the source of their authority. Since the senate maintained that the board had no say in an agreement made between senate, committee, and students, and since the majority of the committee agreed, Mrs Burwash was isolated. Nevertheless, she was adamant and, moreover, had the signing power in virtue of her presidency. Thus she was given leave to seek the view of the board as a private individual.[56] Meanwhile, she did not sign.

The question was left suspended during the rest of 1911, leaving room for the emergence of a crisis of a different kind. In December 1911, a waitress in the dining room who complained of chills, sore throat, and stiffness was diagnosed with diphtheria. This dread disease involved the growth of a fleshy membrane in the throat, pain in swallowing, fetid discharges, depression, and general weakness that could lead to paralysis or death. It was liable to spread rapidly in institutions where utensils and living space were shared. Swabs were immediately taken of all residents, and fifteen other infected individuals were discovered: three officials, two maids, and ten students. Fortunately, an antitoxin available since 1894 could arrest the disease. Dr MacMurchy worked heroically to administer the treatment, assisted by Will Addison (who in the next year was to work on Toronto's milk commission to secure the pasteurization of milk, one of the suspected carriers of diphtheria bacteria). The doctors and their helpers, after isolating the sufferers in the splendid infirmary and surrounding rooms, thoroughly disinfected their original quarters. These measures were sufficient to contain the outbreak. Addison, worked to the bone, drew comfort from the fact that the uninfected girls rallied splendidly. Rather than pining to go home, they accepted their quarantine state and helped to keep the residence running by washing dishes and clearing tables. *Acta* reported that the quarantine brought a welcome cessation of lectures, term tests, and "all brain-cracking labour," and that the infirm passed their time by playing Parcheesi, checkers, and Old Foxy Grandpa, while healthy friends shouted messages to them from the balconies below.[57]

When the epidemic had passed its peak, discussion once again turned to the vexing question of residence government. On 2 February 1912, Professor Robertson moved that the senate now authorize the chancellor to sign the new agreements regarding Annesley Hall. But to his chagrin, Professors Bell of Classics and McLaughlin of Orientals – surely acting in cahoots with the diehard Dr Burwash – moved a substitute motion: that the chancellor and the deans of arts and theology should form a committee to confer with the dean of Annesley Hall on certain reports that had come to the ears of the senate regarding late nights, dances, theatres, and so on. Their motion was carried, and the whole matter blew open again.

Addison's main response was to draw up a "Report of the Administration of the Rules and Regulations of Annesley Hall, from September 27, 1911 to February 1, 1912," a "Report Concerning the Attendance at the Theatre for the 16 Weeks of the First Term," and a "Report Concerning the Attendance at Dances" for the same period.[58] Here her almost obsessive record-keeping served her well, for she was able to show that such liberties as were allowed under the new rules had not been abused. She reported only a few cases of students failing to return by 12:30 p.m., which were punished by fines ranging from 25 to 50 cents. In fact, most of the rules had never been disobeyed. With typical Addisonian thoroughness she broke down the plays attended into Shakespearean and non-Shakespearean, noting that "the plays of Shakespeare were reckoned as equivalent to lectures, and the students were permitted to attend as many as they wished during the week that Robert Mantell played in Toronto."[59] Only one person had attended as many as six non-Shakespearean plays. In all, seven dances were attended by six people (four Methodists and two Presbyterians, all in good academic standing). A comparison of marks showed that those in residence did as well as, or better than, the non-residents. Obviously, Addison felt that she and the student government had no reason to be ashamed.

Dr Burwash, too, had not been idle. In late February 1912, he sent out a letter asking several church figures and alumnae whether they supported student government and whether they thought there should be changes in the rules of conduct. Although he received some replies taking a liberal view – including one from graduate Cora Hewitt pointing out that the students could not be treated like school children – his concerns were echoed by Albert Carman, still general superintendent of the Methodist Church. Carman was ever an authoritarian figure, and his reply is delightfully typical of old-time Methodism:

When I read of "night watch keys" for girls, of students returning to their rooms from amusements "after midnight," of their "attendance upon theatres and dances," I am strongly inclined to say: "This is not Methodism: I fear it is leagues aside: this is not the pathway of healthful discipline or of sound and safe scholarship; it is not the beaten road of intellectual improvement and spiritual power." That is what I had supposed Methodist colleges to mean; and I fear, the statements of the Report if known abroad will not aid the Secretary-of-Education in his work.[60]

On 15 March 1912, Addison's vindication came at a well-attended meeting of the senate. After hearing all the reports and statements, the senate rejected a last-minute motion from Professor Bell and Chancellor Burwash to reconsider the rules regarding dances, theatres, and chaperones; authorized the chancellor and registrar to sign the agreement; and passed a motion strongly endorsing the dean's conduct of the residence. They also took a further and even more important step: they recommended to the committee of management that all the officers of the Hall should be placed under the dean, rather than reporting directly to the committee. As Martha Bain had written in her letter of support to Addison, "I said at the start that the weak spot in the administration of Annesley was two equal heads – it could not succeed."[61] In exalting the dean in this way the senate doubly vindicated her conduct: not only did it remove a difficulty that she had had since the beginning of her tenure, it made sure that her vision would prevail.

Although the senate was won over, the battle continued in the committee of management. There Mrs Burwash now attempted once more to have the board of regents weigh in over the head of the senate. Her justification was that the board had entrusted the committee with the responsibility of prescribing the duties of the officers of the Hall, a responsibility that the senate now proposed to transfer to the dean. She was not the only member of the committee who feared a concentration of power in Addison's hands. "I don't think the officers are children," wrote Margaret Eaton, "and to think of them being under a Woman like the Dean, is too much, I for one would *never* sanction such a thing ..."[62] Mrs Burwash drew up a memorial to the board, complaining about the transfer of authority and the laxness in the dean's administration, and saying that Addison had been using her discretionary power too freely in granting exceptions to the rules. The problem, she pointed out almost in so many words, lay not with the student government, but with Margaret Addison's handling of it. Mrs Burwash persuaded six other members of the committee to sign her memorial, including Susie D. Massey, Margaret P. Massey (Chester Daniel's second wife), Lillian Massey

Treble, Mrs Wood, and (oddly, since they had supported Addison a month before) Mrs Sutherland and Mary Carty.[63] But the board found itself disinclined to act on the memorial, which subsequently got lost in a maze of committees.

At a meeting of the committee of management on April 11, Mrs Burwash left the chair to make a statement, declaring that "if this committee introduces or allows anything to creep into Annesley Hall which is contrary to the spirit and practice of Victoria College it is exceeding its commission."[64] On her side, Addison was able to state, as if vindicating the student government, that the residents had voted to restrict leave after 12:30 p.m. to Victoria functions only and, furthermore, had passed a resolution disapproving of public dances. With these two opposing statements the meeting adjourned. On 15 April the committee reconvened, expressed pleasure in the senate's resolution of confidence in the dean, and declared themselves willing to readjust the officers' duties. Effectively, Addison had won her battle, though it was some time before the documents were formally signed. In October 1912 the Burwashes were granted a year's leave; they went on holiday out west, and from there the chancellor sent in his resignation.[65] Early in 1913 they went to Japan. In October 1913, Mrs Burwash resigned from the committee of management. Perhaps the last word should go to Margaret Proctor, with her ringing prediction: "If the D——d DEAN wants to run the poor housekeeper and have her under her direction, Let her by all means, and then hear the tales that rise to the heavens, IT is the best way to settle it, Give a man enough rope and She'll hang herself."[66] That the damned dean hung in there instead was not due to any encouragement on Margaret Proctor's part.

Annesley Hall was a time-consuming preoccupation, but it must not be thought that Addison had no private life. As always, she read avidly. Though there is no record of the particular books she read during these early years, she was beginning to amass a large collection, having no resistance where books were concerned. One later graduate remarked that "she bought, loaned and gave away more books than anyone the graduate had ever known."[67] She also spent time in prayer, which was of course completely private. Psychologically she was developing, learning to some extent to modify her expectations, or at least the expression of them. In person she was becoming more stately and impressive. Pheme Wood, it seems, had imparted some of her worldly *savoir faire*; by introducing Addison to an excellent dressmaker and offering suggestions on deportment, she had helped to transform a diffident provincial schoolteacher into a gracious woman who could hold her own in any gathering.[68]

Addison was constantly supported by her family, which during these years expanded considerably. Arthur, a minister whose postings included North Bay, Alliston, and Newmarket, had four children: his oldest daughter Louise, born in 1901, was followed by Bill, Peter, and George. In 1903 Will married Janie Hillock, a graduate of the University of Toronto in mathematics and physics who was unable to teach her chosen subject because of her sex, and who eventually became a governess to Joseph Flavelle's children. Although the couple lived in Penetanguishine for a while, by 1907 they were back in Toronto to supervise the building of their house at 431 Broadview Avenue; there Will ran his medical practice while also serving as company doctor for Flavelle's William Davies Company. They had a daughter, Mary, in 1904, a son Peter in 1907 (he was known as "Black" Peter for his hair colour and to distinguish him from his cousin, Arthur's "Red" Peter), and then Julia and Jack. Margaret used to invite these nephews and nieces to dinner in Annesley Hall when the girls had gone, so that the halls rang for a change with high voices and childish footsteps.[69] The children loved to investigate Aunt Margaret's room on the ground floor of the Hall, and to accompany her as she toured through the abandoned bedrooms and assessed their state.

Margaret was particularly close to her sister Charlotte in these years. After the death of their mother in 1905, the family had considered having Charlotte stay home to look after her father, Peter Addison. But Margaret had refused to let Charlotte's career be sacrificed in this way and urged the plan eventually adopted: the family home on Markham Street was sold, and Peter and Charlotte went to live with one or other of the brothers during the year. Grandfather Addison fit into his sons' families very well, peacefully sitting by the fire reading and peeling platefuls of apples sent to him from the Bemans' farm, or, still strong of arm, chopping wood or shovelling snow with one of his grandsons. In the summer, Margaret herself looked after her father at the Orchard Beach cottage, where he had become accustomed to sleeping in a tent on a wooden platform so his family could fit into the main building.

Unfortunately, circumstances put an end to Charlotte's career as a music teacher. Perhaps because of diphtheria, she became seriously deaf in 1908. Although her first recourse was to enrol in University College, she turned to the study of household science from 1909 to 1911, preparing to become a dietician. As her deafness was a barrier there too, Margaret attended lectures with her and took notes. Charlotte was often at Annesley Hall for meals, amusing the girls with the definiteness of her opinions.

Margaret and Charlotte enjoyed being at the cottage together during the summer, usually a time of relaxation. In the summer of 1909, however, Margaret was stricken by a shadowy illness, perhaps gastrointestinal, that necessitated an operation and a long convalescence at the cottage, spent mostly in bed. Managing to totter back to work in the fall, she told the committee that "I had not expected to be here this year. I thought my life on earth was finished."[70] For more than a year thereafter she suffered from dizziness and needed to lie down for an hour or two in the afternoon. Her health never really recovered.

The summer of 1912 presented an opportunity to travel abroad that was particularly welcome after the battles of the previous two years. There were two important congresses that year: a meeting of the World's YWCA in Swanwick, Derbyshire, England (of which little is known); and the Congress of the Universities of the Empire, convened in London to share information on university administration. Margaret was accredited to both bodies; as always, she jumped at the chance to gain an international perspective and to meet Europeans. She had long felt that Canada suffered from an inflated notion of its own importance and an appalling lack of cosmopolitan knowledge; as she told the alumnae, the nation was in a state of adolescence, "and we as a part of it suffer from immaturity, and self-consciousness."[71]

In attending the Congress of the Universities from July 2 to 5, Addison was part of a very distinguished group of people, playfully characterized by Prince Arthur of Connaught as "the quintessence of the wisdom of the ages, and the brain power of today."[72] The chancellors of all the British universities were there, as well as officials from forty-nine of the fifty-three degree-granting institutions in the empire. The University of Toronto had sent President Falconer, Vice-President Ramsay Wright, Dean Pakenham, Professor J.C. Robertson of Victoria, and Professor A.H. Young of Trinity; Addison represented the United Alumnae. The conference, the first such gathering, was widely reported in the press, and its delegates were treated to luncheon at the Savoy, a reception at the Mansion House, dinner at the British Academy, and other marks of favour.

For Addison it renewed memories of her 1900 trip. The sessions took place in the Imperial Institute, which she had visited in 1900 to see the University of London. Among those giving addresses was Mrs Sidgwick of Newnham, who was at least familiar to her by name, and Professor J.A.R. Marriott, whom she had met at Oxford. The opening address was given by Lord Rosebery, chancellor of the University of London, whose talk on the London local elections she had tried to hear in 1900, though she had arrived too late to get a seat.

Clearly, he was a popular and apposite speaker. In a speech to the congress that must have struck an answering chord in Addison despite its non-inclusive language, he stressed the universities' role in developing the men of principle that the empire needed – "a form of Imperialism," he noted, "to which not the least Englander could take exception."[73] Nearly ten years later Margaret could still remember his words: "You cannot have a class of character or a class of morals; but you can imbue and infuse character and morals and energy and patriotism by the tone and atmosphere of your universities and of your professors. We need men whose character and virtues can influence and inspire others."[74] Of particular interest to her were the sessions on university extension work, ably addressed by working-man Albert Mansbridge, and the one on the position of women in universities.[75]

During the session on women, on the last day of the congress, Addison had a chance literally to stand up for her principles. Miss H.M. White, principal of Alexandra College, had given a paper on women's concerns which was statistically inaccurate. Besides, according to Professor Young in his report for the Toronto *Globe*,

She showed that she had entirely failed to grasp the significance of the distinction between the honour and the pass courses of the University of Toronto. She also seemed inclined to make merry, almost to wax satirical, over the honour course in domestic science, which gave Miss Addison of Annesley Hall an excellent opportunity to set her right and to tell the Congress what an important part in public health and private comfort domestic science was playing and will further play in Canada, besides offering women highly paid employment.[76]

Addison was a well-informed critic: not only had she studied the teaching of household science in England and encouraged its introduction in Canada, but she had just sat through the course of lectures with Charlotte and knew whereof she spoke. Unfortunately, no record remains of the words in which she defended her vision of educated womanhood in the service of home and country. After the convention she had the opportunity to visit sites such as the University of Birmingham and the Royal Holloway College for Women, the latter unaccountably omitted in her 1900 tour. It must have been uncommonly satisfying to reflect how the holidaying high-school teacher of 1900 had become 1912's official delegate from the University of Toronto, the recipient of red-carpet treatment, and a recognized part of the brain power of today, if not of the quintessence of the wisdom of the ages.

CHAPTER SEVEN

War Years

After the battles of 1911–12, Addison faced a fluid and uncertain situation in the 1913–14 school year. The Burwashes's departure precipitated a drastic turnover, from top to bottom, in the staff and officials of her world. Victoria's new principal and chancellor, Richard Pinch Bowles, was inducted in the fall of 1913. At the same time, Mrs R.N. Burns replaced Mrs Burwash as president of the committee of management. She was the former Mary Crossen, the first student at Brookhurst Academy in Cobourg to attend lectures at Victoria. Although she was to serve as president for sixteen years, she was a neophyte at that time, having joined the committee only in January 1912. In January 1914 – no doubt in sympathy with Mrs Burwash – Margaret Eaton, Pheme Wood, and Margaret Massey resigned from the committee. Martha Bain, though a supporter and friend of Addison's, also sent in her resignation; she was now a seventy-six-year-old widow and had moved to Winnipeg. Since death removed Susie Chown soon after she was appointed in 1912, and later Mrs Treble as well, one-third of the committee were newcomers. To add to the difficulty of learning to work together, they had also to become accustomed to the workings of a new constitution. This reorganization, imposed as a result of Addison's gaining more authority over the Hall officers, decentralized the committee; subcommittees were formed to deal with separate areas such as finances and furnishing.

At the Hall itself, changes occurred as well. Mrs Scott Raff sent in her resignation; though there is little documentation on the matter, it appears that she found it difficult to accept Addison's increased authority and her own official subordination. The classes she had run in the gym since the inception of Annesley Hall were discontinued. Fortunately, the Household Science building had opened next door with a small pool and a gym in the basement, open to all University of Toronto women. The Annesley housekeeper, the invaluable Miss Richardson, said to be opposed to a plan to have two pupil dieticians in residence but no doubt also unhappy at becoming answerable to

the dean, was invited by the committee to take six months' paid leave
of absence from July 1913 to regain her health.[1] The two pupil dieticians, Alice Prangley and Olive Cruikshank, arrived in the fall of 1914
but departed again in December, on the grounds that they were not
learning as much as they had expected to. Even the faithful janitor,
James Mullin, had left in June 1912 when his wife became ill; his
replacement, Mr Light, died in April 1913.

Some of the difficulties of dealing with the domestic staff may be
gauged by letters passing between Mrs Burwash and Mrs Sheffield,
head of South Hall, regarding the hiring of Eleanor Bowden. She was
an English maid who had "borne a great sorrow" – a euphemism, it
would appear, for a baby. Mrs Sheffield's letter suggests a chilly social
climate:

Personally the "sorrow" to which you refer would not be an impediment,
as I would be only to glad to render a helping hand. The fact that she "feels
very keenly" seems to be assurance that she would be careful to conceal
from the maids of both halls anything that it would be wise to withhold
from them. That is, as far as I can see, the only danger point. Should the
others [i.e., other maids] even suspect anything wrong, the demand for her
dismissal, or the fashionable *strike*, would probably follow, with all that
would mean.[2]

In December 1913, a sad incident occurred in which a Finnish maid,
Anni Jokinen, disappeared from the Hall and was found two weeks
later just before she died, having perhaps lost her memory. Addison
and MacMurchy attended her funeral on the afternoon of Christmas
Day in a bitter wind. In January two servants were dismissed, after
a rash of thefts.[3] Clearly, the position of head of the Hall employees
involved more headaches than joy. Moreover, as Addison noted in
her Annual Report to the Committee of Management, in the unsettled
climate of 1913–14 she had been mired down in administrative detail;
thus she had had little opportunity for her real work: to "quicken the
lives of the young women, spiritually and mentally."[4]

It proved particularly difficult for Addison to find a replacement
for Miss Richardson, with whom (she felt) she had worked so har-
moniously. The woman who succeeded Miss Richardson in July 1913,
Helen G. Reid (Mrs Esson Reid), was not a happy choice. After an
initial contretemps in which she balked at learning that she was to
be responsible to both the dean and Mrs Sheffield and resigned her
post before it had really been taken up, she was mollified by the new
title of dietician and director of household. She was allowed to move

into residence with her two daughters, aged sixteen and nineteen. But by September, Addison was annoyed to discover that the older daughter, Marjorie, who was starting university, had enroled in University College rather than Victoria, and thus was technically ineligible for a place in Annesley Hall. She swallowed her chagrin, however, when Mrs Reid argued that she thought an exception had been made for her family, inasmuch as all her relatives had gone to University College. But her difficulties with Mrs Reid did not end there. The household never did run smoothly and, as early as October, rumblings of discontent were heard about the quality of the meals and their tardiness. Eventually, the girls sent a delegation to the committee to complain; finally, on 29 October, Mrs Reid, commenting scornfully on false gossip from the servants' hall, sent in her resignation.[5] In 1915 Addison noted that Mrs Reid was causing the University College Alumnae the same trouble that she had caused at Victoria: they "have had to close their tea rooms, and are not at all sure that they will be able to get their furniture."[6]

Mrs Reid left a fine mess behind her: the storerooms were dirty and disordered, "nothing in either house was under lock and key, and the domestics lived high."[7] Fortunately, another new officer had been hired – a nurse, Marion L. Clark, who was a gem. As Miss Richardson showed no inclination to return, Miss Clark helped Addison to run the household until a new housekeeper could be found. And when Jessie Elliott was hired in December 1913, she too proved to be a "keeper." In her October 1914 report, Addison spoke highly of Miss Elliott's qualities: "But no Committee, and no report, can tell how valuable Miss Elliott is to our Residences in the spirit which she has introduced into her share of the work. She considers in every way the best interests of the young women, making them feel how much this is a home for them, and yet is very firm if they exceed their rights."[8] Addison also emphasized the new harmony attainable when all the officers were under the same management, namely hers: "There is now enough organization in the household to carry out our plans with the least waste of energy on the part of each worker, and yet all arrangements are elastic enough to do away with any feeling of restraint." Miss Clark and Miss Elliott, she said elsewhere, realized that in the theatre of life "it is not enough that each enact her own role, but that each enact it with due regard to the unity and perfection of the whole."[9] Even the maids now felt themselves part of the community and exhibited their new spirit by listening to the prayers in the dining hall, or at least standing still and appearing to do so, rather than using the pause as an opportunity to unload the crockery.

With Miss Elliott's help, Addison organized a mighty, cathartic cleanup after the departure of the peccant Mrs Reid. The rooms were cleaned and painted, couches re-covered, the supply of linens and dishes renewed, and repairs made, so that all would be spic and span for the fall of 1914. Addison also addressed the continuing problem of overcrowding. Crowding in the dining room particularly distressed her, because it made for a noisy and frenetic atmosphere. Since October 1913 she had arranged for meals to be served in South Hall – cooked in Annesley and carried over in a fireless cooker – so that a more family-like atmosphere prevailed. As a further relief, for the 1914–15 year another satellite building was obtained, encircling Annesley along with South Hall and the rented Bloor Street boarding house. This was "the Annex" at 81 Charles Street West, bought by the board of regents and furnished by the Victoria Women's Association (as the VWREA was now called). Here sixteen "energetic and merry" freshies[10] were lodged under the direction of Miss Cruikshank. In January 1915, Miss Cruikshank was succeeded by Clara Clinkscale, a brilliant graduate of 1912, who had won the James Loudon gold medal in physics and been in charge of the Bloor Street house since November 1913.

In the years immediately preceding the war, the Victoria campus expanded in other ways. The Birge-Carnegie Library had arisen to the west of the main college during 1910, its Collegiate Gothic style reminiscent of the great English universities. To the east, the long-awaited men's residence, named Burwash Hall after the departing chancellor, was begun in 1911 and formally opened on 17 October 1913. Although Addison may not have been wholly delighted at the prospect of such a concentration of turbulent male energy so close at hand, the VWA had long since agreed that the need for men's residences was so pressing as to take precedence over the expansion of the women's building. The men's dean of residence was the future governor-general, Vincent Massey. He was the son of the donor of the residence, C.D. Massey, and of the latter's first wife Anna, who had served briefly on the committee of management until her death in 1903. Vincent, a great anglophile who had just returned from Balliol College, Oxford, hoped to bring the refinements of an older culture to bear on what he considered the "rather fearsome crudity" of the young men of Victoria.[11] The civilizing process included the introduction of Oxford rituals such as Latin grace before meals to the residence, which had been built as a series of "houses" designed to recall the "staircases" of an Oxford college.[12] Given Massey's belief in English tradition and in the English notion that education should

form the character, there were theoretical grounds at least for a sense
of shared mission between the deans.

It was a minor irony that just as the residence was prepared to open
on a firm footing in 1914, newly refurbished and with a harmonious
slate of officials, war should break out and render all such considerations insignificant. Addison was reticent about the war, but of course
it affected her both personally and professionally. Immediately after
war was declared in August, twenty-two girls withdrew their applications for residence, and she began to fear that the purchase of the
Annex might prove unnecessary. The Victoria campus was a quieter
and more sombre place in the fall of 1914. President Bowles in his
message to returning students urged "simplicity of life and frugality
of social functions." "Seriousness, gravity, duty, the blast of the
bugle," he admonished, "remember these things this year."[13] The
Senior Dinner, the Senior Reception, and the Conversazione or "At
Home" were all cancelled and replaced by one simpler reception. At
first few college men enlisted, although they toyed with the possibility and formed a Victoria company of the Canadian Officers' Training
Corps. Several times a week the Annesley girls were awakened by a
bugle call as the company drilled on the grounds behind their residence before classes. All over the campus were columns of trainees
marching past.

Gradually, the young men disappeared, some for ever. By the fall
of 1915, ninety Victoria men still remained in first year; by the fall of
1916, however, only ninety remained in the whole college and a mere
seventeen of these were freshmen. Burwash Hall, partially emptied,
became an army barracks for officers and non-commissioned officers
in training.[14] The sight of rows of young men at a college function
brought a lump to Margaret's throat: "I could hardly keep from
weeping when I thought of how many of these young fellows would
probably have laid down their lives ere another year has passed."[15]
In March 1915 she went to the Exhibition grounds to see the muster-
ing of the soldiers who were leaving for Europe with the Second
Contingent; a group of them were entertained at tea at Annesley. In
January 1916 she was attending a service in Convocation Hall, when
to her dismay it was announced that Ross Taylor had been killed the
week before. She had taught at Stratford CI with his father, Wilson
Taylor, and had held Ross when he was a baby; he was a fine student,

she wrote in a letter to friends, and "particularly lovable, as well as clever."[16] He had been entertaining *Acta* readers with accounts of his travels in Italy during off-duty hours. In a heartbreaking gesture, reported Addison, "the mothers of the two who rest in Flanders were present at [the 1916] graduation and at the reception – they thought that their boys would have liked them to meet their classmates."[17]

Amidst the horror and carnage was one possible redemptive feature: the new spirit of seriousness that swept the nation. In the pre-war years everything had been too easy, Addison thought; prosperity had bred the featherheaded type of character who lacked internal discipline and thought only of momentary pleasure.[18] In early 1914, for instance, the whole university had been seized with a craze for the tango (the Lambada of the early century). Addison was probably not amused by a report in the *Varsity* that Victoria students had been surreptitiously tangoing in the basement gym of Annesley Hall, and that she herself had been driven "to confess that she could see no harm in a little after-dinner 'hop' as an aid to digestion."[19] As she wrote to her sister, these worldly distractions tended to cheat the students out of "a real consciousness of what God might be to them":

I work up to a high degree – or a *low* degree would be better – of despair every February, when the winter sports are on, when the earnest students who bear the burden of their societies can scarcely find time even to skate on the rink, and the more flighty students can scarcely find time to stay in the house. They toboggan, and nearly break their pretty heads; they snow-shoe in the moon-light, and nearly break their dear hearts; while the band on the rink lures them out at least two nights a week. In vain I storm within, but nobody seems to sympathize with me much.[20]

War achieved what moral exhortation could not do, sweeping away these frivolities and allowing the important things of life to come to the fore. Could it be, Addison wondered, that this was the start of that new era of self-sacrifice and spiritual power, so long awaited and prayed for? Early on she wrote to Miss Rouse, now English secretary of the YWCA, "It is hardly possible for us to feel the results of the war as keenly as you do in England, and yet it is making a great difference even here. None of us can be untouched by it. Hearts are softer and more tender than they were, and naturally materialism has not the same hold upon the people."[21] In November 1915 she reported that "there is a deeper sense of the power of prayer this year, more faith, and a larger number keeping the morning watch than for some time."[22]

The women's spiritual discipline was the age-old one of patience, waiting, and passive suffering. As Addison saw it,

I think the reason why women suffer so much is because they have no choice in the matter of going or staying. It requires much reasoning with oneself to be content to keep on at the same tasks that one has performed all one's life, with a little knitting added thereto, and a little Red Cross work, to feel that one is offering something that is of any use to the country. Of course, we know that the constructive work of education is as much needed just now as the destructive work of battle.[23]

In compassion she bent some of the rules a little. For instance, though normally frowning on reading at the breakfast table, she arranged for a paper to be provided at each table in the dining hall every morning so that one girl could read the war news out loud. War news was also posted daily in the women's study at the college, and the Annesley Hall prayers included a period of silent intercession for the men at the front.

Many of the women at Victoria sought a more active role and cast about for ways to show themselves worthy of the sacrifices of the men. There was talk of forming a female corps and learning to march in formation, but the idea was rejected as of limited usefulness.[24] The Women's Literary Society sent a circular letter pleading for economy and simplicity: "We leave it to each girl to draw the line between what is legitimate expenditure and what is extravagance, suggesting only the abstinence from obvious extravagances such as candy, flowers and elaborate dress."[25] Some gave up going to the theatre for the duration of the war; many bought fewer and less elaborate Christmas presents, in order to donate more to the allied cause. The women of the college began a Patriotic Tea Room, offering a 10- or 15-cent tea in the women's study three times a week, with the profits going to the Red Cross. Eighty women also enrolled in a St. John Ambulance course in first aid for the injured.

In Annesley Hall, the women made and packed candy for the men at the front, in addition to making scrapbooks for soldiers in hospital. As the Red Cross had an almost unlimited need for clothing and supplies, the girls knitted and sewed in every free moment, at social circles and even at Bible study groups. They were particularly adept at a new kind of sock, "like a little bag," explained Margaret, describing to Charlotte what would now be called a tube sock; it "has no heel, but you can make a heel anywhere – all the way around – which greatly saves darning."[26]

The university women, the vwa, and the University Women's Club also worked tirelessly for the University Hospital Supply Committee.[27] The University of Toronto had committed itself to provide a 1040-bed hospital, known as No. 4 Canadian General Hospital, to operate in Salonica. Addison could see some irony in the situation: "If it were not so gruesome, one would find it humorous to think of men being trained for months and months and months to shoot down other men, and then to have hospitals established to care for the men that were not quite killed."[28] Nevertheless, she threw herself into the committee work necessary to raise money and to provide the needed supplies. The hospital was seeking donations of $3,300 a month, as well as twelve thousand sheets; six thousand surgical nightshirts; and a corresponding number of pyjamas, slippers, socks, hot-water-bottle covers, caps, gowns, masks, and so on. From March to May 1915, the Biology building was open every week day from ten to five so that women could sew supplies on forty sewing machines, or cut out garments for others to sew at home. In these three months they were able to provide the complete initial needs of the hospital. Later in the war, the hospital found it easier to obtain supplies from the Red Cross in Britain than to wait for uncertain transport from Canada; in exchange, the products of the Biology Building were sent to the Canadian Red Cross for use in French hospitals. By 1917 the women had shipped 1,394 cases of goods; a typical week's output was 192 pairs of pyjamas, 84 day shirts, 90 surgical shirts, 11 dressing gowns, and 362 pairs of socks.

As the war progressed, labour was in ever shorter supply. President Bowles described himself as acting as his own hired man on his farm, forking hay in the blazing sun.[29] Meanwhile, the girls of Annesley Hall took the place of some of the maids in washing dishes and cleaning the Hall. By the summer of 1917, it was necessary to call on women university students to help bring in the fruit crop. Fifty-nine Victoria women answered this appeal and spent their summer holidays in camps at Niagara or at Winona, twelve miles east of Hamilton, near the E.D. Smith cannery. According to a vivid account of the experience by Hilda Collins, an Annesley Hall resident, many predicted that educated girls were too soft and luxury loving for the scheme to succeed.[30] There were pointed warnings that the work was hard; the Dominion Council of the ywca, organizing tent cities, sent letters admonishing the fruit pickers to realize "that they are not to be housed in luxurious hotels" and must bring their own bedding and towels and be prepared to pitch in with the housework, besides paying $4 a week for board.[31]

At the camp at Winona the women – mostly from the University of Toronto, with a sprinkling of high school and Queen's girls – rose at 5:15 a.m. and were taken in wagons to the jam factory, where they worked from 7:00 a.m. to 6:00 p.m. with an hour off for lunch. For three weeks they sat on stools and hulled strawberries, varying the monotony with song:

My thumbs they are wobbly and weary;
My eyes they are blood-shot and bleary;
My back it is broken, and that is a token
I'm tired of hulling strawberries.

For the rest of the summer, they hoed clay fields in the blazing sun and picked fruit. Not the least of their satisfactions was in confounding the doubters, including the farmers, who had been as enthusiastic about receiving their help as a recruiting sergeant confronted with a posse of nursemaids. In fact they were able to complete tasks that had defeated inexperienced male workers.

The YWCA positively encouraged the fruit pickers to leave their bulky clothes at home and wear the working uniform of a shady hat, middy blouses, and bloomers. As Hilda Collins put it, "How could anyone work expeditiously and comfortably in heavy skirts, and how could thin, flimsy, cool skirts endure the impact with thorns and briar bushes?"[32] Addison did not find it easy to condone this new freedom in dress – even years later she was rebuking Edna Ash for appearing on the stage of the Victoria College chapel wearing men's pants while playing the part of one of the witches in *Macbeth*.[33] She had given her niece Louise some bloomers, left behind at Annesley Hall, but she was horrified when Louise (then a high-school student) proposed to wear them in public while picking cherries. Nevertheless, Louise persisted, and the garment – a coulotte of heavy and prickly blue wool reaching below her knees – became a token of liberation.

At the same time as she was encouraging the Annesley girls to do war work, Addison, through her membership in a network of women's organizations and her seemingly inexhaustible capacity for committee meetings, was also involved with the movement to mobilize the talents of women in society at large. As is well known, World War I marks the first entry of women into the general work force and into previously male jobs, and women's groups such as the YWCA organized their recruitment. Neither manufacturers nor labour were enthusiastic about this innovation; organized labour, in particular, feared that employers would take advantage of the emergency to replace regular workers with low-paid females and to roll back hard-won concessions such as sanitary requirements and limitation of hours.[34] Through her position on the Dominion Council of the YWCA, Addison was one of those involved in making the arrangements and calming fears.

She was, for instance, a committee member on the Women's Emergency Corps, a Toronto group formed to register women for war work in January 1916. She and four other committee members met representatives of the Trades and Labour Union of Toronto at the Labour Temple to assure them that they were not trying to displace the male labour force, but simply drawing up a list of women who could step in when men were unavailable. The union men wanted all vacant positions to be offered first to returning soldiers, then to men too old or unfit to go to the front, and only lastly to women. They recommended that the women's committee speak to the secretary of the Dominion Labour Congress (Paddy Draper), who was coming to town, and on Monday 31 January they went down to Elliott House to do so. Draper, "a heavily-built man, with a stern face," received them courteously, but said he was strongly opposed to women doing heavy work in munitions; he added that the principle of equal pay for equal work should be rigorously upheld so that the women did not undercut the men. He suggested that, as the shortage of workers was mainly a Toronto phenomenon, the women might make a local arrangement with the union.[35] This was apparently done to the satisfaction of both parties; nevertheless, as the war progressed, women were inevitably drawn into munitions and other factory work. Since the manufacturers maintained that they could not look after the women recruited from outlying areas, the Munitions Board of Ottawa called on the YWCA to take charge of their housing and feeding. Addison, as a member of the YWCA Committee for Military Purposes, as well as a former resident of Lindsay, helped with the arrangements for several hundred women brought in to work at the arsenal in Lindsay.[36]

This was not her only involvement with the needs of women outside the university during these years. Her interest in broader social problems can be seen, for instance, in her attendence at the Conference on Social Problems in New York in April 1914 as a delegate of the student YWCA. In particular, she worked for the welfare of domestic servants, whose lot she thought would be much improved by more solid credentials. During her trip to England in 1900, she had studied British and continental provision of technical training for women. Such training had become more feasible in Ontario with the passage of the Industrial Education Act of 1911, and Addison was a member of a subcommittee of the University Women's Club formed to institute a course for maids. Part of her task was to pick out promising maids whose mistresses were willing to pay the tuition fee and give them three half-days off a week to attend classes at the Technical High School. In the fall of 1915, the school, now known as Central Technical School, moved to its new quarters, at two million dollars the most expensive school building in the province. Among its labs and shops was a completely equipped model apartment for housekeeping practice.

In March of 1915, when one of the chosen maids was troubled to the point of possible violence, Addison put her up in her own bedroom over the weekend until the hospital could take her in. The sight of this hapless woman being carted off stirred her conscience:

It is some progress to have any place such as a hospital [she wrote], but it is also too bad that some of us have things so much in abundance and to others are denied the necessities of life. One becomes quite tangled up in one's thought about it, and I suppose the most one can do is to do the best one can where one is, and have the spirit of democracy in one's heart, even if there is little evidence of it outside of one's heart.[37]

Charity did begin at home with her sympathetic attitude to the maids at Annesley Hall. Among her annual admonitions to the girls was a plea to be considerate of the servants: many of them, she explained, were immigrants who had no parents or settled home in this country and led unimaginably lonely and unsupported lives.[38] When they had nowhere but Annesley Hall in which to spend Christmas, she made sure that she or someone senior was on hand to fill their stockings and provide seasonal treats.[39]

Addison worked to improve the education of the more privileged classes, too, through her connection with the Ontario Ladies' College. Though she had taught there for only two years, she maintained links with the institution through its alumnae association, the Trafalgar Daughters. In March 1915, thinking it "too good a lark to miss,"[40] she travelled to Whitby in a special railway car with thirty other men and women to attend an overnight reunion there. In spite of having miscalculated and brought only her second-best gown and consequently "look[ing] appallingly simple beside all these grandees from Toronto and Whitby, to say nothing of the students," she enjoyed herself immensely and stayed up talking to other women in the halls till 2:00 a.m. about the possible future of the school. 1915 was a pivotal year in its history, since Dr Hare was resigning as principal after forty-one years in April, and a new lady principal (his second-in-command) was also needed. Although Hare would have loved to hire Addison for this position, he rightly judged that she would not entertain the offer. She in turn argued that a woman should take Dr Hare's place, though the directors did not agree.[41] She did, however, serve on the committee of the Trafalgar Daughters to search for a new lady principal. Once again there was talk of letting the school evolve into a women's college, and Addison, though on the whole preferring coeducational and more broadly based institutions, was not averse to the plan. Colleges such as the OLC provided the only education that some society women in Canada were likely to receive, and a dogmatic prejudice against them was counterproductive, declared Addison. "Education is a means to an end," she argued, "and there are many roads to Rome."[42]

She also kept up her interest in high-school teaching through membership in the Ontario Educational Association, serving as chair of the Modern Languages Section in 1915. "A presidential address hangs over me like a dark cloud," she confided to her friends,[43] though by now she was an accomplished speaker. Among the teachers she saw when she could were the two Marty sisters: Sophie, her successor at Stratford; and Aletta Elise, also a teacher of moderns, who had taught at her old school at Lindsay. Sophie evidently kept her informed as to teachers' salaries, while Aletta, who was to become Toronto's first female school inspector and receive an honorary doctorate from Queen's, was perhaps inspired by her friend Margaret when she helped to found Ban Righ Hall at Queen's.

On the Toronto university campus, the needs of women had become more pressing. Contrary to fears in early 1914, generated by the sudden withdrawal of applications, the war had actually encouraged the enrolment of women: by the 1916–17 year, a record 179 were studying at Victoria. Annesley Hall was host to two exotic visitors, both taking Toronto's renowned Household Science course: Doris Ding of China, who was sent by Ethel Wallace as a replacement for Marjorie Hung; and Hanago Sakamoto, a Japanese protegé of Emma Kaufman of the YWCA. Even before the war, in January 1913, the United Alumnae had drawn up a memorial for the board of governors of the university protesting the lack of facilities for the growing number of women. Residence space was grossly inadequate. The University of Toronto Schools, an elite high school to be operated in connection with the faculty of Education, had opened in 1910 for boys only. Hart House, a magnificent structure which was arising on the front campus thanks to the generosity of the Massey family, would provide a complete social and athletic centre, but again for men only.[44] When the existing dining hall was moved from University College to Hart House, the memorial pointed out, there would be no central place on campus where non-resident women could obtain

Margaret Addison seated on the Annesley staircase with residents

meals. Neither was there a recreation ground for women, and little provision had been made for physical training.[45]

During the war the demands for facilities were naturally put into abeyance, though they revived with the United Alumnae's submission to the Royal Universities Commission in 1920. Addison did, however, continue to work for a more adequate course in physical education. The university's physical education program, for some years in a state of latency, had been revived with the appointment of Ivy Coventry as its directress in 1911. At the time it seemed ripe to urge that the course be given a higher profile and that some exercise be required from all students. In May 1915 Addison caused the United Alumnae to form a committee to look into this question; one of her expedients was to assign each member of the United Alumnae executive the name of a prominent college, with instructions to determine the arrangements each made for physical training.[46] It was not until 1934, however, that an hour's physical education per week became a requirement for all first-year women.[47]

At Victoria College, Addison was very conscious of a widening gap between the women in residence and the growing number who lived in Toronto and commuted to the university. The VWA, recognizing the latter's need, had in 1911–12 furnished a women's study in the main college building where they could obtain rest and refreshment. Addison did her best to make them welcome in the Hall: since its inception

Margaret Addison in the Annesley common room with residents

residents had been allowed to have fellow students as guests to any
meal on payment of a small fee, but, in addition, she made a point of
having teas and even dinners at which all the women of a specific
year could be together at Annesley. She also instituted weekend parties just before the start of term for which the female freshies could
come into residence, along with members of the upper years; the leaders of the women's college societies used this weekend to plan the
coming year's program. In the fall of 1914, Addison tried out another
idea, dividing the first- and second-year women into small groups
who were then entertained by individual faculty wives at home.

Despite these social efforts – which, in Addison's mind, should
have made rival organizations unnecessary – the sorority question
reared its head again in 1916. The group which had appeared in
Torontonensis in 1911 as "Xi Zeta Gamma Sorority of Victoria College"
had subsequently become the Beta Psi Chapter of Kappa Kappa
Gamma. By 1915 the women's student council of Victoria was finding
it a divisive force and petitioned the senate against it. Addison
agreed, going so far in a letter as to say that it was unchristian for
the sorority to separate from the main body in a spirit of exclusive-
ness.[48] In February 1915, through a process of negotiation now
untraceable, the sorority agreed to disband, provided that the senate

South Hall Women's Union

passed a resolution disallowing any other sorority at Victoria. In March, however, they withdrew their promise, infuriating Addison by their reliance on what she considered a mere quibble: "Thursday I was so wrought up and indignant and angry that I could hardly contain myself. I do not often get at white heat, but when I do the heat is so white that it stays for a long time ... It has been exceedingly cleverly done. It has been most shrewd. It has taken us who trusted them unawares. It may be legally right, but it is ethically bad."[49] Although she does not explain the nature of the quibble, the terms of the sorority's agreement were in fact never met. The senate did not outlaw other sororities, fearing to "cause an irreconcilable difference among the students of Victoria College,"[50] and the sorority question remained to cause future unrest.

In truth the Toronto students did need a centre for their activities, and, in early 1917, no doubt with the insidious appeal of the sorority in mind, a committee that included Addison, Vincent Massey's wife Alice, and Nellie Rowell looked into the feasibility of forming a student union. Although for some years Addison had dreamed of an extension to the residence or a new building, she saw, in the meantime, the possibility of rearranging the existing facilities. South Hall had recently become an adjunct of Annesley Hall rather than a separate unit; Mrs Sheffield, whose salary had consequently been reduced, had, with the added plea of ill health, resigned. The committee decided not to replace her, but to turn South Hall into a women's student union, with library, meeting rooms, a guest bedroom, and a dining hall. As this would decrease the already inadequate supply of residence places, third-year students were asked to remove themselves to boarding houses for a single year. The committee then hired May Skinner, a Victoria graduate of 1898 who had been active in the Alumnae Association, to live in the union as its supervisor.

The new union was modelled on those Addison had visited at such British universities as Edinburgh, St. Andrews, Manchester, and Birmingham. Under Miss Skinner's supervision it became a lively social centre. The public rooms were the site of meetings, rehearsals, public lectures, and discussion groups such as Professor Edgar's on contemporary literature.[51] Since women had won the Ontario vote in April 1917, to be followed by the federal vote in May 1918, there was particular interest in the talks and study groups on citizenship, as well as in the investigation of new fields of employment for women. The dining hall served three meals a day, with up to fifty-eight girls at lunch, the most popular meal. Victoria could feel that it had a facility to match the Women's Union of University College, which had recently opened at St. George and Hoskin under the direction of Miss Wrong and was fostering, as Addison had heard, "a new birth of life among the women there."[52]

These stressful years of war took their toll on Addison. She was beginning to age. Ruefully she described to her family a meeting with the tall, white-haired Dr Bell, once her professor but now nearly a contemporary: "As he looked down upon me, he said: 'I see you use the same kind of hair vigor that I do.' I replied to him: 'And it is as ineffective with me as it has been with you.' I begin to feel how old I am getting to be. I have gone through the shock of admitting to myself that I am growing older, but it was rather a blow to find that outside people admitted it, too. For my hair is really getting very white."[53] Her youthful figure was long gone, too, her flesh filling out like dough slowly rising in the oven. Little lines of perplexity in her face became permanent.

Addison's work load became ever heavier; she complained that her presence with an oil can was required night and day to prevent friction.[54] In addition to her normal duties as dean, she undertook to lead two Bible study groups, in South Hall and the Annex, in order to get to know the freshies housed there better. She fielded so many queries about employment, from institutions seeking graduates as well as from the girls themselves, that she claimed Annesley Hall was a virtual employment agency. Her secretarial duties were endless; in 1915 she counted 1739 letters written during the school year. Fortunately she was able, at her own expense, to hire a stenographer for two hours every Saturday morning to take down letters from dictation. The saving of time was considerable and would have been even greater had Addison not seized the opportunity to enlarge the circle of her correspondents. She began writing an annual letter to graduates, to keep them in touch with Annesley Hall activities, as well as a general letter, monthly or even weekly, for friends and family. Keeping a chronicle became, intermittently, as obsessive an activity as recording the number of letters written, phone calls made, and visits received. One happy incidental result, though, is that from this time on her activities can be followed in considerable detail.

Her health, never robust, deteriorated steadily under this relentless activity. An exact diagnosis is impossible now, as perhaps it was then, but she was troubled by both headaches and intestinal disorders. Bodily woes combined with a more general malaise, a sense that her best work might be over and her purpose no longer clear. "This is the year, of all years," she wrote shortly after the outbreak of war, "when one feels that one must stop and consider whether all that one is doing is worth while doing." The result was that "one does not feel very well content with things as they are, and least of all with one's self as one is. We seem to have bungled awfully."[55] Her activities she deemed pointless: "I think there must surely be something wrong, somewhere, when we are driven so hard that we find it difficult to keep our poise, and to have a really sane outlook upon life. A life of rush leaves one rather depressed, and feeling that there is a lack of the sense of proportion, somewhere."[56] She began to feel that she did not have the vision to carry the residences forward into the future. The first ten years at Annesley, she mused to her correspondents in early 1916, had been spent in establishing traditions, while the past two were preoccupied with a necessary reorganization in the household and the committee of management. "Now all this organizing has been finished," she wrote, "and I have been asking myself what next? All this time I have been devoting myself to details, and I feel that now we need a bigger outlook, and I do not feel myself at all equal to the future – especially intellectually ... What is one's duty?"[57]

As she had realized long ago when she left Oxford, she needed detachment, along with that exercise that she was always urging on others. She tended to focus too exclusively on what she was doing and to calculate too anxiously the consequences. At the end of the war, her brother Dr Will Addison sent her to see Dr McPhedran, who in turn sent her to the hospital for x-rays. Finding that food did not leave her stomach under six hours, he agreed with her suspicion that the tensions of her situation were partly to blame. According to Addison, "Dr. McPhedran says that no man or woman could possibly live the life I do and be well; that no one can be on the alert for so many hours in the day, live with so many persons, and have so little resource that is intellectual, without paying a heavy penalty."[58]

Sometimes a long walk in the fresh air was enough to restore her sanity, as one diary fragment reveals: "I was so ... miserable and depressed after three days of headache and pain, and poor nights of sleep, and the prospect looked so gloomy, I felt unequal to the duties of this evening. But a walk in the Riverdale Park, and a couple of hours in God's great out of doors, gave me some rest, and He has been so wonderfully gracious to me, has given me strength as I needed it."[59] Her attention was also diverted by the antics of a series of dogs (sad-eyed Paddy, frisky Teddy, and Vic) who lived with her in the residence and were taken out for walks by her or the janitor. She loved to go out for a social evening or tea, usually with a group of women. Tea with Miss Withrow sounds as lively as a night out at the pub: once Miss Withrow had invited two friends and a companion, all of whom were great talkers, "and so are Miss Withrow and I, and we talked so hard and so loud and so fast that we could scarcely hear each other."[60] A little club of friends centred around Helena Coleman met regularly to have dinner together and discuss learned topics such as Hilaire Belloc's writings or Bergson's philosophy; but they also chatted and listened to music. Another circle she belonged to, in which she and Mrs Pakenham (wife of the dean of the Faculty of Education) met with some of the Faculty of Education students on a Saturday night to knit and socialize, sounds a little too close to her work to be truly relaxing.

Like most busy administrators, Addison longed for the summer holidays. "I love the students until it is time for them to go," she confessed, "and then they cannot go fast enough."[61] She was still accustomed to spending part of her holidays, especially at Christmas, with the Bemans in Newcastle; when she arrived she was sometimes so exhausted that she would crawl straight into bed and stay there till the last day of her visit.[62] She also had a new retreat, on the shores of Georgian Bay. In about 1912 the Addisons had bought some land in Tiny Township, and by 1914 they had constructed three cottages: one for Will's family; one for Art's; and between them one shared by

Margaret, Charlotte, and their father. It was a spot as remote as any nature-lover could wish. Northwards the shore stretched uninhabited except for a few fishermen's shacks, and behind the cottages were woods dense enough to absorb effortlessly Peter's craving for chopping. The family would load up with provisions for the whole summer ordered from Eaton's, take the Penetang Flyer to Penetanguishene, and from there lumber to the beach with all their goods in two horse-drawn wagons like a pioneer family searching for greener pastures, not to leave until September. The little settlement of Lafontaine, across a mosquito-filled woodland, was home to a number of French Canadian farmers; one named Joe Beausoleil drove by regularly in his wagon with supplies of milk, eggs, and vegetables.

Margaret's cottage was a focus for family life. Here she became better acquainted with her nephews and nieces. And if she unwittingly slighted the latter by considering it exclusively a boy's job to bicycle out for the mail and thus receive the 25-cent tip, they nevertheless loved to be hugged to her ample bosom. From the first she held a Sunday service for the whole family, with the children sitting on cushions on the floor. Charlotte played the organ and Margaret read a short sermon, or rather bellowed it into a speaking tube for the benefit of her father, who had become very deaf. After supper she read aloud to the children, often classics such as Thoreau's *The Maine Woods*. Evenings were spent talking and reading round the huge fireplace. Over the mantle Margaret's brother Arthur had carved the legend "How now, what dost thou here? Truly Sir, I take mine ease": a Jacobean-sounding sentiment that apparently he made up himself.[63] When Bessie and Lydia Dent from Stratford visited, Margaret and Charlotte would laugh with them till the tears ran down their cheeks. "Those old women," the farmer would say, shaking his head, as shrieks of mirth emanated from the middle cabin.

Of course the cottage was not a completely separate world, and Margaret was not one to take too much ease. She packed her Annesley Hall correspondence in her baggage, set up a card table on the screened-in porch, and for many hours of the summer day could be found writing letters. She did not just answer queries about residence rooms in a business-like manner, but took the time to respond to each girl's personal concerns, not neglecting the opportunity to underline a moral or sow the seeds of a wholesome attitude. A letter to Chester Massey written during a holiday at Newcastle suggests the obsessiveness with which she approached her task. In it she explains that the bill for the support of Doris Ding sent to him a year ago was wrongly itemized. Painstakingly she relists the items of expenditure, making minor adjustments in the amounts for room and board and laboratory fees, even though the total amount of $347 remained the same and had long ago been paid by Massey.[64]

Perhaps because of this inability to let Annesley Hall go, she did not build up enough stamina during the summers to carry her through a school year. The late winter was the most difficult time. In February 1915, she had to take two weeks off for a rest cure at Clifton Springs Sanatarium, a sulphur-water spa in New York State's Finger Lakes area much patronized by Toronto Methodists. Here, in a mansion surrounded by extensive grounds, she was pampered until, as she put it, "one feels quite above all one's friends, and cannot tolerate the thought of even writing to them."[65] Since she took breakfast in bed, and the patients had all retired by 9:00 p.m., she spent many peaceful hours alone in her room, reading or dozing or gazing out of her two large windows. Medical treatments included salt rubs, electro-thermal baths, massages, and gentle walks.

The next winter, though, in spite of heeding her doctor's orders to cut out all committee meetings and social functions, her condition was so poor that she had to take three weeks off in March. In the 1916–17 school year, it was even worse: she became ill before Christmas, and was away for much of December and January. By this time she realized that she was becoming an absentee dean and would not be able to act effectively the next year. She therefore asked for, and was granted, a year's leave of absence. During the year of 1917–18, the first in which the union was operating in South Hall, the women were under an acting dean, Marjory Curlette, a 1900 graduate of St. Hilda's who had recently been principal of Westbourne School on Bloor Street. Addison spent her time recuperating at Clifton Springs, before visiting North Carolina and California.

These repeated absences provided some perspective and forced her to let go of the small details, though as an inveterate letter writer and organizer she was incapable of complete isolation. Typically, she used part of the time she spent among the pillows musing on the larger picture, trying to find structural reasons why her job seemed so difficult. Her analysis appears principally in two documents of early 1917, the Report to the Committee of Management of February 1917, and the Annual Report to the Senate for the year 1916–17. According to these reports, a dean of residence was pulled in two directions. On the one hand, she must be active and knowledgeable in the world outside the college, bringing the world into the college in order to answer the girls' questions about careers, opportunities, and social conditions, and bringing the college before the world in order to attract funds. On the other hand, she was responsible for all the minutiae of daily life in the residence. In Addison's view, Canadian girls needed a special degree of oversight and protection; brought up mainly in the country or small towns, they were liable to come to grief in the capital of the province. So a dean's internal duties were twice as onerous as they were in, say, the English colleges, where social traditions were secure and residences relatively insulated from the town. She concluded to the committee that it was not possible for one person to do both parts of the job adequately:

After long experience I am quite sure that the disintegrating and uninterest-ing doling out of evening permissions, the enquiries into chaperones, gentlemen escorts and places of amusement are as necessary in administering a Canadian College residence for women as the provision of breakfast, lunch and dinner. And I am also certain that these matters, stupid as they cannot fail to be to the person in authority, cannot be delegated to an inexperienced person, for they call for wide discrimination and quick decision, and often indeed for hours of reasoning and many heart to heart talks. I have come to the conclusion, then, after long years of the most careful consideration, that we are attempting to do what it is impossible to do, that we are trying to make bricks without straw, when we think one person can stand before the public, with the prestige she ought to have, and at the same time deal with the innumerable details which make for the comfort and happiness of a home life in residence.[66]

Addison characteristically found a partial solution to her dilemma in the practices of the English women's colleges, though she recog-nized that social differences had to be taken into account. In these colleges the head was often a remote figure preoccupied with repre-senting the college before the world, but she was assisted in her intellectual work among the girls by other women. There were women on the college staff – something which Victoria sorely needed – to provide mentors for both resident and non-resident women. Moreover, there were women in the residences whom we would now call "dons": "Birmingham has ten such women, or one woman to every five students in residence."[67] These young people, university graduates now employed in outside occupations, would bring in "freshness and vigour of mind," said Addison, and she looked for-ward to the time when a new and enlarged building could accommodate them.[68]

In the back of her mind was the thought that she should be doing more, through her position in the residences, to foster intellectual and spiritual life. The present was a time of unprecedented opportunity, she told the senate in the 1917 report. War had led to an intellectual awakening among the women: "They ask more questions, and are showing a wholesome dissatisfaction with many institutions which they have before accepted without query." Their aspirations could be seen in the five discussion groups they had formed, in the choral concerts and plays they put on, and in their war work. Yet Canada faced the same problems as the United States in the weakening hold of religion and the lack of training in self-discipline. Young women were searching for guidance, Addison explained; never had they been more willing to listen to those older and more experienced.[69] To this end, she had in the past invited older women into the residence as guest speakers and discussion group leaders, and had suggested, though apparently without following it up, that the girls might get to know the committee of management better;[70] more recently she had mobilized faculty wives to meet new students. May Skinner's presence in the union during the next school year,, aided by other women, would be another step towards providing a more mature perspective. But nothing could quite replace having graduates living in the residence, where they could both take over some of the administrative duties and exert a salutary personal influence.

Older women were not the only possible sources of intellectual stimulus. Perhaps as a result of the unnatural absence of men during the war, Addison was especially willing at the time to acknowledge the value of social intercourse with men. She began to wonder whether she should abandon her model of a community of women and revert, on a university level, to that of the family, where generations and sexes lived together and learned from each other: "From time to time we have made efforts to bring the young women into closer acquaintanceship with the wives of the Faculty. What if we were today to bring both men and women into closer union with both Faculty and their wives? We have been put in homes, men and women, and young and old. May not this plan be a better one than our more artificial one?"[71] To the senate she confided her hopes for a comradeship between men and women based on common intellectual interests rather than on sports or social concerns, so that "the tone of the college women will be more elevated and more earnest."[72] As well, during her enforced leisure of 1918, she renewed her commitment to religious work. "I should like to take prompt and decisive action," she wrote to President Bowles from Clifton Springs, "against slackness, want of self-discipline, sabbath breaking, dissipation of time, energy, mind and soul, and to substitute as far as possible a simple and quiet life for that which is restless and full of strain."

Convinced that the time was ripe for exercising a wholesome influence, she determined that "the major part of my work next year must be personal evangelism."[73]

Determined to carry on but by no means completely restored to health, Margaret Addison returned to her Hall in September 1918. The campus was a different place that fall, as the war drew to a close. Wartime shortages meant that the residences were perpetually short of maids; the cook, a feckless individual, took off a few days after the girls arrived; and once again the students were in the kitchen washing dishes and helping to wait at table. The residence had been enlarged by the purchase of a house at 113 Bloor Street West, known as Oaklawn, to replace the rooms lost when South Hall became a student union. To head this house (which contained mostly third-year students), Miss Curlette had been able to secure the services of Mary Rowell, just the type of person Addison was seeking for work among the girls: a Victoria graduate of 1898, sister-in-law of Nellie Rowell, she was a respected academic who had just resigned her post as dean of women and teacher of French at Wesley College in Winnipeg. Next year, making belated amends for Addison's aborted career as a lecturer, the college hired Rowell in the French department as their first permanent female faculty member. Soon the soldiers would be returning – "at last, real undergraduates," one of the professors was heard to remark[74] – and a whole new atmosphere would prevail.

In the meantime came the influenza epidemic of October 1918. This flu, unlike the glorified cold that bears its name today, was a killer disease that caused fifty thousand deaths in Canada during 1918–19, and perhaps forty million worldwide. In early October it arrived in the residence, and by the 10th nineteen people were in bed, including the nurse, Miss Gregory. Eleanor Wyllie, the sickest student, developed pneumonia in one lung. The dean spent hours on the phone trying to round up nurses, with little success; she counted herself lucky when Professor Bell's wife, a trained nurse, agreed to pitch in. As pneumonia spread to Miss Wyllie's other lung, and the number of cases rose towards the final tally of thirty-three, there were frantic consultations with the doctor in charge, Dr Henderson, and the college authorities. As a result, all the girls not afflicted were advised to go home immediately, while other patients from the student union, the Annex, and Oaklawn were gathered together in Annesley Hall, where they filled the infirmary and overflowed into the surrounding bedrooms. Then followed days when Annesley Hall seemed under siege, when Addison and Miss Elliott, cooking and nursing and mopping up, worked like stokers in a boiler room. Miss Wyllie's family was sent for; but on 15 October, while her brother was downstairs eating dinner and her father was on the way, she died quietly during a nervous chill – "the first time," said a devastated Addison, "that a young spirit has taken its flight within our walls."[75] This was the nadir of the epidemic, which gradually worked itself out, and after which the Hall was closed for three weeks while things were put to rights.

After tragedy, triumph: the end of the war was celebrated on Monday, 11 November 1918, after a celebration the Thursday before had been found to be premature. Almost everyone in Annesley had lost someone during the war – if not a brother or a sweetheart, then a classmate or neighbour or hometown boy – and they celebrated the end of loss, if not the achievement of any great gain. The sophomores formed a band and paraded through the halls whistling through combs and waving flags, and the girls poured out of the residence to join the University College girls in a march to the UC Union. In the evening, Miss Addison hosted a formal dinner, where the girls dressed in evening gowns and tossed back toasts in temperance punch. Afterwards, the Kaiser was burned in effigy on the front lawn of the Hall, and there were skits and stunts, hymns and songs, and refreshments.

Unfortunately – as might have been predicted – the spiritual awakening that Addison discerned during the war did not last. On the contrary, there was an outburst of frenzied pleasure seeking among the survivors of the carnage. The girls themselves had enjoyed a degree of freedom as they engaged in war work in the fields or in teaching out west; for a year and a half they had not been under the eagle eye of Miss Addison. The young men returning from abroad had been through unimaginable experiences, had met freely with women, and were in no mood to countenance restrictions on Victoria girls that seemed to resemble those of a Methodist boarding school. As Addison saw it, "All the grievances of the ages seem[ed] to have come to the surface, and destructive criticism was rife. Minorities everywhere clamoured for their rights, too often so limited by personal desires as to preclude all sense of social obligation."[76]

As usual, the grievances focused on the rules. The matter came to a head in early 1919 when Addison had to discipline three young women who had eaten in a downtown restaurant late at night. The students demanded to know why they were not allowed to do this or to go to public dances, as many perfectly respectable people did.

At a mass meeting on 13 January, Addison explained the rationale for the rules, which, she admitted, belonged to the domain of relative rather than absolute truth. Only the heads of her discourse remain, but these sufficiently suggest the thrust of her arguments: "disappearance of Smith College girl; Wellesley girls in house of ill fame; a certain nurse; weak persons; white slave traffic; standard to be maintained."[77] After hearing her, the girls withdrew the request to eat at downtown restaurants after attending plays or concerts. They did, however, suggest that they might safely be allowed to attend Columbus Hall, a well-conducted dance hall at the Knights of Columbus building on Sherbourne Street, or failing that to hold dances in Annesley itself. They also wanted permission to stay out until 11:30 instead of 11:00 on skating nights, so that they could eat at the uptown establishments of Hunt's or the Regent Inn, and they asked that second-year students be allowed a second late night a week.

The prohibition against such activities was not simply Addison's foible. The heads of Annesley, St. Hilda's, and Queen's Hall, and of the University College and Victoria College women's unions, were all concerned that manners were becoming too free and standards of social conduct were slipping. Addison's solution, predictably, was to form a committee, a permanent body under her convenorship to take action when necessary. The committee met on 28 January 1919 at Annesley Hall with other concerned women such as Miss Laird and Dr Clara Benson of Household Science. Resolutions were drawn up in favour of limiting social functions; creating a simpler standard in matters such as flowers, taxis, and refreshments; and discouraging attendance at dance halls and downtown restaurants. After a further meeting, attended by the university's President Falconer and college officials, all women of the university were forbidden to visit outside dance halls, "irrespective of the excellent reputation of Columbus Hall."[78]

Meanwhile, at Annesley Hall, negotiations were taking place between the students, the dean, and the joint committee on Annesley Hall. The joint committee agreed to allow the girls to eat at Hunt's and Regent's Inn up to 11:30 p.m. after skating and to take a taxi from the Hall to a party. The dean agreed to support a modest request that late leaves for second year could *average* one night a week, rather than being confined to Friday night. After a final address by Chancellor Bowles and Lady Falconer, the president's wife, at a mass meeting at Annesley Hall on 4 February 1919, a vote was taken in which only fourteen very brave girls now supported the right to attend Columbus Hall. For Addison, who saw it as a demonstration of the ability of the majority to recognize a compelling argument when they heard one, it highlighted the duty of the administration to provide guidance. "Does it not mean," she asked the committee, "that in the swinging of the pendulum from one [of] strictness to license, we who are older have in the main been too occupied to take a wise stand to make public opinion?" Disappointed by the lack of support from male administrators, who adopted a laissez-faire attitude, she noted that women had faith in the possibility of improvement through wise, consensual regulation. "Can we really sit still and see our young women failing in health and in character too, because they have no time for the best things of life? They are, of course, entitled to the best of recreation – what we wish to have them saved from is dissipation."[79]

During the 1919–20 year, bearing in mind the discussions of the spring of 1919, Annesley students modernized their rules in a way that had Addison's full approval. Students were allowed to eat in the evenings at certain restaurants and hotels, to be specified; special privileges were granted to facilitate attendance at university dances; and on producing a letter from her parents, a girl might even be allowed to go to a limited number of public dance halls such as Columbus Hall (this provision apparently overruling the university's prohibition). As well, late leaves were granted somewhat more liberally, though the authorities still wanted to know the whereabouts of every first- and second-year girl who was outside the residence after 7:00 p.m. Moreover, it was now possible to go walking or motoring with men in the evening, providing another woman was present.

With these revisions Annesley became a shade more permissive than University College. Addison, though, was ecstatic with their moderation. Once again, they had provided a vindication of student government and a sign that truth would prevail, that "the Dean is only a human sympathetic finger post pointing to the principles, universal and eternal, upon which law is based." As she proudly reported: "There has been no coercion on my part, and only one trifling change in the original draft. This fact is mentioned, as we have been the recipients of a great deal of super solicitude on the part of our young men champions which really is quite unmerited. As one young woman remarked, 'Outsiders see only the restrictions, they do not see the life we have, and they do not know that we believe in our own rules.'"[80] That all the young women shared this attitude is doubtful, but the 1920 revision did at any rate take place without much friction. Addison discerned, too, a new spirit in the women towards the end of the year: more enthusiasm for Bible study and the student societies; a determination to buckle down to school work; even a sense of the barrenness of the coveted social life.[81] After the disappointments of the immediate post-war years – "I think last year was the most godless of any in our residence history," Addison remarked in early 1920 –[82] the annual report for 1919–20 declared that the year was closing with more hopefulness than in any one year since the war began.

CHAPTER EIGHT

Turmoil and Recovery

The upbeat note at the end of Addison's annual report in April 1920 was perhaps a whistling in the dark; the spirit of the students may have been improving, but administratively problems abounded. The most immediate was financial. For some reason, despite letting out rooms to conferences during the summer holiday, the residences were no longer paying their way; in February the committee had written to Chancellor Bowles confessing a shortfall in revenue that might reach $4000 by the end of the year.[1] Addison's overwork was also a problem. Reinforcing the themes of her 1917 reports, she repeated in the spring of 1920 that "we are still following the short-sighted policy of laying upon those who should give intellectual and spiritual stimulus to the young women who are to be, or ought to become, the leaders of your church and country a burden of detail that dwarfs the women's side of our college life."[2] More help was urgently needed. Annesley Hall was becoming ever more crowded, too, yet the committee that had been set up to look into the possibility of obtaining an addition or a new building felt that it was impossible to proceed until the policy regarding city students had been clarified.[3] Once a small minority, these students now numbered 75, as opposed to 124 in residence. As Addison had pointed out when the question of a dean of women first surfaced, they were far too easily swayed by their contemporaries in their choice of courses and needed someone to counsel them.[4] Although the union in South Hall had been a success in terms of extracurricular needs, it was too small and represented an additional financial drain. Now that the seriously ill Miss Skinner of the union had resigned (in the spring of 1920), it was a good time both financially and psychologically to make a change.

During the spring a subcommittee including Addison, Louise Starr, Nellie Rowell, Mrs Langford, and Mrs Lang met with representatives of the board of regents to discuss better ways to manage the residences. The upshot of the negotiations was a radical revamping of the machinery of residence.[5] It was the greatest change in the organization of women's affairs at Victoria since the introduction of Annesley student government: a change born in conflict, mired in controversy, and ultimately to some extent unworkable. The one permanent and valuable feature was the creation of the long-awaited post of dean of women, to look after the welfare of both the residents and non-residents. Margaret Addison accepted the position, at an annual salary of $2500.

Although Addison's new post was a promotion, in another sense it was a lateral slide: it involved her vacating her quarters in the Hall, where she had presided for seventeen years. Unfortunately, no new dean of residence was hired to take her place. Indeed, Annesley Hall ceased to exist officially as a residential unit. In order to integrate the city students with the residents, the union moved from South Hall into the lower two floors of Annesley. To accommodate it, the basement gym had to be sacrificed. Stripped of apparatus, it acquired a working fireplace and easy chairs and became a lunch room for commuters. Where the changing room used to be, a kitchen was installed for brewing tea and coffee and heating soup. On the ground floor, what had originally been envisaged as the reception rooms of a gracious home became women's student lounges and meeting rooms for campus organizations. And in the Annesley dining room, tables were now set for 170 at lunch, to accommodate city students needing a hot meal. The top two floors of the Hall, now Upper Annesley and Lower Annesley, became separate residential units, each under a don. They operated on a par with the three other units and their dons: South Hall (now reconverted into a residence), the Annex at 81 Charles Street, and Oaklawn at 113 Bloor Street West.

Meanwhile, the committee of management's powers were severely curtailed. The college office took over the accounting and bookkeeping. The committee no longer hired the servants of the residence, nor was it to have a say in the appointment of the dean of women or the dons. The board of regents now chose the dean. A committee comprising the dean of women, the dean of the Faculty of Arts, and the college president together chose the five dons. The dean of women and the president chose a dietitian to run the food services and housekeeping, and the dietitian, in turn, engaged the underservants in both the dormitories and common rooms. The committee of management was left with responsibility for the furniture, an advisory role in the choice of a dietitian, and the opportunity to proffer general advice. The student union which, like the residence units, lacked an overall head, was to be supervised by the newly christened Women's Undergraduate Association. A dean's council, composed of the dean of women and the five dons, had general supervisory authority over the undergraduate association and the residences.

These changes had several positive effects. They improved the lot of the city women, as the dean was now formally charged with representing their interests. They encouraged an easier fellowship between residents and non-residents, since all shared the same building and could eat lunch together in the Annesley dining room. They also introduced into the residences more of the young dons who could provide intellectual stimulation. Oaklawn was particularly fortunate in this regard; its supervisor, Dr Cornelia Harcum, was a woman of wide experience, who had been dean of women at Rockford, Illinois, before becoming curator of the classical collection at the Royal Ontario Museum. She was a popular lecturer on such topics as domestic life in ancient Greece.[6] The other dons, more recent graduates, were working women who brought a fresh perspective. For Addison personally, the new arrangements provided one thing she had long coveted: as dean of women she became a member of faculty by virtue of her own position, rather than through the merely nominal title of lecturer in German.

Nevertheless, for Addison and many of her women associates the plan was radically flawed. The committee of management naturally did not take kindly to being demoted; nor, in spite of some past struggles with its innate conservatism, did Addison really want to give up working closely with this body of women who represented the community. By weakening the control of the committee to such an extent, the college authorities had taken women's affairs out of the hands of women and merged them into the general college administration. To Addison, the lack of one older woman, either as dean of all the residences or as head of Annesley Hall, seemed a mistake from every point of view. Her experience as an administrator told her that a single decision-maker was needed to keep order. As well, the absence of such an individual had symbolic implications. It made a mockery of Annesley's claim to be a second home, a repository of courtesy and civilized living. How could it function without a mature resident head to act as hostess, mother figure, and guardian of standards? The Hall would become a Grand Central Station of noise and bustle, with its ground floor open to the comings and goings of a transient population; in the crowded dining room it would be impossible to have a dignified meal. It was a far cry from the Oxford ideal she had initially envisaged. As Addison had complained when the numbers first started to grow, "the large number gathered together formed a company, not a family."[7] The whole arrangement filled her with foreboding:

The Deanless residence will work, no doubt, but in place of a fine home life, yielding its aid to the best type of education for women for our Canadian homes, we shall have a very common and ordinary life, bereft of that which can make the finest contribution to enlightened and devoted character. There should be someone in my place, and I hope and trust that the year will make that plain. The women want it and they should be the judges as to what best fits women's needs.[8]

In order to understand how changes in some ways so inimical to Addison's notions came about, it is necessary to look at the per-

Vincent and Alice Massey

sonalities and views of two somewhat shadowy, background figures: Mr and Mrs Vincent Massey. As liberal benefactors of the college, the two were bound to exercise considerable weight. Although the evidence is rather sketchy (since official minutes and letters are discreet), from a diary Addison kept in 1920–1 and from stray hints one gathers that the Masseys were determined to give the residences a new character. They disapproved of the cosy corporate life of Annesley Hall; what they saw as Addison's old-fashioned regime was, to their eyes, past due for a shakeup. By vigorous lobbying and even, as Addison came to believe, by "the misrepresentation and misinterpretation of Mrs. M,"[9] they won Chancellor Bowles and the college authorities to their view. The details of the rearrangement simply carried out their agenda.

Vincent Massey was still dean of the men's residence with the official title of senior tutor; preoccupied with other things, however, he did not draw his full salary and left the day-to-day administration to an acting dean. War work had called him away in 1915; then, after the war ended, he devoted most of his energies to Hart House, which formally opened on 11 November 1919, and to the family business. He nevertheless continued to live on the Victoria campus, in a house at 71 Queen's Park Crescent, and to take an interest in the college. Unfortunately, the rapport that might have been expected between him and Addison never really developed. Perhaps they were too unlike in temperament: Margaret Addison too democratic (for all her love of gracious manners) to be other than irritated at the pretensions of this smooth and aloof young man; Vincent Massey too aristocratic (for all his political liberalism) to be sympathetic towards a representative of the earnest, plebian Methodism that he was trying hard to put behind him. Though brought up within the bosom of the Methodist church, he had deliberately attended the supposedly godless University College rather than Victoria[10] and, not surprisingly, he eventually joined the Anglican Church, where good taste and tradition reigned. While still an undergraduate he had declared Methodist institutions "the apotheosis of mediocrity"; the work he had been doing on the Massey Foundation's Commission on the Secondary Schools and Colleges of the Methodist Church in Canada, which would issue its final report in 1921, did not alter his opinion.[11]

The wife Vincent married in 1915 came from a very different sphere than Addison's. The former Alice Parkin, she was the daughter of Sir George Parkin, an anglophile Canadian who served as principal of Upper Canada College, secretary of the Rhodes Trust, and a member of the Imperial Federation League, and who had many friends in high places in England. Alice herself was not highly educated – Vincent's biographer mildly remarked that "there was no likelihood of her being called a bluestocking"[12] – but she believed in the advancement of women and had charm, managerial ability, and an energetic will to carry out her ideas. In the school year before her marriage (1914–15), she had served as head of Queen's Hall, the University College women's residence. According to Addison, her tenure there had drawn forth diverse opinions: whereas the students of the hall were generally devoted to her, the UC alumnae were "fairly seething," apparently at her lack of scholarly attainments.[13] Addison herself was somewhat ambivalent; after she had finally entertained her colleague at Annesley late in the school year in March 1915, she remarked to Charlotte, in terms that hardly suggest an eager hostess, that she was "tremendously relieved to have Miss Parkin off my mind."[14] Her comments on Alice's tenure at Queen's Hall have a distinct edge:

Miss Parkin is a remarkably optimistic person. She has made almost as many discoveries in this one year as Miss Cartwright and I have done in twelve, and has apparently reached the solution of the difficulties more readily than Miss Cartwright and I. She has planned a new building as a residence for University College, which is to have a dining-room, a cafeteria, an assembly hall, and offices, a large gymnasium, and is to be built of stone, like Burwash Hall. It is *not* to have class-rooms. She sees some of the money already in sight, and expects the rest ... But who knows? she may be able to accomplish what all the rest of us have been unable to do.[15]

As Mrs Vincent Massey, Alice continued to forward her own as well as her husband's ideals. Having joined the committee of management in late 1915, as a replacement for the decreased Lillian Massey Treble, she soon was taking much upon herself. In June 1917, for instance, when Addison had only just embarked on her year's leave of absence, she wrote to Vincent from Winnipeg that she had met a Miss Jones, who "impresses me as just the person to become Dean of Women at Vic." Already she had seized the opportunity to broach that possibility with Miss Jones. "I am particularly anxious to start agitating for the future appointment at once," she explained to her husband, "so that from the first no one will consider Miss Skinner a permanent appointment."[16] Apparently she had very strong views "about people and about their qualifications for special jobs."[17]

Both the Masseys became convinced that the model of Annesley Hall as a "home from home" had had its day. As Mrs Massey wrote in October 1921, the prevailing theory that "the Head should be 'in loco parentis,' and the students, although perhaps living under some form of 'student government,' should be under the close supervision of older women," had the disadvantage that "the residence will probably have little or no relation to the intellectual life of the student." According to her:

The fact is recognized that when women come to a University they are to a large extent – at least after their freshman year – freed from the necessary restrictions of the High School period. On this assumption the senior members of the community should be of an age and training which render them companions rather than supervisors, and the individual student should be encouraged to regard herself as a responsible person possessing an independent mind, in her movements as free as possible, and hampered by the minimum of rules.[18]

To her it followed that a committee of women, and mature or even elderly women at that, should not have complete control over the residence. The men students might sleep in Burwash, the women in Annesley Hall, she argued, but the two residences could well be supervised by a single committee of men and women – a committee that would further the common intellectual life of both sexes.[19]

Addison felt deeply the injustice of being cast in the role of an obstacle to progress. It was incredible, she thought, that people could say she was opposed to freedom. Had she not introduced student government over strenuous objections? True, she did not believe that college women could be treated as full adults; nevertheless, she wanted them to have as much liberty as they were capable of handling.[20] At this time she thought much about the nature of liberty, which for her, as for Milton, has more to do with following the dictates of right reason than with mere licence. The respected Matthew Arnold pointed in the same direction, valuing the choice of rational conduct over the anarchic "doing as one pleases." Thus to abandon standards of conduct and to leave the students entirely to their own devices was to adopt that lax continental concern for the intellect alone, against which Lord Rosebery had so memorably spoken at the Congress of the Universities of the Empire.[21] Besides, there was a practical consideration: the need to keep in mind the demands of her wider constituency, the Methodist Church. As Addison wrote in her Dean's Report of 1922, a certain sacrifice was exacted in return for the support and loyalty of the church body: "It has always been so for the women – women are even yet on sufferance in any institution which began with men and to which later women were admitted, and women have been told from the beginning that upon their good behaviour depended their remaining in such colleges. They could never be in advance of public opinion concerning their freedom. But as public opinion changed, so could their freedom expand."[22]

The disagreement stemmed in part from a different reading of the women's movement. According to the Masseys, it was time to abandon the old timid restrictions on women, to cut the umbilical cord as it were, and to advance boldly to a more unisex present. To Addison, this was to be "caught by a fallacy long ago outworn and outlived, viz. that women must be like men and do the same things; that equality signifies uniformity." In her comments on such shallow thinkers she obviously had the Masseys in mind:

They wish to make Annesley Hall like Burwash Hall, the men's residence. They do not see that the former long, long ago passed the stage at which the latter now is, and they cannot remember that women wish to develop their own personalities in their own way, and according to their own genius. This point of view was for a time, and is still at times depressing, inasmuch as it is so antiquated and so out of joint with modern progress.[23]

Unfortunately, for a good many years at least, modern progress was to move in the unisex direction envisaged by the Masseys; Addison was premature in her notion that, equality having been achieved, it was time to assert difference. The ideal she espoused nevertheless had much to recommend it. She put a positive spin on the old notion of women's distinctive character, seeing it not as a barrier to achievement but as a strength. In particular, she maintained, women had a genius for creating a co-operative environment, something sorely needed in the world. Thus Annesley's rules and prescribed rituals existed not to oppress its inmates or to treat them as children, but to produce harmony. In a talk to the girls about the regulations in February 1920, Addison called the residence a unique preparation for community life, an ambience in which "free students of a free college" give up some of their self-regarding ways for the sake of the larger whole. The girls dressed for dinner, she told them, because they owed it to each other, when they had finished lectures and withdrawn into home life, to put off their work-a-day clothes; they observed quiet hours because it would be selfish to disturb those who were studying.[24] Such courtesies and practices, she maintained, had been found to reduce friction in communities. Undoubtedly, Addison thought they should be observed by both men and women, as they were rooted in Christian ethics, although she claimed that women with their talents for relationship and beauty were particularly fitted to bring these practices to fruition. In another talk, answering her own rhetorical question to the girls regarding their unseemly demonstrations of affection on dates ("Why should couples *not* stand ranged all along the roadway and standing at doors?"), she rose into the empyrian as she contemplated women's potential for forging a better lifestyle. In her words, "We are to be artists – physical, mental, spiritual artists – that beauty and goodness and truth may dwell among us, and flourish in our college, our University, our country, and internationally."[25]

Whereas this view of Annesley's rules and regulations was somewhat idealized, the Masseys' hopes for individual freedom were somewhat naive. Many of the girls undoubtedly did chafe at the elaborate system of leaves, safeguards, and rules and would do so increasingly as the twenties roared along. Mrs Fudger of the committee wrote to Mrs Burns that "the mothering and missioning system in Annesley Hall will have to go eventually, if only because most of the students resent it."[26] But the resident girls had an easy dualism, bending the rules a little in a spirit of youthful adventure while also fully appreciating Miss Addison and her concern. Ruth Lawson and some friends, for instance, although they cheerfully slid out to a prohibited dance hall, accepted the justice of their punishment when, in the cloakroom afterwards, they found Miss Addison, no doubt with her crocodile smile, waiting to escort them home.[27] Jean Cameron, who graduated in 1927, recalls being hauled up before ASGA for returning late from a function at Burwash, but feeling it was well worth it: everyone had stayed late because the news was circulating like wildfire that don Lester Pearson had just asked Maryon to marry him.[28] As early as 10 October 1920, a number of Annesley students headed by Gertrude Rutherford sent the board of regents a petition asking that Miss Addison be allowed to come back and live in Annesley Hall, an action that scarcely suggests deep resentment of her system.[29]

During that winter Addison watched events unfold from the sidelines, having found lodging, it appears, with Helena Coleman, who kept house for her brother Professor Arthur Coleman at 476 Huron Street. Still hoping that new residence buildings would necessitate yet another rearrangement, she wrote optimistically on 5 May 1920 that "it seems desirable to try out the experiment for this year, for I am convinced that we shall learn a great deal that it is wise that we should learn before new buildings are erected." By 28 October her tone was somewhat less sanguine: "The experiment is expected to give wisdom to those whose experience of residence life is limited." In pursuit of her new duties as dean of women she kept office hours in what used to be the ladies' study at the college from 9:45 a.m. to 1:30 p.m. As a compromise measure, she also spent from 1:30 to 2:00 p.m. in Annesley Hall, in an office well supplied with phones. (Upper and Lower Annesley were also wired with their own phones. "Think of it," she wrote to the alumnae, "ye, who used to stand in a long line outside of the door of the solitary telephone in the house."[30]) Miss Bain, daughter of Professor and Mrs Bain, acted as a very competent secretary to lessen the drudgery.

Addison continued to be involved in residence activities, occasionally even addressing the girls when requested to do so by ASGA, or when administrative matters seemed to demand it. She watched over the founding pangs of the new Student Christian Movement, which took over the evangelical functions of the YM/YWCA in the college. Though she seldom played the piano now, her love of music remained; one of her favourite duties was always the escorting of girls to concerts. In 1919 she had helped to found the Victoria orchestra, of which she was the honourary president, and started the tradition of hosting an annual reception at Annesley after the spring concert. The young people fulfilled her highest ideals of culture as they made their own music right at home, under the baton of Frank Blachford.

Dr MacMurchy had left Toronto in 1920, called away to Ottawa to become the first head of the Department of Health's new Department of Child Welfare. Fortunately, the residence was able to secure the services of another distinguished medical woman, Dr Edna Guest (later an O.B.E.). She was founder and first head of the Special Department of Venereal Disease at Women's College Hospital. As residence doctor she offered lectures to the women in the fall of 1920 on the origin of life and on venereal diseases. "Such a meeting," said Addison, was "to be optional and for mature students."[31] Although Violet

Trench, a travelling member of the British National Committee for Combating Venereal Diseases, was willing to give a similar course at the college, Addison, Miss Wrong, and Miss Cartwright consulted together and decided to have the lecture series offered university-wide. Pursuing as liberal a way as possible, Addison was also a patroness at two dances, at an OLC alumnae gathering and at a sorority. "This is a new departure," she wrote, "but after most careful thought it seemed wiser in these days, since public opinion has so greatly changed, to give a wide latitude to those things which are matters of decision for individual consciences."[32]

At this time a curious incident occurred which, though cloaked in obscurity, sheds some light on the continuing difference of outlook between Addison and the Masseys. In December 1920 Vincent received a letter from the Rev. Robert Milliken, of Third Avenue Methodist Church in Saskatoon, complaining of Miss Addison though never mentioning her by name. According to the covering letter with which Massey forwarded the complaint to Dr Bowles, Milliken "was nursing a feeling of resentment against Annesley Hall, arising out of an incident in which the friendship between his daughter and another girl was interfered with, by the authorities, on the grounds that it was not good for it to continue." Massey wrote back to Milliken in suggestive generalities, saying that his letter "throws a very important light on certain aspects of the present regime," and is helpful to "those of us, who are interested in progress"; he hoped, he said, to use it confidentially to encourage "a better atmosphere, among the women students." It appeared that he, his wife, and Dr Bowles had often discussed "the problem."[33]

Milliken's original, five-page, handwritten letter of complaint resides among some unsorted papers of Chancellor Bowles in the Victoria University Archives.[34] It protests bitterly against mistaken zeal among those "who cherish certain ideals narrowly and intensely, and look upon these and these alone as essential to one's salvation." Such zealots – to wit, we must conclude, Miss Addison – are incapable, it says, of appreciating the broader ideals of an age of transition and become cruel and unjust in their compulsion to offset whatever militates against their own narrow conception of the good life. It is not clear what, in this case, Miss Addison objected to in the friendship. Perhaps the friend was simply considered a bad influence, morally or intellectually; the subtext could also be that Addison was being accused of a paranoid or hysterical fear of lesbianism. In fact, even the breaking up of the friendship is not specifically mentioned. Since Milliken's resentment had originally surfaced in informal conversations

with a Mrs Robson in Saskatoon, who subsequently talked it over with
the Masseys before suggesting that he put his feelings in writing, no
details at all survive in the written record.

The issue of potential lesbianism among the girls could well have
been a preoccupation of Addison's. According to the researches of
Caroll Smith-Rosenberg, the medical establishment since the 1890s
had been attacking the kind of close female friendship which had
been accepted uncritically in Victorian times. Such relationships,
labelled as inversions or perversions, were considered typically
"unnatural" characteristics of the "new woman" who rejected her
traditional role. According to writers such as Havelock Ellis, female
boarding schools and colleges were hotbeds of lesbianism, where
"congenital" homosexuals were likely to seduce and pervert those
whose tendencies were ambivalent.[35]

More overtly, Milliken's letter expresses at great length the indig-
nation of a parent who saw the young soul of his daughter, as he put
it, "away from home and from any possibility of advice and comfort,"
in "a position of almost ostracism because it chose to follow its own
conceptions of life." It seems all too likely that Addison could have
been leaning heavily on the young woman, when one recalls Kathleen Cowan's 1907–11 diary with its chronicle of the dean's icy stares
and ambiguous smirks. After all, even such a stalwart defender of
liberty as John Stuart Mill admitted the legitimacy of moral suasion
and of the exhibition of distaste or even contempt for mistaken
courses. These means were especially appropriate for those in a state
of pupillage. Addison probably underestimated the crushing weight
of her disapproval on sensitive souls like Miss Milliken, who were
unable to shrug it off as Miss Cowan did with a robust "ah pshaw."
Milliken's complaint suggests that Addison did not always manage
to strike a balance between allowing the freedom that makes choice
meaningful, and what she saw as her duty to draw young souls
towards the light. She remained a child of her upbringing in that the
latter was always paramount.

By the spring of 1921, it was apparent to many people that the new
arrangement was not as satisfactory as the old. Ethel Patterson, one
of the two nominees for president of ASGA for the following year,
came to Miss Addison on 12 March to ask if she could withdraw her
candidacy; the rules, she said, were being broken right and left, and
"there was such a spirit as made the burden of the presidency too

great."[36] On 21 March the two dons of Annesley, Winifred Barnstead and Lillian Smith (a Vic graduate of 1910), friends and librarians at the Toronto Public Library who would later both have distinguished careers in librarianship, came to the dean with a litany of complaints. Although realizing that Annesley Hall had not been well run during the past year, they blamed Addison for not properly introducing them, for not spelling out their duties, and for addressing the girls when they were not present; besides, they said, their position had been eroded when the dietitian took the head of the table at Sunday tea.[37] Addison tried to answer these and other concerns, but apparently not persuasively, as both dons sent in their resignations shortly after. As well, Dr Bowles, aware that the year had not gone smoothly, partly blamed the failure on Addison's lack of enthusiastic support for the new arrangements. In March, he sent a letter to ASGA, asking them to signify their perfect satisfaction with existing affairs; they, however, refused to do so.[38]

Dissatisfaction was the prevailing mood at the Alumnae Association as well. At a meeting on 28 April, after heated discussion, the women passed a motion declaring that a change was needed in the residence system. A committee was formed to request a discussion with the chancellor on the residence situation and to draw up a letter of appreciation for Miss Addison's work as dean of residence.[39]

The committee of management, too, was restive. At a meeting of 12 May (where the four absentees significantly included Alice Massey and Hannah Fudger), they discussed the fact that "life in Annesley Hall did not satisfy the mothers of the students, that it had lost its dignity, because there was no resident head to act as hostess and as a controlling presence, and that the conduct of the students was unsatisfactory." They were concerned too about their own lack of authority, both in setting general policy and in supervising the servants. For instance, there was a crying need for someone to have a word with the dietitian, Miss Morris, who though a delightful person was inadequately trained and insouciant. It was unclear, however, whether the committee of management had this responsibility. There was talk of possible resignations as well. During this meeting, which Addison later described in her diary as "the best, most thoughtful, most jolly and most earnest meeting we have had during the year," Addison felt a heightened female camaraderie with the committee. "In its essence," she wrote, "the whole discussion was a protest against the autocracy of men in the affairs of women." It seems that although she had sometimes resented the committee in the past, she now saw it as a bulwark of female power that a male administration wanted to sweep away.[40] According to her diary, she defended it vigorously in a discussion with Chancellor Bowles: "It was urged that women could best think for women, and the Committee was needed – that much of the success of the past was due to their efforts, in presenting the outside point of view – that Victoria College should lead in the idea that women know better how to manage women's education than men."[41]

Addison had suggested to the chancellor in early May that her resignation might be the best course. Poor Bowles: caught between a wealthy supporter of the college, whose advice he valued and whom he wished to retain as honorary dean, and a dean of women whose services had been stellar and who had much support among the women. Whatever his private sympathies in the matter, the wise policy demanded that he placate both. On 10 May he wrote to Vincent, detailing the pressure he was under to have the dean of women return to Annesley Hall and take charge of the situation: pressure from a committee of students, from a delegation of the women's student government, from the alumnae association, from some of the committee of management, and even from some board members. "You will appreciate," he wrote to Massey, "that I have been in a very delicate and difficult situation."[42] He and Dean Robertson had hit upon the expedient of reuniting the two Annesley units under one head, thus preventing a complete reversion while correcting the most glaring deficiency of the present arrangement. On 14 May he met with Addison and prevailed upon her to accept this compromise of the appointment of a head of Annesley. She did so, although she continued to believe that an overall head of all the residence units, such as she had been previously, was needed.

In this conversation Bowles convinced Addison that for now the union must stay in Annesley Hall. His argument was that because Mrs Massey had contributed so much money to the Hall, she had a valid claim to influencing its affairs. "If someone would give money for a union," he reasonably pointed out, "that would make a great change in outlook." According to her diary, Addison also "found out [from Bowles] that the Board [of Regents] know how hard Mrs. M. is to get along with, and that was much comfort to me." The talk as a whole seemed a breakthrough to her: "We got up on to the plane which is above personalities, and considered matters with a larger freedom." They parted in amity, with Bowles suggesting that Addison might bring her wide experience to bear by writing a book on residences, with a history of Annesley Hall.[43]

Bowles may have had more on his mind at this 14 May 1921 meeting than Addison realized or the official record reveals. Years later Northrop Frye, recording in his diary some staff gossip about the college's attempts to attract donations, wrote that "we missed the Massey money because Mrs. M. took offence when her offer to build a women's residence, subject to putting Lillian Smith in as dean of women, was refused."[44] Frye does not indicate a date for Victoria's costly vote of confidence in Addison, but it may well have occurred in the spring of 1921. Certainly it is reasonable to suppose that the offer of funds occurred during the period of the Masseys' greatest involvement with the college, between 1915 and 1921. The committee of management had formally requested new buildings in a communication to the board of regents that was read at a meeting of 14 February 1919 – a meeting the board had invited the Masseys to attend as "corresponding members."[45] On 2 December 1919, the board established a committee to secure an architect and obtain plans. "Just where the money is coming from," Addison wrote to her friends, "is a mystery still to us."[46] But then, according to Addison, the committee discovered that the whole policy regarding women students – including the relation of the student union to the residence – needed to be clarified before the buildings could be designed; hence the reorganization of spring 1920 intervened.[47] In September 1920, the board was still discussing plans.[48] Since Lillian Smith was don of lower Annesley during the ensuing academic year, and increasingly disaffected, this seems a likely time for her to have caught Mrs Massey's eye as someone with excellent qualifications for replacing Addison. If this is so, then Bowles was taking a considerable gamble, or perhaps a leap of faith, when he refused Addison's proffered resignation and persuaded her to accept a single head of Annesley.

Shortly afterwards, the board appointed Gertrude Rutherford to the position of general head of Annesley Hall, with supervisory powers over the union as well as the dormitories. Besides having Miss Addison's entire confidence, Miss Rutherford, a graduate of the previous year and a former member of ASGA, was young and active enough to appeal to the progressives. Miraculously, the committee of management was given the authority to resume supervision of the residences, though financial affairs remained in the hands of the college. At the fall meeting at which this concession was announced, the committee, which had been wondering whether it might not just as well disband, proceeded to elect its officers and form subcommittees.[49] At some point Addison evidently moved back into her residence quarters, though she was determined not to interfere with Miss Rutherford's administration. In June of 1923, she regained the title of dean of residences, adding to that of dean of women.

The natural sequel, as affairs gradually reverted towards what they had been in 1919, was the resignation of Alice Massey from the committee of management. She had often felt herself a minority of one on this body, she wrote to its chairman, Mrs Burns, in her surprisingly eloquent letter of resignation in October 1921. But, she continued, as long as her views were discussed on their merits she had been willing to advance them for the sake of the residence. Now, however, she felt that "a permanent issue has been joined between my fellow-members and myself," and that only embarrassment would ensue from her remaining. In parting she reiterated a warning that was general in form but pointed in its intended application: "Nothing will so thwart development as a disposition to accept the status quo as an ultimate achievement."[50] In December of 1924, Vincent Massey stepped down as senior tutor (though retaining the title of honorary dean of residence until 1932), and in 1926 he sold his house on Queen's Park Crescent to the college. Thus the Masseys' active involvement with the college ended.

With Annesley Hall under Miss Rutherford's eye, Addison settled into her duties as dean of women with an easier mind. She enjoyed many aspects of the job, including her position on the faculty and on the Victoria senate and university bodies: not for her the modern administrator's weariness with committees and boards. In the fall of 1921, she became president of the Victoria Women's Association, an organization she cultivated and cherished. Because it brought together non-academics, friends of the college, and mothers of students, the association helped to fulfil one of her chief aims: to make the college known in the wider community. She also conscientiously attended meetings of the women's student societies. Nevertheless she found the hoped-for contact with Toronto students elusive: "Most of the city girls are too busy to be laid hold upon; there is nothing that is not casual to bring them close to a Dean."[51] She missed the closeness with young people, the constant chats and discussions that had been the chief delight of her position as dean of residence.

In 1922 there were several opportunities to view her work in the context of a wider society. In February, she travelled to the Conference of the National Association of Women Deans in Chicago in the company of Minnie Bollert, recently appointed dean of women at the University of British Columbia and formerly principal of Regina College, a Methodist institution. The program included a tour of the residence, Ida Noyes Hall, and discussions of fundraising and careers for women. Addison was glad to report that the American deans shared her way of thinking: "Emphasis was laid upon the necessity of making halls of residence approximate home life, if we wish the young women when they leave college to prefer home life to hotel life."[52]

In April of 1922, Addison embarked on four months' leave to visit Europe – "the most restful and carefree holiday I have ever had."[53] As with her previous European trips, it was a necessary remove from the scene of her labours. Each summer she had retreated to her cottage where, surrounded by trees and water and the calming influences of nature, she won through to a resolve to live on a higher plane on her return to the city. And each fall she fell back into the same mind-numbing grind. Dr Guest said she had "brain-fag" and urged a complete change. But again, as with previous European trips, this was not a mere pleasure jaunt. Just as along with detective novels she took piles of books on educational theory and Christianity to the cottage, so she incorporated a serious purpose into her 1922 itinerary: attendance at the conference of the World's YWCA at St. Wolfgang, Austria, and at the meeting of the International Federation of University Women in Paris.

At the YWCA conference, Addison participated as a voting delegate from Canada, along with Nellie and Mary Rowell. The main business of the meeting was to analyze the results of a questionnaire sent out to every national association on the nature of the contemporary young woman – her attitude to religion, church, family, community, and national and international responsibilities. Not surprisingly, the conference found, along with the growing economic independence of women in the developing world, the restlessness of an age of transition.[54] The Paris gathering, which took place from July 15 to 18 at the centre for American university women in Montparnasse, was a less formal affair. The federation of university women had been founded two years ago with the general purpose of promoting understanding, friendship, and the interchange of information. General sessions with prepared papers were held and – though she was not disabused of her previous impression that Parisians were somewhat brusque – Addison enjoyed the receptions and excursions laid on, which included a production of Molière's *L'avare*.[55]

Addison's itinerary also included a trip to Italy. In a letter to Louise in 1928, when Louise was herself going to Italy, her aunt told her that she would love the Italians for their spontaneous kindness and responsiveness; Addison noted that she herself had lost her heart to nearly every Italian she met. Amusingly, the particular Italians she described to prove her point were chiefly attractive males: the modest youth at the post office who helped to register her parcel and to negotiate at the bank; the brown-eyed lad in Capri, not above pressing for generous remuneration; the tall, handsome man in Rome who swept off his hat and bowed with the dignity of a descendant of the Caesars.[56] Once again she found in Europe a freedom and gaiety lacking in Canadian life.

There was, of course, another side to Europe: the post-war rubble, the bereavement and displacement, the bitterness. Margaret could not see the labour of reconstruction without giving her own time, labour, and organizational skills to the cause. A letter to the *Varsity* in 1924, for instance, reveals that she was in touch with women in Vienna (no doubt met on her holiday), arranging for the sale of needlework done by students and the unemployed to support themselves.[57] With her co-operation the Victoria women raised money for European student relief; the services they offered included "darning, sewing, dressmaking, laundry work, dyeing, manicuring, shampooing, hairdressing, shoe shining, shopping, copying notes, running errands, candy making, catering for parties, serving refreshments after the rink, and serving tea to the Burwash Hall men, for whom tea is not provided on Sundays."[58] They even found a surprisingly lucrative niche market in taking and selling snapshots of professors. By these efforts they raised $345, which – as $1.25 provided one meal a day for a month – must have made a considerable difference. "As to the sound economic basis of making money out of each other," Addison commented, "one may have considerable doubt, but as to the enthusiasm awakened on behalf of the European students and the thought of them, there can be no question."[59]

To Addison it was important to let the antagonisms of the war die out: "We should never forget the men that lie asleep in Flanders Fields, but we want no more men to be put to sleep there."[60] Typically, she believed that only the spirit of Christianity was strong enough to effect this reconciliation and to bring about a lasting peace. She had experienced the power of this spirit at the YWCA conference, where nations so recently at war had come together in friendliness and co-operation at a communion service conducted by a German pastor and attended by representatives of all thirty nations present, including France. At the university women's gathering, on the other hand, France had vetoed the idea of a German presence. "Under the sway of intellectuality," commented Addison to a Toronto *Globe* reporter on her return, "harmony among the nations seemed impossible, but at St. Wolfgang, there was positive proof of the power of the Spirit of Christ to draw the nations together in peace and understanding."[61]

This reliance on religious commitment was also apparent in her approach to post-war social problems at home. In essence, she felt that they could only be tackled with the help of divine grace working through individuals. Not that she ignored secular and pragmatic solutions; on the contrary, she made sure that Victoria women were aware of the latest forms of social work. She had already introduced them to her friend Dr Margaret Patterson, a former medical missionary and the first woman magistrate in Toronto, who had addressed the girls on Red Cross work during the war. Then in December 1924, Dr Patterson gave an interesting presentation on her work in the Domestic Relations and Morals Court at City Hall, where she had presided since 1922. In this "Women's Court" she dealt mainly with sex offences such as prostitution and pimping and, in what sounds like enlightened early criminology, attempted to use a combination of medicine, psychiatry, and law to approach social problems.[62] Addison hoped that some of the young women might see Dr Patterson as a role model, although she was convinced that such labours were futile without a moral and basically Christian regeneration in society.

The problem was brought home to her vividly by a chance encounter in early 1925, when she was struck by the sight of a desolate woman leaning motionless against a post on College Street. Hesitating only a moment before approaching the woman to see if she was in trouble, Addison found that she was a married woman, Russian by birth, who had left her American husband and run off to Toronto with an Assyrian, who had since deserted her. Margaret escorted her back to her lodging and enlisted the help of Vera Parks of the Social Service Exchange to send her home to New Hampshire. The incident left her rather depressed, thinking "that she is only one of tens of thousands – a bright girl, a loving girl, uneducated, with no background of morals – just the kind of person to be a prey to any emotion that was passing ... What can be done for such people?"[63] The lack of real Christianity in society gave Addison moments of despair: "I think it is one of the reasons why when we rap at the door of ourselves and enter hoping to find buoyancy, we find sitting on the hearth fatigue and dulness."[64] She herself could find renewal and a sense of perspective in "earnest, continuous prayer" of a meditative kind – "the direct contact between the spirit of the eternal Father and our own spirits" – yet even the Victoria women closest to her seemed not to avail themselves of this resource.[65] This she considered the heart of her mission; in this she was carrying on the evangelism of her father, a responsibility shouldered by her whole family. If her college girls lacked commitment, the blame must partly be placed on the lack of heroism among those, such as herself, who should be their spiritual leaders.

Of course the 1920 rearrangement had brought in auxiliaries, in the person of the dons, and Addison realized the help they could be:

I find it very difficult to put into words the value of a Don, because if she is a poor Don she is not the least use, and if she is a good Don it is like trying to put into words something of one's Christian experience – a very difficult matter. Houses are tidier, students better behaved, but who is going to define what tidiness and behaviour mean, let alone the great question of the moulding of character, for which there is no measure.

From this letter it appears that in her choice of dons, their Christian life was a chief factor. These dons – women like Marion McCamus, Sadie Bush, Hazel Cleaver, and Rose Beatty – she saw not merely as educational workers, bringing the best self of each girl to fruition, but as fellow-evangelists, whose basic aim was "to try to make the Kingdom of God prevail right here at home": "We may become members of the League of Nations, and propagate the cause, but if we can live at peace in our own community and cultivate the spirit of love and friendship, that is the best contribution we can make to the peace of nations and to no more war."[66]

In this context of the building of a Christian community, the vexed question of the sorority had a special resonance. Although the Kappa Kappa Gammas had continued to exist, tolerated but resented, in February 1924 a group of girls petitioned the senate for permission to form a second sorority. Another group of girls immediately sent in a counter-petition, objecting.[67] Addison and the committee of management, fearing a threat to "the ideals upon which our whole life is founded – a common sisterhood,"[68] asked the senate to form a committee to study the question. The committee, which included Mrs Dingman of the committee of management and Mrs Blewett, one of the first female members of the board of regents, consulted widely with the interested groups. On 3 October the committee presented its conclusions: while no reasonable grounds existed upon which to deny the petition for a second sorority and to allow only one in the college, sororities tended to be divisive and to provoke jealousy and recrimination; it would therefore be much better to have none.[69] After heated debate, carried over to 17 October, the senate went on record with the opinion that no sorority or fraternity should exist within the student body of Victoria – a recommendation that endures to this day. Understandably, the Kappas were reluctant to disband. Addison wrote to a number of deans of women in early 1925 for their opinions on sororities and received overwhelmingly unfavourable replies, which she showed to the leaders of the Kappas, Mary Rowell and Beth Hiltz.[70] After another meeting with the whole sorority, they agreed to stop initiating new members for the sake of peace. Eventually, the Kappas ceased to exist as a unit at the college.

The desire of some girls to form a sorority seemed to point to some failure of community life, some shortage of facilities or opportunities for fellowship. Addison thought it basically a psychological problem, one exacerbated by physical overcrowding. Annesley Hall, built to house fifty-five girls, now accommodated seventy-one; as for the dining room, it was stuffed with what Addison described as 164 chairs and 169 persons to sit on them.[71] She and the committee of management had already formed a building committee which, by April of 1923, had persuaded the board of regents to form a similar committee to consult with them. But the joint committee did not meet until January 1925.[72] During that January Addison attended a missionary conference in Washington; on the way back, she visited a number of American colleges such as Johns Hopkins, Goucher, Bryn Mawr, Wellesley, and Radcliffe. All these colleges had single rooms, she reported, whereas Victoria now had three or even four girls in some former doubles. They also had libraries with fireplaces and whole suites of rooms for guests, even though in many cases they were seeking to raise six million dollars in endowment.[73] Victoria set its own goal at a modest $250,000, and on 28 February 1925 the Alumnae Association, the Victoria Women's Association, and the Women's Undergraduate Association combined to launch the campaign at a dinner at the King Edward Hotel. In her address to this gathering Addison elaborated on the needs which she had already defined succinctly in an earlier report, when, with a fine blend of piety and practicality, she had called for "a larger faith that He, whose work this is, and who is master of all wealth, will touch some heart to respond to His call for His work. We want a Union, two residential units, and an extension to the kitchen and the stories above it."[74]

Her prayer was answered fairly briskly, for the campaign had scarcely got underway when Mr and Mrs E.R. Wood responded with a munificent gift: their stately town home, Wymilwood. This lovely residence – fortuitously in the same architectural style as Annesley Hall, and designed by Sproatt and Rolph, the architects of Burwash Hall – had stood on the west side of Queen's Park Crescent since 1895. In fact it may be seen there still, though it is now called Falconer Hall and belongs to the university. Its unusual name was formed from Wood and the shortened names of the Woods' two children, William and Mildred.[75] Inside, it had a gorgeous entrance hall and mahogany staircase, fine details such as carved ceilings and mantle-pieces, fluted pillars, walnut panelling, murals and frescoes, and other appurtenances of gracious living such as a library, billiard room, and sunroom. Initially, Edward Wood had suggested that the building, probably worth $150,000 in the current market,[76] might be bought by the college for $50,000; his wife, however, persuaded him that they should make it a donation, for the use and benefit of Victoria women.

To adapt this mansion to student use and to furnish it, a gift of $60,000 was offered by Clara Flavelle of the committee of management (now Lady Flavelle), on condition that the sum would be matched by another $60,000 obtained through fundraising. Addison and her committee spent long hours deciding on the most advantageous disposition of the new space. Eventually, dormer windows were made in the roof so that thirty women students could be housed on the second and third floors, along with their don, Rose Beatty. A new wing included an extra staircase and washrooms. The ground floor was to house the women's student union, which for five years had huddled in Annesley Hall; in spite of its female orientation, campus organizations that included both sexes were encouraged to use it. This floor included a cafeteria under the direction of a dietitian, Miss Beemer.

To Addison's joy, she was able to engage Dorothy Kilpatrick, whom she had known for many years, as head of the union. In her description to Charlotte, she endowed Miss Kilpatrick with all the virtues she felt she herself lacked:

She has a marvellous way of getting on with people. She is so sweet and clever and sunny and sympathetic. She walks into people's hearts and in return they give her anything she wants. The students all think everything of her but she is far too high-minded and beautiful to do other than allow their regard for her to lead them on to higher plains [sic]. I cannot tell you how happy I am to have somebody who will do personal work which is the very essence of real education and which I, overborne with care and limited in so many ways, cannot do.[77]

Wymilwood was officially opened in January 1926. Large numbers of people came to marvel at the tastefully decorated rooms. The ease with which the house had been furnished (in colour-schemes coordinated by an interior designer) showed an encouraging progress since the days of the furnishing of Annesley Hall, when Mrs Burwash had sent out appeals for feathers to stuff the pillows or for a donation towards wastepaper baskets. Apparently no residual puritanism hampered the Victoria community's appreciation of Wymilwood. When a reporter from *Saturday Night* asked whether all this elegance might inspire covetousness and unreal standards in Canada's future housewives, Mrs Wood explained that the aim was rather to create a love of beauty and harmony that the girls could carry into their own homes. "The question of money does not enter into the making of a true home," she maintained with the unworldliness of a rich woman, "but the essential qualities are order, exquisite cleanliness, refinement of taste and a loving heart."[78] Addison, too, believed that lovely surroundings could influence character. She was delighted that, through the gift of Wymilwood, Annesley Hall could return to its former status as a homelike residence. The most galling continuing legacy of the 1920 rearrangement was finally removed.

CHAPTER NINE

Dean of Women

Addison was fifty-one when she became dean of women in 1920, and sixty-two when she retired in 1931. She was, then, a mature woman when she became the official advisor to all the young women in Victoria University. Understanding between generations is never easy, but its inherent difficulties were increased by the far-reaching changes that had taken place since Addison's own youth, as society moved from the Victorian to the modern era, from an agricultural to an urban economy, and from professed Christianity to a growing secularism. Addison's generation, even more than that of most people in their fifties, had to beware of falling into nostalgic longing for the days of yore, when life was simpler. As for the younger generation, World War I had revealed the bankruptcy of the old dispensation and legitimized a certain amount of revolt. Unlike previous young people, who on the whole had accepted their role as adults in training, this generation tended to set themselves consciously against their elders, either in hedonism or in promoting radical political change through such movements as Communism or anarchism. Of course, there is an element of exaggeration in the popular notion of a reckless and doomed generation; as Northrop Frye recalled, "A very conventional friend of mine once remarked to me rather wistfully that he wished he had known that he was one of the rebellious flaming youth of the roaring twenties!"[1] But there is no denying that the decade was wild and difficult, one in which young people strained the limits as never before, even in staid and godly Toronto.

By and large, Addison responded well to the challenge of post-war changes. Although she held fast to her values, she realized that some things she had taken for ends were only means and could be altered without disaster. As Gertrude Rutherford testified, the girls were sometimes tempted to dismiss Miss Addison as "belonging to the earlier life of the college," or as "too narrowly Methodist in outlook," yet they were unable to do so honestly.[2] She remained open to truth from whatever quarter; according to Kay Coburn, a don from 1929 to 1930, "what compelled the regard of the young, and what sooner or later won over even the most difficult student, was her own fearless honesty of mind and her obvious respect for it in others, even when unpalatable or disturbing in its conclusions."[3]

One of the sources of her strength was a genuine love for young people. "I am realizing," she wrote in 1924, "what a tremendous advantage it is to live among young people ... As a rule young people do not do so much hating. They prefer the way of kindness and goodness and peace."[4] She often recalled her own youth, especially now that her ninety-year-old father was visibly failing. Strangely enough, though she appears to have been a model child, her chief remembrance seems to be a spirit of rebellion against the injustices of the world, and an annoyance at the patronizing attitude of adults who assured her she would know better later. To her mind, a refusal to accept the *status quo* was one of the assets of every thinking young person: "I would not take from youth one whit of revolt, or smile a superior smile. Nothing could be more fatal than that youth should take everything in the world as youth finds it."[5] Thus she could sympathize with her young charges, and perhaps even envy the overt gestures with which they made their non-compliance clear.

Not that Addison wished she were young again herself; on the contrary, another source of her strength was her wholehearted acceptance of change in her own life. Along with wrinkles and grey hair had come maturity and a stronger faith. Out of the turbulence of her childhood and the awkwardness, even dumpiness, of her adolescent years had come what seemed her natural persona: a large, stately woman, with neatly waved grey hair and steely glasses – a sterner, updated version of her twinkling mother. When she entered a room, one knew immediately that someone of importance had arrived; her brother Will's family secretly called her the duchess.[6] But it was not presence that she valued so much as a new, though intermittent, serenity of spirit. "I think one is so much happier as one grows older," she wrote, "despite the infirmities that come with the years and despite all that which accompanies the turn that means one is going down the hill instead of going up."[7] She would never be able to shrug off troubles and responsibilities or her own individual duty to improve the world, but she no longer despaired because of her lack of success. Brief periods of despondency were more than balanced by periods of joy and confidence. "I think God meant us to love life," she wrote, "and love everything, as well as to love him with all our being."[8]

Thus Addison managed to keep a surprising equanimity before the phenomenon of the flapper, the girl with the boyish bob and expanse of vivid stockings. In January 1926, she was interviewed by a reporter from the Toronto *Star* for her opinion of the modern girl. She remarked that the war had produced a gulf between the generations that made judgment very perilous; but she then went on to praise the modern girl for her frankness, practicality, and lack of sentimentality. She even alluded with apparent aplomb to the petting party – which modern readers might have supposed came in around the time of *Peyton Place* – saying she thought it was popular because the present-day girl lacked a sense of beauty. For her, random public expressions of affection were the sign of a disregard for the fitness of things. But the excesses of the jazz age, she felt, were a passing phenomenon, and, on the whole, the modern girl was "rather an improvement on previous generations."[9]

Of course the changes were far deeper and more significant than the mere advent of the flapper. In her last report to the committee before retirement, Addison tried to sum up the gains and losses for women that had taken place since she first became dean. Young women of today, she wrote,

have more culture, more freedom, more independence; they grow in ability and self-reliance, are more tolerant, easier to live with, since their interests in life are so many ... This present generation of young people are very frank and honest; they are especially amiable and energetic and unsentimental; they are also selfish and irresponsible. There is little faith in God, less faith in prayer, a groping after a new revelation of God, and difficulty in finding such expressions of it as they can understand. Their need is great, and their desires in many cases are for something which they do not find.[10]

She could only deplore this spiritual vacuum, and the plight of a minority "who have repudiated church and early training and are at loose ends, with no anchorage, and no stability."[11] But, though she never wavered in the belief that Christianity was the answer to the dilemma, she did not hanker for a return to the more closed religious climate of her youth. Rather she had faith in a progressive revelation; she believed that the new openness would lead to a stronger and more persuasive Christianity.

In a talk in 1920, Addison had defined the four most pressing problems of the age as "the repatriation of the soldier, the foreigner in our midst, the relation between capital and labour, and woman's place in the world."[12] She continued to read in all these areas, lapping up such works as Keynes's *Economic Consequences of the Peace* and Bertrand Russell's *Education and the Good Life*. She concentrated, though, on the topic of women's place, which she considered the most far-reaching problem. Keeping an open mind about what the future would bring for women, she was not committed to retaining women's place in the home, nor was she striving to create a new woman completely freed from domesticity. Indeed, her task would have been simpler if she had had such a definite ideology. "If only one could forsee what a woman will do in the future," she remarked in a report to the committee of management in 1926," whether she will be in a home of her own, or whether she will follow a profession. This doubt plays a large part in the question of the education of women."[13]

Her only fixed point of reference was that women, whatever they undertook, should do it in a womanly way, capitalizing on their particular strengths and gifts. In an interview with a reporter from *Saturday Night* in 1925, she enlarged on this theme, even suggesting that Canada should now have a college for women. Though she had opposed a separate college at the University of Toronto in 1909, she reasoned that those were the earlier days of women's higher education, when such a college might well have entailed a subordinate status. Now, she felt, there was scope for an independent institution, similar to Wellesley or Bryn Mawr, where a genuinely alternative, woman-centred experiment in education might take place. Her thinking had been much influenced by a British study that she mentioned to the *Saturday Night* reporter:

The Report of a British Commission on "Differentiation of Curricula between the Sexes in Secondary Schools" points out that in the early days before higher education was open to women, there was a difference of education based on the supposed inequality of mental capacity in men and women; that after higher education was open to women, there was an identity of curricula in which women proved that they had mental capacities equal to those of men. It would seem now, the report continues, as if there might be a differentiation of curricula based on equality of men and women, but taking into consideration those differences in function that must always distinguish women from men.[14]

The report reinforced her argument with the Masseys in 1920, that equality does not entail uniformity.

In the *Star* interview, Addison had commented that although "the girl of today wants to make a man's contribution to life because she has been given a man's education," this would soon change. To the *Saturday Night* reporter, she emphasized that women will always be the mothers of the next generation and the guardians of beauty. Thus women needed not to abandon their intellectual endeavours but to balance them with the imaginative side of life, as the curriculum of

OLC had sought to do. Addison had been impressed by Benjamin Kidd's *The Science of Power* (1918), an indictment of the bankruptcy of Western civilization in the light of the World War, which blamed the West's troubles on its glorification of the qualities of the fighting male. According to Kidd, the world could evolve only by tapping powers found primarily in women: altruism, care for the race rather than the individual, emotional power rather than reason, and the ability to work towards a distant ideal.[15] The very course of history demanded that women should become more themselves.

Unfortunately, the twenties was not a propitious time for the establishment of a women's college. Indeed, Addison's advocacy of it is a clear manifestation of the generation gap. The women's movement had lost its impetus and was experiencing a sense of anti-climax, after winning the vote and securing recognition of women's right to be educated. Unfortunately, it had proved all to easy for members of the younger generation to forget the struges and sacrifices of the pioneering women who had secured these victories. As a contemporary of Addison's remarked of the flapper, "Nothing is so dead as the won causes of yesterday; there is no reason why she should think of herself as a feminist; she has inherited feminism."[16] Far from identifying with their older, unmarried teachers, such young women tended to see them as frumpish and rejected the specifically female culture championed by them.[17] Embracing sex wholeheartedly, they saw no need for the sharp demarcations of yesteryear. Thus they were less interested in defining their womanhood than in adopting some of the enviable habits of men; there was a definite trend to boyishness. At Victoria University, the tendency to the integration of the sexes may be seen even in religious matters. For instance, after 1920, the students gave up the student YMCA and YWCA and joined together in the unisex Student Christian Movement.

Slowly the residence rules were changed to accommodate the tide of modernism. By 1927 Annesley Hall had a more generous late leave (1:00 a.m.) than either University College (12:30) or St. Hilda's (11:30).[18] One of Addison's letters of 1923 is concerned with a report that Victoria College women have been smoking – "a nasty accusation to have brought in."[19] Sensibly, she recognized that regulations, though they have their place in maintaining standards, cannot "do a great deal to stem the tide of freedom for women that has been the outcome of their new position politically." The only hope, she felt, was to instill principles that would show a better way.

In the matter of dancing, that traditional Methodist paradigm for the devil's worldly brew, Addison came to see that it was not necessarily a highway to perdition. "When the war ended," she told her correspondents, "dancing came in like a mighty tidal wave, before which we were powerless."[20] Increasingly the traditional "promenades" were out of touch with the spirit of the twenties, to judge from a 1926 graduate's description: "The women lined up on one side of the main hall, with the men on the other side getting up their courage to cross and seek partners for a succession of 'proms.' This involved walking about and talking, on the first and second floors, while the band played a number. A few really daring couples crept surreptitiously to the dark third floor, where they wickedly *danced* to the music."[21] The authorities seemed hypocritical in maintaining a blanket prohibition while quite aware of the capers cut behind their backs; far better to allow dances in the college buildings, under supervision and in controlled circumstances. The first such dance took place in Annesley Hall in November 1926, with only a slight awkwardness as it was unclear whether the girls had invited Miss Addison or not. It was followed by other college-sanctioned events. "Imagine Chancellor Bowles, Mrs. Starr, the President of the Alumnae – Miss Thompson – and myself receiving for [the Victoria At-Home] in Hart House!" marvelled Addison, no doubt thinking of the staid promenades of her own youth. "The only thing I did not like, was the dancing of some young girl from somebody's studio who turned two or three handsprings during the dance."[22]

Although the Methodist conscience could enlarge to encompass dancing and to contemplate smoking, it drew the line at drinking, which it continued to see as the root of many social problems. There is no evidence that the women of Annesley differed from their elders in this regard. Ontario had been officially "dry" since the war years; that is, the public sale of alcoholic beverages was forbidden, though its manufacture for sale elsewhere was still permitted, and actual consumption continued steadily (and sometimes literally) under the table. Gradually, however, other provinces were repealing their prohibition: British Columbia became "wet" in 1920, followed by Manitoba and Alberta in 1923. The fate of the Ontario Temperance Act, or OTA, became problematical with the election of Conservative Premier Howard Ferguson in June of 1923. Ultimately it was his winning of the 1926 election on a platform advocating the government-controlled sale of liquor that signalled the end of prohibition. However, the question was first put to the electorate in 1924 in a plebiscite on 23 October.

On this significant day, lectures at Victoria College were cancelled so that students could serve as scrutineers. Fifty Annesley Hall girls breakfasted early and went to the polls by 7:40 a.m., some arriving home only at 7:15 p.m. By then they were rather a dispirited group, as every single Toronto district went wet. "In one polling booth there were 150 wet votes and one dry – the poor girl who was there came home and collapsed for the night," wrote Addison.[23] But she despaired too soon: as the votes came in from outlying areas, the original majority for government control was whittled away and, by one in the morning, the tide had turned and a majority had built up for the OTA. At Arthur Addison's, where a group was listening to the results on the radio, they woke up old Peter Addison to tell him the good news. And at breakfast the next morning, the Annesley girls replaced their usual prayers with the Doxology: "Praise God from whom all blessings flow."

Some time later, in the run-up to the election of November 1926, Premier Ferguson got into hot water by a widely reported remark to the effect that "no girl would hardly speak to a fellow at a dance who had not liquor on his breath." At a mass meeting at Annesley Hall, the following resolution was passed and sent on to Ferguson: "Be it resolved that the women of the Victoria College residences go on record as being opposed to any association, including that of dancing, with any man who bears signs of liquor on his breath or on his person."[24] Unfortunately (from the Methodist point of view), the majority of Ontarians were less fastidious: Ferguson won the election, and it was only a matter of time before prohibition was repealed.

Finally – to complete the list of sins – sexual mores were altering rapidly. Addison was delighted to see her nieces and nephews married, and she cut out all her former residents' engagement and marriage notices from the newspaper to stick in her scrapbook; but she was no fan of sex in the abstract. Only a stern sense of duty compelled her, one summer holiday, to take her nose out of books on education and mysticism and to catch up on the latest thoughts on the subject of men and women. "It really needed the blue skies and water, the trees and sunshine, and the absolute compulsion of the necessity of reading such books," she told the committee of management, "to make it possible to wade through them."[25] But wade she did, being convinced of the need for a dean of women to be abreast of all that affected the women's movement and position. She did not mention the titles of the books in question; if she was reading Havelock Ellis and others on the dangers of lesbianism, her glumness is explained.

She continued, however, to bring to the residence speakers on sexual matters, and to encourage discussion. Particularly popular was a voluntary group in eugenics, which about a quarter of the girls attended. No doubt, Addison was influenced here by the work of Helen MacMurchy and the federal government to stop what MacMurchy considered the avoidable hereditary transmission of feeble-mindedness, criminality, and even pauperism.[26] But the term eugenics, which had not yet acquired its Nazi overtones, was also used as a euphemism for the teaching of enlightened sexual practices and avoidance of venereal disease. The thirteenth edition of the *Encyclopaedia Britannica* in 1926 called this "positive eugenics": "greater enthusiasm for health and a heightened biological patriotism." Such at least is the implication of Addison's explanation of the need for such courses: "We have our choice, either of giving them wise, sane, unsensational information or of having them get it in other and probably in objectionable form."[27]

Addison used a similar justification when asked to comment on an article by Dr. Ernest Thomas, "Marriage: Discipline or Adventure," in *The New Outlook* of 21 December 1927. Some ministers had objected to this article – surprisingly, since it praises lifelong Christian marriage as a challenge and an adventure. Perhaps they objected to the mere acknowledgement, in the official church paper, of growing promiscuity – the "succession of adventurous exploits in temporary mating" that the smart set held to be less boring and more imaginative than monogamy. Perhaps, too, they were offended by Dr. Thomas's suggestion that to attempt to foist the church's ideal on lives not basically Christian was to invite conflict. Undoubtedly, some disliked his approval of planned parenthood. But Addison, appealed to as an authority by the Board of Evangelism and Social Service, gave such discussions as Dr. Thomas's her blessing:

It is necessary for the followers of Jesus to know the world in which they live, if they are to serve it, and those who have to do with young people today know that there is the frankest possible discussion on all matters which pertain to the propagation of the race. If the Christian Church will see in this possibilities for good, and will sympathetically place before youth the scientific bases of a better race, made glorious by the spiritual beauty and significance of marriage as Jesus set it forth, youth may be saved from receiving replies to their questionings from sources that are gross and materialistic.[28]

As society changed, so – or soon after – did the Methodist church. In 1925 came the last and greatest change, as it folded itself, along with Presbyterians and Congregationalists, into the United Church of Canada. At the ceremony in the Mutual Street Arena on June 10, Peter Addison was honoured as the oldest Methodist minister in the Toronto Conference and a representative of the bygone, heroic generation of saddlebag preachers. Margaret never forgot the sight of her dear father trudging slowly down the long aisle of the arena to the platform in what was to be his last public appearance. She loved his endurance, his faith, the great spirit that even at ninety-three could welcome a bold experiment in the life of the church.

Not that the formation of the United Church was a sudden development: negotiations had been going on since 1902, and the doctrinal basis of agreement had been drawn up by a subcommittee headed by President Burwash before the war.[29] Nevertheless, when the time came it was not easy for Methodists to give up their historic identity. Margaret, who found it hard to become accustomed to the Presbyterian form of service, confessed that she was "longing for the old stirring words that belong to the Anglican form, which we former Methodists adopted."[30] But she embraced this opportunity to sacrifice for the greater good, speaking of "the thrilling experience that comes from sinking one's personal feelings and past traditions in a great spiritual vision."[31] Church union was a small step towards that vision, the reunification of all Christendom, and, ultimately, the Christianization of the world.

Church union affected Victoria University in a practical way. Although the Methodist theological students had for many years been taught on the third floor of the main Victoria building, this space became hopelessly inadequate when students from the former Presbyterian and Congregational churches swelled their number to over two hundred. The expectation that the United Church would inherit Knox, the Presbyterian theological college, was dashed in 1926, when the Ontario legislature awarded the building, charter, and most of the endowment to the Presbyterians staying outside the union. There seemed nothing for it but to build a new facility. By an act of 1928, Victoria's theological faculty and the uniting members of Knox were formed into a new college within Victoria University. After much discussion the name Emmanuel or "God with us" was chosen; according to a student verse quoted by Sissons,

'Tis done, the great transaction's done,
The name's euphonious, orthodox;
The meaning's best of all, bar none –
The lord's with us, and not with Knox.[32]

The campaign to raise money for the Emmanuel College building, as well as residences for theological students, included, and eventually pre-empted, the women's campaign launched in 1925. The women had continued to seek funds after the acquisition of Wymilwood because that building, though it had solved the problem of the student union, in the end had not greatly increased residence space. In return for Wymilwood, the college had taken back South Hall for a theological residence, for a net gain to the women of only five beds. In some of the Bloor Street houses, there were even rooms for four. By 1927 women were being housed in the United Church Training School on St. Clair Avenue, more than two kilometres from the college, and at the former Presbyterian deaconess home on Grosvenor Street, a brisk walk away. The Annesley dining hall continued to be too small, and twenty-eight girls had to be sent over in rotation to eat at Wymilwood. So the Victoria campaign, launched in 1929 with a goal of $1.2 million, included in its plans new women's residence space along with a theological college, a chapel, and theological residences.

The glossy campaign brochure, *The Spirit of '29*, pictured a new and rather Anglicized Victoria campus. On the north side of Charles Street, Annesley Hall was to be enlarged by a new dining room to the north and a residence extension to the east, thereby forming a large, hollow square around a central courtyard; the existing Annesley Hall served as the western edge. The new residences were to be arranged as five separate "houses" much like the Burwash arrangement. South of Charles Street was to be the larger Victoria quadrangle, with the college in the centre surrounded, like a cathedral, by a square of buildings. To the south of the Birge-Carnegie library, Emmanuel College was to take the position it now occupies, while an imposing chapel and the Emmanuel residences would form a solid wall on the south of the quadrangle, linking Emmanuel to the existing men's residences on the east.

Addison was active in the building campaign, speaking at the Embassy Club luncheon in April 1929, for instance, to publicize the appeal. In November 1929, she hosted three fund-raising teas at which over a thousand women were led through the college buildings; perhaps they found the buildings opulent enough already, however, for the net profit appears to have been a meagre $8.96.[33] She participated simultaneously in a similar campaign by the women of the University of Toronto, who were working for a women's union comparable to Hart House. Although the initial committee was made up of women on the university staff and faculty wives, they hoped to involve representatives of government and their wives, the board of governors and their wives, prominent citizens, and alumnae. They envisioned a magnificent building with amenities such as meeting and common rooms, a kitchen, a dining room, a small concert hall, a gymnasium, a swimming pool, offices for the YWCA and other organizations, three guest bedrooms, two or three staff suites, and a health service.[34]

Unfortunately, both the university women's building and the new women's residences were to remain just that – a vision – until the late 1950s. After the stock market crash of October 1929, the collapsing economy was not favourable to large gifts; in mid 1930 the Victoria appeal was terminated, having raised a disappointing $737,000. This money was allocated chiefly to the building of Emmanuel and the theological residences. The chapel itself was abandoned, and the new residences re-situated as a result – an arrangement which conveniently enlarged the campus and left room for the new buildings of the 1960s. The women received $50,000 to renovate the Bloor Street houses and make them suitable for an indefinite occupation. Addison remarked philosophically that the women had to wait in the interests of the greater whole, and that "waiting is a source of much discipline."[35]

Crowded conditions, not to mention the general growth of the student body after the war, gave rise to the thought that perhaps the size of the college should be capped. In late 1927, the senate appointed a committee to look into this subject. Addison herself felt the college was becoming too large; in 1927 there were 405 women, whereas in her opinion total enrolment should not exceed 600, divided equally between women and men. Her ideal was a community, not a mob. All her favourite educational writers, and particularly Newman and Thomas Jesse Jones, stressed the fact that college education was a matter of personal contact between teacher and student, to the benefit of both parties; as expanding numbers made this impossible, education risked becoming merely an intellectual matter, as in the impoverished continental model. Little was gained, Addison felt, by offering to the multitude an experience so watered down that it hardly deserved the name of education. Seeking to explain this elitist-sounding point of view to her correspondents – and not advocating, as one might expect, the creation of more small colleges – she instanced the case of Christ and his twelve hand-picked disciples, from whom knowledge percolated down.

On 8 December, the Alumnae Association discussed the subject. Professor Sissons of the senate committee attended, arguing that "a college education is only for those who have both character and ability sufficient to make their life agreeable and profitable in a cultural atmosphere." Addison also "produced many documents and quoted many educationists favouring limitation."[36] The minute-taker who recorded their arguments felt constrained to note "I don't agree" in a balloon in the margin, but many of the women students did agree. Unlike the majority of the men, they voted in favour of the limitation of college enrolment in the student debate on the subject – according to Addison, because they were more community-minded than the men and felt more responsible for each other.[37] But their views proved politically impossible to adopt. The spirit of the age favoured a wider availability of education, and the college continued to grow.

Given the lack of new residence space, Addison devoted much of her energy during her last years as dean to the creative integration of the Bloor Street houses and Wymilwood. Regarding Wymilwood there was some friction. The first warden, the admirable Miss Kilpatrick, resigned in September 1926, after less than a year on the job, to return to India. Her replacement, acting head Vera Sparling, had an even shorter tenure, as she left to get married at Christmas 1926. Addison found she did not always see eye to eye with the new warden, Miss Muriel Manning, who took over in January 1927; she would have preferred to be in charge of the union herself, with a dietitian to take care of the practical details.[38] But the warden proved to be a survivor, eventually staying at Victoria for twenty years, and the two strong-willed women had to resolve their differences as best they could.

Arrangements for the Bloor Street houses were more harmonious. By the end of Addison's tenure, Victoria owned four houses on Bloor – Tait House (no. 147), Pugsley or New House (137), Waldie House (127), and Oaklawn (113) – as well as, intermittently, some houses on Charles Street. The girls on Bloor Street had a regular "milk run" out of their back doors, through the garden, and along an alley to Annesley Hall where they took their meals. Their dons were chosen from a variety of fields, including teaching, research, library work, the YWCA, and social services. Some of them became permanent members of the Victoria teaching staff: Laure Rièse of the French department; Ruth Jenking, originally in classics; and Kathleen Coburn, later an eminent scholar in the English department. Along with Alta Lind Cook of the French department, they were the first women to join the faculty after Mary Rowell's appointment in 1919.

In 1928, in an early and innovative attempt at French immersion for twenty Ontario university students, Addison transformed Waldie House at 127 Bloor Street West into a "French house." From her high school teaching days, and indeed her own adventures in Europe, she was well aware of the vast gap between high-school or even university study of French literature and grammar, and fluency in speaking. By great good luck she was able to secure as don the eighteen-year-old Laure Rièse, a French-speaking Swiss girl who had enroled as an undergraduate at Victoria College in 1929, but who worked as an

Portrait of Margaret Addison
by McGillivray Knowles, 1925

instructor in the French Department as early as 1930–31. By
speaking French in the house,
heading a French table in the
Annesley dining hall, and inviting French-speaking guests, Mlle
Rièse did a great deal to loosen
the vocal chords of her initially
very English-speaking charges.

By this time the residences had
existed long enough to have
developed traditions; in fact Miss
Addison was one of them. From
October 1925 her portrait by
MacGillivray Knowles had hung
in Annesley's reception area, so
that even when she was bodily
absent her image brooded over
the Hall, glancing into the future
with a gaze at once far-sighted and serene.[39] Her long prayers before
meals were legendary as well. As she called on the Lord for world
peace, racking her brains for ever more countries to be blessed,
latecomers waiting at the door would sometimes decide to slip away
instead to Bloor Street, for a meal.[40] The evening dinner remained
formal, with a seating plan that was changed regularly to break up
cliques and promote social mingling. The annual pre-university
house party – all incoming first-year women were invited into residence for a weekend to get to know the senior students, the college,
and each other – was another tradition that proved to be a valuable
and permanent part of the college proceedings, all the more fun
because the girls had to double up and sleep on the floor.

Among the other rituals, Addison was particularly moved by the
annual Lamp of Learning ceremony at the end of the initiation
period. In an evening gathering of first- and second-year girls in
Wymilwood, sophomores carrying lighted candles read out the oath
of allegiance to the college. Then the girls processed two by two, each
sophomore with a freshie, to the college chapel, where they heard
about the origin of the lamp of learning, the icon that symbolizes
theology in the college crest. A lighted lamp was passed from the
president of the second year to the president of the first; each sophomore then gave her lighted candle to her corresponding freshie, and
the girls moved in procession back to Wymilwood. Addison did not
record how the candles were kept alight during the open-air journey,

but she found their sparkling light movingly symbolic.[41] Of course, before this ceremony the sophomores had celebrated by causing the freshies to dress up as goats, with appended horns and tails, and do penance for their misdemeanours. The whole residence liked to join in the Annesley Hall yell, beginning "Rickety cuss, rickety cuss, What the heck's the matter with us?"[42]

Cultural events in the residences continued. Addison was much more knowledgeable about music than about art, where her tastes were conservative: she had not warmed to the Impressionists on her 1900 tour and had never reconciled herself to the development of Cubism. But Annesley Hall was acquiring art through its picture committee. Until 1932 it was known as the Currelly Picture Fund, inasmuch as that energetic museum director had both founded and directed it. Thanks to his wide acquaintanceship among Canadian painters, Currelly was able to persuade one or two artists a year to donate a work to Annesley, in consideration of an honorarium of $100 sent by the Women's Undergraduate Association. In this way the residence obtained some remarkable contemporary Canadian paintings, including an A.Y. Jackson and a J.E.H. Macdonald.[43]

Along with art appreciation Addison tried to foster social awareness, with the co-operation of Miss Manning. Wymilwood was the setting for discussion groups on such topics as Christian citizenship, Hinduism, and the life of Jesus. Women's opportunities and responsibilities were widening; in the famous "persons" case of 1929, women, now admitted to be persons in the eyes of the law, became eligible for such offices as senator, previously restricted to men. Grace Hunter, a prominent lawyer, addressed the women about the implications of this case. In December 1929, Annesley hosted a conference on vocations for women, spread over five evenings. Each day a prominent speaker, such as the witty Dr George Locke, Toronto librarian and long-time member of the board of regents, came to dinner, met the students over coffee, and then gave a more formal address at Wymilwood. The first speaker covered public health and nursing, social service, and church work; the second, business; and the others literary work, teaching, and library work. Presumably senatorship was tucked in somewhere.

Addison was proud of the fact that Annesley was the only residence in Canada to boast a resident nurse as well as a consultant physician. These officials earned their keep when smallpox struck the college in the fall of 1927. The disease affected some half-dozen young men in first year; the whole freshman class was placed in quarantine though, as the first-year women had been working closely with the men on the Bob. For two days, as part of a scheme to have

the whole college vaccinated, the basement tea room became a vac-
cination room; for the next two weeks, only those who had been
previously vaccinated were allowed to attend lectures. Social events
came to a standstill. Thanks to these prompt measures, the epidemic
was much less severe than the earlier dreadful outbreaks of diphtheria and influenza. No women were infected, and among the men "not
one of the six invalids was even dangerously ill."[44]

As early as 1927 – despite much success in the residences and despite
her own status as a college icon, presiding in soft blue, grey, or mauve
at numerous functions – Addison began to think that it was time to
retire. By 1928 she would have been dean for twenty-five years, and
she felt a quarter of a century was long enough for anyone. She
suspected, not for the first time, that she was getting stale in her job
and that her energies were no longer sufficient to respond to the
demands placed upon her. She recognized, as she lamented to her
niece Louise, "how much more my office might have meant to all
these girls had I had more vision, a more cosmopolitan outlook, had
I *drudged* less."[45] Yet she realized by now that she was chronically
unable to let details go. So, not wishing to hang on to office beyond
her due time, she startled the committee of management in September 1927 by telling them that she intended to send in her resignation,
to take effect in June 1928, at the end of the school year.

The committee, caught off guard, wrote in the minutes that "the
women's department of Victoria College centres so much around the
administrative gifts and personal charm of Miss Addison that it seems
unthinkable to go on without her at present."[46] They begged her to
reconsider. Though she did send a formal letter of resignation to
Bowles in October 1927, he too remonstrated, suggesting that she withhold it from the board of regents for a while. Soon Lady Flavelle and
Mrs Dingman of the committee had met with several members of the
board and devised a counter-proposal. Addison had been invited by
Dr Stapleford, president of Regina College in Saskatchewan, to visit
Manitoba and Saskatchewan, all expenses paid, to view the colleges
and address the university women's clubs there. Could she not be
given leave during term-time to accept this invitation, and then to
travel on to the west coast courtesy of the college, after which delightful vacation she might have strength to resume her duties? It proved
to be an offer too good to refuse.

The trip west was in effect a triumphal tour: a reward for Addison's years of labour as well as the inauguration of her final term of office. Even her initial letter of resignation had brought forth accolades; as she remarked caustically in a letter to Louise, "resigning is something like dying – all one's virtues come to the top."[47] As the tour took shape, tokens of appreciation piled up. "I have received more kindness than I have at all deserved," wrote Addison, "and not only that, but kindness beyond all reason, and appreciation that leaves me both humble and amazed."[48] The college presented her with a leather hatbox and suitcase with intricate fittings and accessories of mother-of-pearl and amber; the staff offered a blue silk travelling umbrella; the students of Annesley, at a farewell dinner at the residence, gave her a beaded handbag in her favourite pale blue. Best of all, Karen Lukes, a congenial graduate of 1910 and a future don, decided to accompany her and take care of all the details. On 22 February 1928, they left Union Station in a CPR stateroom with two berths and a private washroom for the long ride to Winnipeg. They were to travel through the scrubby snow-covered country of Northern Ontario and along the majestic north shore of Lake Superior.

Addison's experience at Winnipeg, in temperatures well below zero fahrenheit, was typical of the tour: receptions, luncheons, a tour of the university, talks to the University Women's Club and the Women's Canadian Club, meetings with United Church and YWCA groups, private accommodation with the mother of former Annesley residents, reunions with many of the girls themselves, and bouquets of hothouse roses. "I am living in a world far from real, I can tell you!" she wrote to Louise.[49] Her itinerary over the two months she was away took her to Regina, Moose Jaw, Govan, Saskatoon, Edmonton, Vancouver, Banff, and Calgary. Although she was not in any danger of being swept away by the tide of praise – her own review of the past showed her "sins, blunders, limitations!"[50] – it was encouraging to see the female graduates of Victoria fanned out across the nation and engaged in their multifarious labours as home-makers and workers. To her it was a sign that she and the committee of management had been led by a higher power.[51]

The trip had one bad effect, however: Addison contracted diphtheria, probably in the train coming home in April. After the briefest taste of home life she was on the move again, transferred to an isolation hospital where she received anti-toxin treatment and stayed for two months. By the time she emerged in mid-June, the undergraduates had left Annesley Hall and it was nearly time to move to the cottage.

Addison still enjoyed the benefits of a close-knit family who gathered at Tiny Beach in the summer months. Her father had died in 1925, leaving a great void and causing her to draw even closer to her sister and brothers, and their children. Charlotte, who had bought a Buick and with some difficulty mastered the art of driving, often took Margaret on motoring trips to the States during the summer months. They probably did not endear themselves to the mayors of the towns they visited, given their propensity, after they had passed through, to write letters suggesting where improvements could be made. Restaurant owners, too, were often the beneficiaries of their advice. Margaret's oldest niece, Louise, had passed through Victoria College with distinction and gained a post teaching at Alma College; her place at Victoria had been taken by Mary, Will's oldest child, and then by other nieces and nephews. Whether they realized it or not, Aunt Margaret kept a close eye on them. She even suggested that Peter, Louise's brother, should be taught to dance; evidently she had noticed him dancing with the same young lady at the Annesley and Victoria At Homes and worried that the expression on their faces suggested uncertainty and anxiety, if not downright agony.[52]

In September 1929, Addison's mind turned once again to thoughts of resignation. That same month Mrs Burns had given up her presidency of the committee of management after sixteen years, and in January 1930 Chancellor Bowles was due to step down after the same lengthy term. Addison's own incumbency was beginning to strain the limit. She sent in a letter proposing a retirement date of 31 July 1931, and this time it was accepted.[53] So in October of 1930, "in the belief that the position of Dean of Women of Victoria College requires the services of a younger woman," she formally tendered her resignation.[54]

During the late spring of 1931, Victoria College and other parts of the campus served as flowery sites for a number of farewell teas and banquets. Addison was quite sincere when she wrote that "I go about as in a dream, and feel as if all that was said and done belonged to another person. It does happen that one may occupy a spectacular place, so that public recognition comes – but I am too democratic to enjoy it. Whatever I have done, has been dependent upon the quiet unspectacular work of others."[55] Nevertheless, she could not help but be gratified by the attention accorded her. On 8 April, the Victoria Alumnae Association had a farewell for her at its Easter Tea, presenting her with a silver tea service and a purse of gold and initiating a collection for a fund in her honour. Later, the staffs of Annesley Hall and Burwash combined to buy her a handsome walnut chest, while the women students chose for their tribute a sterling silver vanity set. On 25 April, Dr Edna Guest hosted a dinner at Wymilwood at which the deans of women of Ontario universities and of McGill said farewell to their longest-serving colleague. On 29 May, the VWA was the host of a garden party at which was announced the creation of a $5000 Margaret Addison Fund. The income of this was to go to Addison for life, and, in consultation with the chancellor, she was to decide how it would benefit Victoria women in the future. On 1 June, the University Women's Club held their farewell banquet. On 4 June, a dinner at Hart House was held for seventy-five university women and faculty wives; there tributes were given by Clara Benson; Mossie May Kirkwood of University College; and the new acting dean, Dr Norma Ford. Truly Addison went out on a blaze of glory.

Naturally her retirement was the occasion of much reflection on her twenty-eight years as dean, both in talks and in written reports. At the request of the chancellor, Addison wrote a valuable history of the committee of management, using the minutes of the committee, the VWA, and the board of regents. During its preparation she reread all her own reports to the committee, which she found extremely boring and monotonous: "Fine women students, they run, showing co-operation, and honor, with at the end, the pious hope for better things in the future – hopes, apparently, that remained largely hopes; rejoicing in the small achievements, regrets for failure in the larger ones."[56] In two long reports to the committee submitted in March and June 1931, she summed up the changes that had taken place since her arrival in 1903. Inveterate in the compilation of statistics, she showed the growth of the university (from 1777 students to 6716), its staff, its buildings, and its departments. Victoria College itself had burgeoned from 300 to 965 students.

Two statistical facts stood out about the college. The first was that women now outnumbered men in the arts courses at Victoria, though not at University College and Trinity. The second was that since the 1926–27 school year, more non-resident than resident women were in attendance; by 1931, only 39 percent of the girls were in residence. In her March report, Addison highlighted the problems of the city women: a trip of up to 70 minutes on crowded streetcars, the inability to attend events after 5:00 p.m., and the need for both health services and personal guidance. Though her position as dean of women had given her some responsibility for their welfare, she now suggested the appointment of a separate dean of residence to supervise all residents; even more of the dean of women's energies could then be directed to the commuters. Underlining her lasting respect for British civilization, she wrote privately to Kay Coburn, saying she hoped the committee appointing her successor would look for a Canadian dean of residence, aged forty-five to fifty-five, "and a Dean of Women about forty – *an*

Englishwoman, or a Scotch or Irish graduate. I have such profound admiration for the ideals and quality of English education, and for our women of to-morrow, I want to see far more intellectuality."[57]

At the beginning of Addison's tenure, women's participation in business and public life was still in question. At the end, that right was established, although the most advantageous use of women's talents had not been agreed upon, and roles were in a state of flux. Addison's conclusion was that a dean of women, to provide leadership, needed above all to be cognizant of the history of the women's movement and of experiments in women's work. According to Helen Frye, some years later Addison startled her successor Jessie Macpherson by pushing this agenda: "Miss Addison told Jessie Macpherson last week at a conference of deans of women from all over Ontario that the dean should be writing and doing research and lecturing on women's rights, women's education and goodness knows what. Which somewhat bothered J.M."[58] The dean's responsibility was to see her work in the widest possible context: the needs of the world, the gradual improvement of the human race, and, ultimately, the achievement of the Kingdom of God on earth. In her final report Addison circled back to her home base in an allusion to the Kingdom: "Is there any more hopeful place for it to come than in Victoria College?" This hope – so touching, but in practical terms so very unlikely of achievement – sums up beautifully the radical idealism she brought to her vocation.

CHAPTER TEN

An Active Retirement

During her working years, Addison envisaged her retirement as a long-awaited period of peace and contemplation – except, of course, for a little work on the side for the betterment of humankind. "I expect to retire to a small village," she told her correspondents shortly after handing in her resignation in 1929, "and the height of my ambition when I get there is to be on the School Board and to learn something of the problems of rural education."[1] To this end she bought a house in Newcastle, where she had so many friends and memories. The house was far from palatial – in fact it lacked running water and a furnace – but she hoped to have it renovated and to live there in rural seclusion with Charlotte, when that worthy dietitian reached retirement age.

It might have been predicted that this plan would not come to pass. Events and her own personality conspired to keep Margaret active in the larger world. Charlotte was, in any case, less enthusiastic than her sister: she was used to living in New York or, more recently, Pittsburgh and settling in Newcastle seemed like retreating to a backwater. But before a decision could be made, their plans were disrupted by the premature death of their brother Will in September 1930, at the age of sixty. In spite of his distinguished career as a doctor, as a teacher at the Ontario Veterinary College, and as a member of the Medical Council of Ontario, Will had not become wealthy; in that last year, in response to the hard times of the Depression, he had been opening his practice two days a week for free consultations to the poor. He left a family of four children, of whom the two youngest, Julia and Jack, were still in university. His widow, Janie, who had recently been diagnosed as diabetic, was now on the new and costly regime of insulin injections. The Addisons held many anxious consultations about how the family could be supported. The upshot was that, shortly after her retirement, Margaret left her temporary home with her friend Helena Coleman and moved into Will's house at 431 Broadview Avenue to help supplement the finances with monthly payments.[2]

Margaret was no mere lodger, but an integral member of the family circle. Her nephews and nieces simply replaced the Annesley girls. She indulged in a little match-making, advancing the marriage of her nephew Peter (a recent graduate of the university's forestry program) to Ottelyn Robinson by inviting them both to a young people's party at the cottage. She also did her part to spread culture, taking the young people to concerts and trying to foster international awareness in an attempt – transparent to Ottelyn – to counteract what she considered the excessive Scottishness of Janie's family.[3]

Unconfined to the envisaged rural schoolhouse, Addison intensified her work on councils and in committee rooms. Although her connection with the university did not abruptly cease, the focus of her attention gradually shifted from the college to the church and its extension, the YWCA. In so doing she was pursuing her basic concerns in another key – concentrating now on the religious vision that she had always believed must underpin the academic side of life. From the university she brought to the church her concern for accurate knowledge and sound scholarship. As she wrote in a letter of 1926, "It is not enough in these days to have an emotional religious message; it must be backed up by keen intellectual training, which should enlarge not decrease the spiritual message ... I was much interested in a few words at the beginning of a book called *The Lord of Thought* by Lily Dougall, in which she draws attention to the fact that Jesus was keenly intellectual."[4] Alfred North Whitehead, whose *Aims of Education* Addison was reading in 1929, likewise stressed the connection between knowledge and morality: "Where attainable knowledge could have changed the issue, ignorance has the guilt of vice."[5] In her retirement years Addison characteristically concentrated on the educational aspect of religion and on the provision of scholarships and grants, to facilitate the training that women needed if they were to play a significant role in the church and nation.

Organized religion was not, of course, a new interest, and a survey of her work with the United Church must go back to the time immediately after its formation in June 1925. This was a period of consolidation, during which the organizational structures of the Methodist, Presbyterian, and Congregational churches were meshed and new governing bodies formed. It was an alluring opportunity for someone like Addison, who throve on committee work, spoke readily and well, and welcomed any opportunity to clarify basic principles. As she was one of the relatively few women on the bodies that formulated church policy, her voice was particularly influential. She served in three areas: on the board of education, which was concerned with higher education in the church; on the body that supervised deaconesses and other female workers; and on the Women's Missionary Society or WMS, which sent out women missionaries both to isolated parts of Canada and abroad. Even while running Annesley Hall, Addison gave a great deal of time to these groups; a letter of 1927, for instance, notes a meeting of the Candidate Committee of the WMS from 10:00– 1:00 on Thursday, a meeting with missionaries in the evening, a meeting of the committee on the YWCA constitution from 10:30 to 12:30 on Friday morning, and that of the committee on employed women workers in the church from 2.30 to 5.30 on Friday afternoon.[6] Small wonder that she felt hard-pressed at times.

During the formation of the United Church's board of education in 1926, the VWA sent in a brief which resulted in the inclusion of two women among the thirty-two members; one of them was Margaret Addison.[7] Although the board was concerned largely with the theological education of (male) ministerial candidates, it also supervised the "junior colleges" of the church, the thirteen institutions such as the OLC, Alma College, and Mount Allison Academy which offered a Christian secondary education. Addison and her fellow female member, Mrs R.F. McWilliams of Winnipeg, were probably appointed to the board with particular reference to the secondary institutions; their hidden agenda, however, encompassed the more ready admission of women to the regular theological courses. In a 1930 report, for instance, Addison was careful to point out that "we recognize that the classes and courses given in our Theological Colleges are open to all women who may desire to avail themselves of the same."[8] Ultimately, she envisaged the ordination of women, a goal which she heartily endorsed and forwarded in whatever small ways were open to her. Since this had been mooted in the Methodist Church, proposed for the United Church as early as the first General Council of 1926, and continued to be investigated by a committee, it was a realistic goal that coloured much of her work in the church.

Besides serving on the board itself, Addison was a member of the board of management of one of the schools it supervised, the United Church Training School, from its inception in 1926 to 1932. This institution, which replaced the pre-union deaconess training schools, prepared women to be missionaries, deaconesses, religious education teachers, and Christian social workers. Through her position at Victoria, Addison was ideally situated to strengthen the university ties of the training school by requiring that courses in the Bible and Christian doctrine take place at Emmanuel College or, at the least, be given by Emmanuel professors. It was Addison's hope, as well as that of principal Jean Macdonald, that as the school evolved it would be able to make a university degree a prerequisite for entry and offer theology courses of the same calibre as those taken by ministerial candidates.[9]

As a member of the executive of the board of education, Addison soon proposed, and served on, a commission to study in sweeping fashion the role of the church in national education, and the possible effects of a purely secular state education. In 1929 the commission made a partial report, dealing only with the role of the church's secondary schools and junior colleges. Basically, it endorsed the presence of church-affiliated schools, both to accommodate those who for various reasons could not be adequately served by the public school system, and to provide a pool from which the church could draw for leadership and ministerial candidates. Above all it stressed that, despite the fine work being done in the state system, it was necessary to maintain some church residential schools "in which the training in good habits, and the developing of right attitudes, will be given their paramount place in education, and in which the combination of religious and moral with intellectual education can be demonstrated."[10] The commission articulated five principles to be met before a college could be accredited by the United Church, one being that the character and abilities of the teaching staff should be esteemed more important than the building of programs or the physical equipment.

Unfortunately, the further report of the commission was never delivered. But an opportunity to study the same subject in more depth occurred later. By 1931 the church was feeling the pinch of hard times: Regina College and Albert College both had large debts, and Moose Jaw College was unable to open at all that fall. In the name of economy, the board of education was united with the board of religious education (which dealt with such matters as Sunday schools and youth organizations), to form the board of Christian education; it was to run with a smaller staff and lower salaries. When this board was appointed in September 1932, Chancellor Wallace of Victoria was made chairman and Margaret Addison became a member at large; by April 1934, Addison was on the executive. Since enrolment in the church secondary schools was dropping,[11] she became the convener in 1933 of a Committee to Study the Place and Function of Secondary Schools in the United Church. Her work with this committee was not all drudgery, for it involved meeting with the principals of many of the chief private schools in southern Ontario. In fact, several evenings were spent at Wymilwood in animated discussion with such congenial groups as the headmasters of Ridley, Upper Canada College, and Crescent School, and the headmistresses of Havergal, Branksome, Bishop Strachan, Alma College and the OLC.

In the report presented at the board's second annual meeting of April 1934, Addison's own beliefs are apparent, though the document was probably written collaboratively. As before, the committee endorsed the existence of alternative schools to cater to those with special needs. Because of their small classes and the wide range of subjects offered, private schools were praised as "laboratories of education." The committee especially questioned the need for girls' schools in an era of new freedom for women. Addison had continued to believe that an all-female education offered a viable alternative. The report supported her contention, pointing to "something distinctive and disciplinary in the residential schools," and adding optimistically that "there seems to be the beginning of a reaction against careless manners." As for Christian schools, they offered the only education that was adequately grounded in morals: all the principals agreed that such schools were "a Christian home on a large scale" and at a time of "disintegrating, devitalizing forces and counteracting influences," when real Christian homes were in short supply.[12] Surely here can be detected the voice of Addison herself, who, when congratulated by the board of education on the occasion of her retirement, had responded that "any good in the work which I have done, has been due to the influence of a godly home, in which the parents placed first the great principles of our Lord."[13]

This report – which continued the church schools much as they had been before, and perhaps saved some from closure in the name of economy – was Addison's last major work on the board of education. She did though continue to serve on its executive until 1938. Unfortunately, economic conditions and the rising tide of secularism were ultimately to bring an end to the church connection with most of these schools. To much of the public, confessional affiliation had come to seem more of a straightjacket than a garment of righteousness. Ultimately, having found it increasingly difficult to fill the schools, the church withdrew from the field. Some of the schools, however, such as OLC, were able to continue as independent bodies, still committed to an ethos of character development.

Concurrently with her work on the board of education, Addison served on the successive committees that supervised the paid work of women in the church. Women were employed by the church in various capacities: as secretaries, teachers, and missionaries. But the principal workers were the deaconesses – an order introduced into the Methodist Church by 1892 and into the Presbyterian Church by 1908. Originally recruited to serve among the poor, being "the first case-workers and the first visiting nurses," or what another writer has called "the foot soldiers of Methodist applied Christianity,"[14] by

1925 they could also be found teaching Sunday school; directing camps and programs for children, girls, and women; visiting the congregation; conducting prayer meetings; welcoming immigrants; teaching English; and helping in the church office. In a typical year, about a hundred women served as deaconesses. Whereas Presbyterian deaconesses were paid, Methodist ones originally received nothing, "the work of a deaconess being done for the love of Christ and in His name."[15] Only in 1918 did the Methodists begin to receive a salary; at the same time the austere requirement of group-home living was also relaxed.

Deaconesses were required to resign if they got married, for the church tended to regard their work as a stopgap to their true vocation as wives and mothers. They were often looked upon as secondary figures, auxiliaries rather than principals; one recent feminist thesis calls them "handmaidens," called "to do the low-status, behind-the-scenes and supportive work which would enhance the public, visible ministry of the male ordained."[16] Their service of designation certainly stressed humility: "You are to go about doing good, ministering to the wants of a suffering, sorrowing and sin-laden world. You are to be angels of mercy to the poor, to visit the sick, pray with the dying, care for the orphan, seek the wandering, comfort the afflicted, save the sinning and ever be ready to take up any other duty proper to your calling."[17] Their status is illustrated by the experience of Mary Eadie, secretary of the committee on women workers, when a report of that committee was being presented at the general council of October 1936. Two men sitting in front of her were discussing frankly the salary recommendation, one remarking that "we ought to get a half time secretary for less than $900," and the other offering that "I have a girl who could do it." "Well," wrote Eadie to Gertrude Rutherford, "it was plain to see what they thought of the secretary!" The men, she noted, were mortified when they found out that she herself was the secretary, and that this belittling attitude was one reason she was resigning her position.[18]

Margaret Addison was very much aware of the difficulty of attracting competent women to church work while such conditions prevailed. Committee members (both men and women) were concerned with raising the profile of the deaconesses and ensuring their participation as members of the governing bodies of the churches they served. Again Addison was to emphasize education and more education. Hoping to improve the training of all the women workers, she insisted that only properly trained women should be employed. One senses that, whereas Addison drew on her educational work at Annesley Hall and her experience teaching at OLC in her work with the board of education, she drew more upon her administrative career as a dean, and the difficulties she had had in maintaining her prestige among a male college hierarchy, in her work with the successive committees on women workers.

When the general council appointed the Committee on Employed Women Workers in the Church in June 1926, Addison joined as a representative of the WMS. The committee would set the tone for the treatment of women employees in the new church, as it was asked to survey their position and recommend policies on training, remuneration, and whatever else seemed germane. It was also charged with establishing the framework for the new deaconess order, and with administering that order provisionally until the general council of 1928 could review its work.

By the time the committee reported to the general council of 1928, Addison's participation had ended; she had left for her western tour early in 1928, only to be hospitalized with diphtheria on her return. There is every reason to suppose, however, that the report reflects her work on the committee and her views. The survey revealed that the church employed a total of 951 women as deaconesses, teachers, matrons of homes for children, nurses, secretaries, bookkeepers; in community and foreign missions; and in the church-affiliated universities as administrators, lecturers, clerical workers, dietitians, and librarians.[19] The committee noted that standards were generally rather low and lacking in uniformity across the church; it advocated more rigorous requirements to make these jobs more prestigious and fulfilling.

Regarding the new deaconess order, the committee could report that it had set out interim guidelines for candidacy, training, appointment, and withdrawal; had accepted a design for a distinctive uniform and badge[20]; and had set the scale of remuneration – one which, at a minimum of $1000 a year plus five weeks' holiday, was a distinct advance over previous agreements. The nature of the order was obviously connected with the question of the ordination of women, about which the committee had voiced no opinion. In the meantime. however, they urged the council to establish a new order, an ordained diaconate of women, as a way of encouraging women of talent and dedication to serve the church. The ordained deaconesses would not only be more highly trained than the existing personnel, but would also be a recognized part of the ministry, teaching, preaching, and where necessary baptizing.[21] Failing this, however, they recommended that the requirements for deaconess training (at present a two-year course in the training school) should gradually be raised to approximate that of ministers.

According to the deaconesses' newsletter, the report was unfortunately "given at a time when a serious discussion of its contents was
quite impossible."[22] Without much debate, the general council of 1928
decided against creating an ordained diaconate, as the regular ordination of women was likely to be approved soon. Nevertheless, they
did express the hope that deaconesses would become members of
the official boards and sessions of their churches, as the report recommended. Council also acceded to the report's recommendation
that female workers should hereafter be supervised by an Inter-Board
Committee on Women Workers, with representatives from other relevant bodies of the church.

When this interboard committee was set up by council in 1928,
Addison was not a member. But by July 1929 she was sitting on it as
the board of education's representative. She continued in this capacity until 1932, at which point she became the WMS representative until
1935. It is hard to judge how much she actually participated in the
work of this committee, which concerned itself with the day-to-day
administration of the deaconess order and with the yearly conference
arrangements. According to the report of an internal study group in
1936, the interboard committee "does not appear to have impressed
the church" with its importance, and the representatives of the other
boards seldom attended the meetings.[23] Of twenty-three meetings
surveyed, Addison was present at six.

At the general council of 1936, however, perhaps in response to
this study group's rather negative report, the deaconesses and others
were placed under a new and theoretically more effective body, the
Committee on the Deaconess Order and Women Workers of the
Church. Margaret Addison – now Dr Addison, and 68 years old –
was a member, along with her former Annesley pupil Gertrude
Rutherford. Eventually, she agreed to serve as chair. She was accept-
ing a difficult task: during the thirties the deaconess order was generally perceived to be a dying cause, and its budget was reduced.[24]
Only half a dozen or so new students a year presented themselves
for training. As a history of women in the church remarked, the
interboard committee had been hesitant to appeal to young women
to embrace a career in the church, "when demand for their service
was limited, appointment uncertain, and remuneration inadequate."[25] Perhaps the challenge formed a partial reason for Addison's
acceptance of the position.

But there was another reason for her renewed interest in the question of women in the church: at the general council of 1936, the
ordination of women had finally been approved. Though not many
women actually came forward, the move gave renewed spirit to all

female workers. Lydia Gruchy, the first woman to be ordained (November 1936), served on the committee with Addison and became a good friend. In an obituary tribute in the *United Church Observer*, Gruchy summed up what she saw as Addison's motivation in the committee on the deaconess order:

She firmly believed that women had a greater contribution to make in the life of the Church, and indeed of the Dominion and of the world than they were making, and she accepted the Chairmanship of the Committee in order to assist them in making that contribution. She realized that centuries of tradition and custom had militated against their independence of thought on great issues, and yet she was convinced that they were capable of it ... She stressed repeatedly that responsibility for the care of children and of the manifold tasks of the home had made women practical and capable of close attention to details. She saw the possibility of harnessing these attitudes to the tasks of the Church and the nation.[26]

Once again, then, Addison threw herself into the time-consuming task of administration, being entrusted with the responsibility of directing the deaconess order, recruiting candidates, deciding on their curriculum in co-operation with the training schools in Toronto and Winnipeg, finding appointments for those who were trained, and assisting and promoting the interests of those female workers who were not deaconesses. One of her first major acts was to appeal to the executive committee of the general council to give her committee more funds. The council allowed that she might make an appeal to not more than one hundred individuals, which she did with some success. Unfortunately the time of Addison's tenure – the end of the Depression and the coming of war – was not propitious for the development of a strong order; in fact, the deaconesses never did succeed in shaking off their image as handmaids. The committee nevertheless did what it could, producing a booklet on "The Professional Service of Women in the United Church of Canada" as well as a new deaconess manual. When the Fellowship of Professional Women in the United Church of Canada was formed in 1939, Addison became its honorary president. The deaconess order was to put on record its indebtedness to her wise counsel in the formative years of the fellowship.[27]

In 1938 Addison hoped to benefit the female workers in a tangible way by donating her house in Newcastle to the church. As it was evident that she would never live in it herself, she thought it might be of more use as a church-workers' home and guest house. She arranged for an inspection by Gordon West, the architect who had been called in when she bought the house some ten years earlier. In June of 1940 he reported that it had deteriorated since his last visit: there was now a hole in one wall and some rotten joists, and the kitchen wing would have to be torn down and rebuilt. He estimated that $4000 would be needed for repairs.

Addison volunteered to raise this sum from her friends. An anonymous donor who had a sentimental regard both for her and for Newcastle gave her $3000; and with this and a few lesser amounts in hand, the church accepted her gift. When tenders were called for, however, it seemed the work could not be done for less than $6000. Moreover, the committee decided that without an additional expenditure for the construction of two bedrooms above the kitchen, a residence would not be economically viable. For some years thereafter the house was occupied by tenants who put up with the seediness in return for a very low rent. Eventually, after Addison's death, the property was sold for a mere $1200 and the proceeds used for the committee's work; the donor of the $3000, disappointed, took back his or her gift.[28]

A third area of Addison's work in the United Church involved the Women's Missionary Society, formed from the WMS groups of the Presbyterian and Methodist churches. Long before the ordination of women, this society was sending out women as evangelists, religious educators, doctors, nurses, teachers, and Christian social workers, leading the WMS to be characterized as one of the earliest manifestations of the women's movement.[29] The WMS missionaries were every bit as intrepid as their more celebrated contemporaries and predecessors, the Victorian lady travellers. Although the most exotic postings were in the Far East and other distant fields, many served in Canada. The United Church enterprises there included eight boarding and three day schools for native Canadians, northern residences, outreach missions to Chinese and Japanese Canadians, hospitals in remote areas, and community missions offering night classes and other services. The WMS also had a Department of the Stranger that dealt with welcoming immigrants and helping them to become acclimatized.

Today, many of these activities have been called into question as involving the imposition of a dominant culture on others: forcibly, in the case of Canada's natives; and perhaps insensitively, abroad. Workers in the 1930s were not unaware of this possible criticism. In 1932, for instance, the major Protestant denominations in the United States co-operated in a ten-month, on-site investigation into Christian missions, to determine whether they were now superfluous and whether and how they needed to change. Their report, *Re-Thinking Missions: a Laymen's Inquiry after One Hundred Years*, is a far-reaching and intelligent scrutiny of the missionary endeavour, which gives full weight to the emerging world culture of science and to the viability of indigenous religions. Ultimately, the laymen concluded, as did Addison herself, that missionaries were justified if they proceeded in a spirit of co-operation rather than rivalry, as "a spiritual band of friends and helpers, not an instrument of authority or of foreign control."[30] While Christianity was uniquely capable of uniting the world, they argued, the resulting universal church would not represent the triumph of the West. Rather it would unite native churches true to the spirit of their homeland with a Western church weaned from its superficial activism by learning from Eastern religions. This report was widely studied in the United Church, most assiduously in the WMS.

Addison seems to have felt, with other critics, that the commissioners were too quick to criticize the missionaries from an outsider's point of view; she also noted that the report laid insufficient stress on the figure of Christ.[31] She nevertheless recommended it be taken seriously as "a compilation of the honest thought of forward-looking missionaries on the foreign fields."[32] Without denigrating other religions and cultures, she too believed that only a relationship with God through Jesus was sufficient to inspire brotherly love across racial and class lines. "Can there be anything on earth more fascinating," she had written in 1929 after hearing an inspiring address by Dr Mott, "than the vision of the unity of all things, and the unity of all peoples in following the 'way of Jesus'?"[33]

Addison served the WMS chiefly on the Candidate Committee, which made recommendations to the board regarding the acceptance of missionary candidates and gave them guidance during their training. She was chair of this committee in 1926 and 1927, during which time the standards of training for the missionaries were laid down. Generally, at least junior matriculation was required, together with relevant professional experience and one year at the training school, requirements that Addison hoped would be gradually raised.[34] After a meeting with female missionaries on furlough and missionaries' wives, she remarked upon "the unanimity of those present upon the great importance of sufficient and proper training for those going out to mission posts."[35] As befits a life-long believer in physical education, she was very conscious of the need for a strong body and tended to reject candidates whose health was not up to par.[36] From 1932 to 1934, Addison acted as candidate secretary, carrying much of the work of the committee except during a period spent in Japan.

She also served on the Scholarship and Bursary Committee. This had been established in 1932 when the society received, as a gift from

Dr Victoria Cheung, a sum of money equal to that spent by the Presbyterian Church on her medical education. 1932 was not, of course, a good year for interest to accumulate, and it was 1936 before the first scholarships were awarded. Their main purpose was to increase the involvement of indigenous people in the work of Christianization. Some helped with the training of foreigners, either in their own country or in Canada; others were awarded to Canadians of non-Anglo-Saxon background who wanted to do evangelical work in their own ethnic community in Canada. The bulk of the latter went to Japanese Canadian women or to members of Canada's First Nations, though the recipients included a sprinkling of French Canadians, Blacks, Chinese, and non-Anglo-Saxon Europeans.[37] The committee was aware of how important native leadership was becoming both at home and abroad. It welcomed, too, the cross-fertilization that the presence of foreign students in Canada could provide.

The YWCA was an organization close to Addison's heart, both for its fostering of a distinctly female religious culture, and for its ideals of service and commitment to improve the world.[38] Her involvement, which began in 1904 with membership on the executive of the Dominion Council, took her to two world conferences. Her progressive attitude to the "Y" is nicely depicted in a letter of 1915 concerning her work on the Conference Committee (which planned the annual Elgin House conference). "There is a dear member of this committee who will, I am sure, be a means of grace to me," Addison wrote, "but at the present time she is more of an exasperation. I do not think that anything new has ever been suggested on which she has not thrown buckets of cold water." This "dear woman" objected to the idea that an evening at the conference might be devoted to the women's movement because, explained Addison, she feared rumours that the "Y" was advocating women's suffrage might circulate. While not wishing to advance a particular political platform, Addison nevertheless argued in the same letter that the "Y" should be involved in all the important questions in women's lives:

It seems to me that if the YWCA is going to be vital to young women, it must touch their lives in every department, and not be limited to what has heretofore been called the religious side. As if, in these modern days, we did not feel that, in the life of a Christian, nothing is ever secular ... The life of our young girls is powerfully affected by the present economic position of women, and the changes that have come to be in the last fifty years in women's life and position; and I think to ignore that, and to fail to lay this before them – the Christian obligation resting upon them to make their lives useful, to be intelligent about all that which concerns their lives – would be to do them a wrong.

Her concluding words show why she was such an effective committee worker: "Just let me say I shall bring it up at the next committee, and probably at the next, and probably at the next, until my conservative friend is either converted or overcome. Which, you see, is an exceedingly sweet spirit on my part."[39]

After 1917, when she was ill, Addison's involvement with the "Y" lessened for a few years but, by 1924, she was once again on the Dominion Council, joining friends such as Nellie Rowell, Lady Falconer, and Margaret Patterson. In January 1925, she went to the Foreign Missions Conference in Washington, DC, as the YWCA's representative.[40] She also had an important role in planning the biennial conference in Preston, Ontario, 17 to 22 May 1924.[41] At this conference, attended by over 150 people, she gave a Sunday address from the pulpit of the Methodist Church (as it still was then) on the YWCA's work throughout the world.[42] Truly she could feel, as she surveyed her temporary congregation, that she was carrying on both her father's and her heavenly father's work. And the conference led to what was perhaps her most important contribution to the YWCA, the chairmanship of the membership commission. This commission worked from 1924 to 1927 to clarify the requirements for membership in the organization, and in so doing helped to move it away from its narrow Protestant evangelical base.

The question of membership in the YWCA was a complicated one, involving hair-splitting distinctions between "the basis," "the purpose," and "the aim"; between "acceptance of" and "sympathy with"; and between the rules for local and national bodies – all of which are reminiscent of the most dismal passages of medieval theology and were of more interest to Addison than to most people today. In brief, originally all members were required to belong to a Protestant evangelical church. Within this group, membership was automatic for all women and girls who paid the fees. In 1916, seemingly because of student dissatisfaction with organized churches, the college YWCAs were given an alternative: they could admit members on a personal declaration of faith, though the whole governing cabinet of such a college branch was required to be at least in sympathy with Protestant evangelical principles.[43]

This compromise, however, did not lay the question of membership to rest. Now there was neither uniformity between branches nor agreement on basic principles. As well, the requirement for church membership seemed outmoded and bigoted; it excluded, for instance, Roman Catholic membership. Because the YWCA had spread to many countries where the majority of members belonged to the Eastern Orthodox Church, the international body, the World's YWCA, would not accept as an affiliate any national organization that retained this requirement.[44] Yet the personal declaration of faith required more theological certainty than many young people possessed. As Addison explained, "The careless and indifferent might accept it without understanding, while the thoughtful ones would be afraid to accept it lest they were hypocritical."[45] In practice, the ruling concept in many of the local organizations was that of a "dollar membership" ("pay a dollar a year and use the facilities"), which completely ignored the Christian purpose of the organization and did not demand real spiritual commitment.

To set new guidelines for membership and find a formula that would be Christian without requiring too settled a faith, Addison and her committee studied the practices of such bodies as the World's YWCA, the YWCA of the U.S.A. and Britain, and the Young Men's Christian Association in Canada. They concluded that a personal, not denominational, commitment was required. They therefore defined the purpose of the local associations in terms that held up church membership (Christian, but not necessarily evangelical) as a goal rather than as a requirement: "The purpose of this Association shall be to lead young women into personal loyalty to Jesus Christ as Lord and Saviour and into active membership in the church of their choice; to associate them in the development of their spiritual, intellectual, social and physical well-being; and to make the Association a social force in the advancement of the Kingdom of God."[46]

A "full member," in their new formulation, was one who was in sympathy with the purpose of the association and able to make a fairly simple and non-theological declaration: "I wish to join in the world-wide fellowship of the Y.W.C.A., to declare my faith in our Lord, Jesus Christ, and my desire to serve others in His spirit of love." At the same time, provision was made for associate members – all who wished to share in the activities of the association without making the declaration – as well as for "contributors," that precious group who simply wanted to give money. On the governing board of each local group, however, at least four-fifths of the members were to belong to Protestant evangelical churches. As Addison explained when recommending this remnant of denominationalism to her fellow committee members, "It is in the administration, therefore, that we make sure of having a group of persons with sufficient unity of spiritual purpose to safeguard the spiritual values and basis of the Association."[47]

A tolerant Christianity was expressed in the statement of purpose the committee crafted for the Dominion Council of the YWCA: the council "includes in the field of its activities young women of every class, creed, race or nationality," though at the same time it "reaffirms its faith in Bible Study and Prayer as essential to the life of the Association."[48] The social conscience of the council was also stressed, as it "calls all local Associations to promote Christian principles of social and international conduct." Throughout the statements and definitions runs Addison's belief in the efficacy of the YWCA in promoting the world fellowship of Christianity that was to be the precursor of the Kingdom of God. These ideals were her own, but her sensitivity to the high idealism and theological concerns of young people was the fruit of many a long discussion with the students of Annesley Hall.

So Addison's last decade passed in the same round of administration and committee work that had characterized her working years. During this time she received some signal honours. In June 1932 she was given the honorary degree of LL.D. by the University of Toronto and, henceforth, was known as "Dr Addison." The distinction pleased her immensely, as it validated her full membership in an academic community to which she had sometimes felt peripheral because of her lack of teaching duties. Female graduates were earning doctorates in increasing numbers, and, with her respect for learning, there was no group to which she would rather have belonged. Even within the family the new title helped her self-respect; she had been absurdly conscious, as she wrote to her brother Arthur in 1928, that "the rest of you all have *two* degrees."[49]

In 1934, she was also made a Commander of the Order of the British Empire (CBE), on the recommendation of Dr. Helen Mac-Murchy. According to a nephew, she was unwilling to accept this honour for a while. Eventually, however, she did travel to Ottawa to receive it, with the thought that it was an honour for Victoria rather than for her personally.[50] And in 1936, Addison received a distinction that was more local and personal: the residence at 127 Bloor Street West was named "Addison House."[51]

She continued to spend a great deal of time at the cottage. As transportation improved, it became possible to invite more company to Georgian Bay. Addison liked nothing better than an earnest discussion. She would sit at the breakfast table till 10:00 a.m. or around

Margaret Addison, c. 1940

the fire till past midnight, prob-
ing the great questions of life
with guests such as Professor
Kenneth Cousland of Emmanuel;
Lydia Gruchy; Winnifred Thomas
of the training school; and Ruby
Chown, the ample daughter of
the former Methodist leader.
Not that she let the housekeeping lapse. She usually had one
or two students staying as helpers, and, according to their
accounts, she ran the cottage like
a captain on his bridge. Tuesday,
for instance, was washday. On
Monday, handwashing and
soaking was begun and that
night the bread was kneaded. A
large copper boiler filled with
water from the pump was set on
the stove to warm overnight; the
residual heat caused the dough
to rise. On Tuesday, the wash loads, which could include up to twelve
sheets when there were guests, were put through the washer (agi-
tated by a hand-worked lever), the wringer, and two rinses, and the
bread was baked. Later, the ashes from the stove were conveyed to
serve the privy.[52] The students – they included Laure Rièse, the future
Pauline McGibbon, and Celia Corcoran – had to follow instructions
carefully in this and in other routines such as jam making. Nevertheless, they enjoyed themselves and gave Addison a much-appreciated
look at current attitudes among the young when they discussed such
questions as the nature of duty. As Celia reported, "We youngsters
quite startled Miss Addison" – as well they might – "by saying we
didn't think Christ was any more divine than an ordinary person."[53]

The cottage was also a place where Addison could give practical
expression to her belief in world fellowship. It was always open to
foreign students, as it had been ever since 1913 when Marjorie Hung,
the first full-time Chinese student at Annesley, faced a lonely summer
far from home. As one Japanese student entertained at Georgian Bay
testified, "I always found it hard to meet people, but Dr. Addison has
taught me to try and find something of Christ in every person, and
now it has become easier to meet all kinds of people."[54] Missionaries
home on furlough, the children of missionaries not home on furlough,

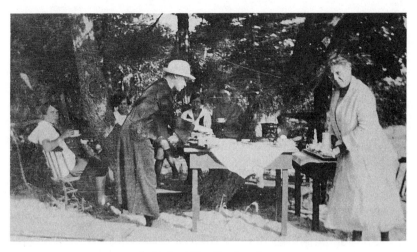

A picnic at Tiny Beach cottage

West Indians, and Oriental students – all made the cottage an international household.

In 1932, Addison's hospitality was returned when she was invited
to visit Japan as the official representative of the WMS and the bearer
of greetings from other Christian organizations: the YWCA; the SCM;
and Simpson Avenue United Church, the church near Broadview
Avenue of which she was now a member. She set sail on 24 September
1932 in the *Empress of Japan*, a magnificent white vessel that was the
pride of the CPR's Pacific fleet and could cross from Victoria to Yoko-
hama in just ten days. The initation had come only a month before, in
a cable from her friend Emma Kaufman, the YWCA worker and home
economist: "Invited visit Japan, October, Kaufman paying travel."[55]
Once there, she engaged in a breathless round of sight-seeing, inspection of schools and institutions, and visiting with old friends in the
missionary movement; she ended the trip with ten days in Korea. An
article she published in *YWCA Notes*, "Our Work in Japan, An Appreciation,"[56] is a rather dry and impersonal summary of statistics and
programs. A series of articles that appeared in the WMS *Missionary
Monthly* gives a much more engaging picture of her activities.[57]

Once she had overcome her cultural shock at the dense traffic and
hordes of bicycles in Tokyo, Addison inspected all three of the girls'
schools run by the WMS: the Toyo Eiwa Jo Gakko in Tokyo (the
original school, established in 1884)[58], and those at Kofu and Shizuoka.
Acutely aware of the scrutiny such schools had received lately from
the laymen who wrote *Re-thinking Missions*, she found the pupils
to be happy and even overly assertive. She visited the Imperial

University, as well as the settlement where Caroline Macdonald had carried on her work until her recent death. She had high praise for the Marlers, Canada's first ambassadors to Japan, who invited her to a luncheon where both Japanese and Caucasian women were guests. Other memorable repasts included a shortened tea ceremony, and a lunch for which she entered, on knees no longer flexible, through a door not three feet high. The social highlight was the emperor's garden party, a top hat and black kimono affair on 8 November: eight thousand people were there, but very few foreigners were accorded the honour. Addison was pleased to see that the emperor, the father of his people, set an example of simplicity and thrift.

In her last article, Addison declared herself cautiously in favour of the liberation of Japanese women, for whom she wished more freedom, more exercise, and wider mental horizons. In some ways their situation reminded her of that found in the English-speaking world some sixty years before, when women had begun to seek more education and influence. Of course, the cultural context was very different. Addison sensed that Asian women played a more important part in the economy than did their Canadian counterparts, working in fields and shops even as married women. But, through no fault of their own, they tended to be intellectually impoverished and psychologically repressed: "Women in the east have been trained to subservience for centuries and now they are in a westernized east where originality, initiative and fearlessness are needed."[59] She was aware of the dangers enfranchisement could pose if Japanese women were to "lose those fine qualities which make them so courteous, so artistic, so beautiful, and take on the aggressiveness of the west." Yet some degree of westernization seemed inevitable, as communication with the rest of the world increased. Without at least a partially westernized education, Japanese women were defenceless: "Women trained for centuries on the assumption they had no souls, and could not be educated, will be susceptible to whatever opinions are thrust upon them. They are open to the wildest views of extreme communists."[60]

More education was therefore necessary in economics, industrial problems, and sociology, as well as in the more traditional disciplines. Although nominally five of the seven Japanese imperial universities were now open to women, the women were so poorly trained in math and science that few were able to fulfil the entrance requirements; even fewer graduated. Addison made a strong plea, therefore, for more effective scientific courses. She argued especially for more theoretical courses in household science, on the model of Toronto's, to open up career opportunities for Japanese women. And since it would be years before Japan could provide teachers in these subjects, she maintained that the WMS should fill the gap: "I am quite convinced from what I have seen that henceforth we should send specially trained women for special work, and highly-trained women." By sharing expertise and training Japanese leaders, such women would be engaging in missionary work "in harmony with new thoughts and new methods."[61]

So Addison left Japan with a gratifying sense that the work at home, in the WMS and the training school, was bearing fruit. Christianity was to her the ultimate message of hope. With its belief in "Jesus and His social programme," it offered a new world order of which extreme Communism was only a parody. Perhaps it would help to mitigate the aggressiveness that she feared for Japanese women. And its gospel of peace would combat the militarism that she saw growing in Japan as much as in Germany. "If Japan does not become Christian," she prophesied at the end of her series in the *Missionary Monthly*, "there is no hope of peace in the east or the west."[62]

At home she continued to take an interest in the fortunes of Victoria University. On her retirement, the board of regents disbanded the committee of management – that body about which she had mixed feelings – and replaced it with a women's council that had only an advisory function. A new dean of women was not immediately appointed, and for three years the distinguished geneticist Dr Norma Ford was acting dean, watched with interest but without interference by her predecessor. In 1934 the college finally hired Jessie Macpherson, a young philosophy student, who was to serve one year longer than Addison, for twenty-nine years, and continued her task of liberalizing the residence rules in accord with evolving mores. There is some evidence that Addison was not happy with a new secularism that was inevitably evolving in the residences,[63] though she made no overt protest. She continued as president of the VWA until April 1933 and served on its executive committee until 1937, taking very seriously her mission to forge links between the college and the community. She returned regularly to college functions and was often invited, as a sort of elder stateswoman, to give advice to other deans at meetings and by letter.

She worked particularly hard to provide scholarships. In 1935, for instance, she was the honorary chairman of the Victoria Alumnae Association's campaign to raise money for scholarships. Her own money was given generously. Craving more knowledge and wider experience for women, she especially tried to enable women to study abroad. As she wrote to her niece Louise, when urging her to pursue a degree in England and see as much as she could, "It is the extra training and experience that give vision, and 'without vision the people perish.' What we need most in Canada are *women* of vision, even more, I think, than men of vision, for too many women are circumscribed by the walls of their homes."[64] When Louise was thinking of prolonging her stay in London in 1928, her maiden aunts were eager to help with finances as well as advice. With apologies to Louise's parents Arthur and Lizzie for "butting in," Margaret urged Louise to accept an instalment or two of the annuity that she herself would not need for a year or two now that her resignation had been declined.[65] She had already sent Louise a cheque at Christmas, to be spent without qualms of conscience. "I have always been sorry for the things I did not see, and the things I did not do, when I was abroad – yes, and the things I did not *buy*," she wrote.[66]

In 1931 she used some of the money from the Alumnae Association's Addison Fund for a loan to Kay Coburn, to help finance postgraduate studies at St. Hugh's College, Oxford. She planned to designate the principal of the VWA's Addison Fund for the provision of travelling scholarships. As she wrote to Coburn,

Did you ever hear of anything either more lovely or more to the point than the scholarship fund? When I pass out, I do so want you all to have that fund made up to $30,000, so that the interest will go to a graduate woman of Victoria College and be available for study abroad – not in the U.S., but in Great Britain, France, Germany, Italy, China, Japan, or India, or in any other country, to which the Alumna would like to go ... If the people of the United States were satisfied with their own educational results, I should have more faith in their ways of thinking. They, like ourselves are young, and experimenting, and I much prefer seeing our women go to older countries.[67]

This wish was granted when, after her death, the Alumnae and the VWA joined their two memorial funds to set up a Margaret Addison Memorial Scholarship, to be awarded every second year to enable a woman graduate of Victoria to pursue graduate study at a university outside Canada. Twenty-eight young women have already benefited from this award. The first scholarship, awarded in 1944, was for $750, and the amount was gradually raised until now it stands at $5000.

The outbreak of the Second World War, near the end of Addison's life, was a cruel blow. World peace had become one of her chief preoccupations: in 1935 she had chaired a mass peace demonstration sponsored by the representatives of sixty women's organizations in Massey Hall.[68] Yet it would not be true to say that the war broke her spirit; throughout her last year, until her death in December 1940, she continued to teach, to exhort, and to work for a post-war order that would represent some improvement over the old one.

Addison was very much aware that Jesus, her exemplar, did not use force, and that there was some logic in a militant pacifism (if such an oxymoron be allowed). Yet, as she wrote to her nephew Peter shortly after the declaration of war, such a stance emphasized divisions made by humans and exacerbated strife. "I am also a member of a community," she explained, "so, I cannot dissociate myself from those gallant souls, who, in giving their lives, protect mine." Declining to be forced into either pacifist or non-pacifist camps, she declared for tolerance and "freedom for all to think as they feel they must think before God. If I claim freedom to make my own decisions, I must also accord that same freedom to my neighbours."[69]

She nevertheless pursued her own peace program in a round of addresses. To a young people's group, for instance, she spoke on "How to live with one's neighbours." "In Time of War Prepare for Peace" was the title of talks given to a home and school council and an evening auxiliary, and also of a series of papers she wrote for the *Missionary Monthly* during 1939 and 1940.[70] These nine articles give a remarkable picture of a woman, now in her early seventies, more radical than most of her contemporaries, arguing vigorously for reform.

For Addison the war was basically a contest between democracy and totalitarianism. She firmly believed that democracy was the form of government most consonant with the Christian view of human beings as an end in themselves, made in the image of God and endowed with individual freedom and responsibility. Yet even in those embattled times she drew attention to areas where Canadian democracy was incomplete. Parliament contained many representatives of business and the law, for instance, but few women or members of the helping professions such as teachers, dentists, doctors, clergy, and social workers. Thus there was little impetus for social reform, and poverty and unemployment continued. "Suppose there had been twenty women or more to speak as our one woman member of the House of Commons spoke in May in the House," she mused, reflecting on the impassioned maiden speech of Mrs Dorise Nielson, a Unity Party member from Saskatchewan who spoke of feeding a family of five on relief of $11.25 a month.[71] It was no use blaming men for the fact that the woman's point of view was seldom heard. Women were not sufficiently alive to their responsibilities, nor sufficiently altruistic: "We have a vote, but it is of value only in so far as the voter possesses strong character, disinterestedness, courage and intelligence and puts them into action."[72]

In her November article, Addison used her allotted space to encourage women to serve on municipal governments and school boards as an introduction to democratic politics. Throughout the series, she urged more serious study of competing social systems in order to deal intelligently with the revolution and upheaval that were sure to dominate the post-war world. She suggested helpful books on capitalism, socialism, democracy, communism, and fascism, such as Gregory Vlastos' *Christian Faith and Democracy.* These volumes had formed the staple of her own reading that last year and were subjects of discussion in her Sunday school class at Simpson Avenue.[73]

Unfortunately, before Addison could write on ways of practising democracy in the family, the economy, and society, the series was broken off by her death. With little warning (except perhaps for her lifelong headaches), on 18 December 1940, she suffered a cerebral haemorrhage – the same malady that had felled her brother Will, and was later to take Arthur and Charlotte. She was taken to Women's College Hospital, where she died a few hours later. It was as she had wished: only two months earlier she had remarked to her nephew Peter, "Blessed are they who go out suddenly!"[74] Not for her a long and slow decline, a twilight of encroaching senility. She died characteristically: writing, reading, and hatching schemes, a committee member to the last.

Immediately, the ceremonial apparatus of Victoria University swung into action. Throughout the morning of the 20th, Addison lay in state in the Victoria College Chapel for visitation; in the afternoon her own pastor, the Rev. Clark Lawson, acted as chief minister at an impressive funeral there. In his memorial address, Principal Walter Brown stressed Addison's immense contributions to what in a happy phrase he called "the cause of educated Christian womanhood."[75] This is surely what had moved the huge crowd of people who watched her casket carried down the wide steps from the second-floor chapel to the main floor of Victoria College, thence to be driven to its final resting place in Mount Pleasant Cemetery. Addison embodied the earlier, religiously inspired life of the college – its idealism, certainly some of its limitations, but perhaps above all its amazing capacity to absorb new points of view.

From the longer perspective of today, we can see more clearly Addison's importance as a transitional figure. If on the one hand she brought the values of an earlier era into the twentieth century, on the other she brought into the university some of the ideals articulated in the twentieth century: a woman's right to develop her intellect and study any subject on the college curriculum; careers for women in new spheres; a religion freed from narrowly moralistic prohibitions; and free choice and responsibility for college students within practicable limits. She worked within the existing framework, having no desire to destroy traditions or cultural norms but rather seeking to help them evolve. Such unspectacular workers are not always given enough credit; the flamboyant rebels, the Emma Goldmans of this world, provide more fascinating copy. But from her position of authority, Addison was able to influence a whole generation of Canadian college women: the "Annesley girls" fanned out across the nation and beyond, inspired by her brand of intellectual probity, activism, and duty.

Her view of the sexes is partly of its time, yet not to be dismissed out of hand. Though unlikely to be hailed as a soulmate by radical feminists, she has some kinship with other contemporary theorists who stress that the priorities of women are different from those of men and have been undervalued in unconsciously gendered formulations. When reading Carol Gilligan's *In a Different Voice*, for instance, one might well be reminded of Addison's stress on women's ethics of care, skill in relationships, and sense of personal responsibility for the welfare of others. These were notions that Addison had imbibed in her youth and that, for her, were based on a religious sense of a divine order of creation in which each sex had its distinctive nature and role. But her strength was that she did not accept a simple correlation between essential nature and current social structure. On the contrary, she was as adamant as many a recent theorist on the need for women's distinctive qualities to be used in the public sphere. In upholding these ideals even in the relatively slack period, for the women's movement, of the 1920s and '30s, she has a large claim to be considered ahead of her time.

Margaret Addison, while grateful for the recognition that came her way, always felt that she could have done more. Sometimes she blamed herself, recognizing that she dissipated her energies and got diverted from larger questions by her propensity to roll up her sleeves and pitch into the sea of mundane tasks that were always needing attention. But sometimes she situated her difficulties in the matrix of women's position in society. Even the overconcern with details could be attributed to the fact that the women's side of the college was understaffed, or to the expectation that women would take care of such matters.[76] In the largest perspective, she saw that it all boiled down to a question of power, and that women did not have enough of it. As has been suggested, she began to embrace an embryonic women's separatism in education in her later years. Writing to Chancellor Wallace from Japan in 1932, looking back upon the past "with the detachment which leisure and distance give," she tried to explain why she had come to support the notion of a separate college for women. A president's mission, she argued, is to formulate the ideals of his (or her) college; "If this is true, in reality, Mrs. Burwash was president for the first ten years, and I for the following eighteen" (an admission which is less startling if we take her to mean president of a virtual women's college, Annesley Hall, rather than the real power behind the throne in Victoria University). Her position was thus anomalous:

Not infrequently I found myself faced with the choice – to do what I knew to be best, from the first hand knowledge I had, which, as it had often to do with human relationships, was not of a character to be revealed to others ... or, to seem to be seeking power, which did not lawfully belong to me. Rightly or wrongly, I chose the former, but had I been President of a college, instead of Dean of Women, it would have been my business to make the decision.[77]

The somewhat confused syntax here perhaps betrays a slight hesitation in saying what she thinks – for would not doing what she knew to be best entail assuming power rather than being an alternative to it? Nevertheless, her main drift is clear: she should have had a commanding position such as that of college president. Though such a position would scarcely have been possible in Canada given the cultural values of the era, she was obviously laying the groundwork for a time when women would have more authority. As Principal Gertrude Rutherford said in a memorial service at the United Church Training School, "Ordered, systematic, unhurried, consistent, thorough – she worked and planned with the future always in her mind."[78]

Kathleen Coburn, in her autobiographical reminiscence *In Pursuit of Coleridge*, recalls a significant moment in her life in 1933, when Addison came to see her to urge her to take up a position that was being offered in Japan. They went for a walk around Queen's Park where "Miss Addison loved to scuffle the dry fallen leaves with her big broad feet," while Coburn explained why she wanted to reject the Japanese position and stay at Victoria even in the teeth of Principal Walter Brown's entrenched anti-feminism.

Long silence, long strides, for perhaps a quarter of a mile.
"Well, dear," she said with that complete finality of which she was capable, "if you see that clearly, and are prepared to fight it out, I would like to see you stay. I'll tell you this," she gave a shocked chuckle at having the thought, "time is on your side."[79]

The episode is delightfully emblematic of Addison: her success in seeking out advantageous posts for her students; her ability to listen to their opposing points of view; and, above all, her long perspective on the women's movement. Time has been on her side too. Throughout her life she worked tirelessly to advance what she believed was God's plan for a more equitable society. And she was prepared for peace.

Notes

INTRODUCTION

1 Gertrude Rutherford, "Dean of Women," *United Church Observer,* 15 Jan. 1941, 22; letter of Judith Grant, 9 Apr. 1997, regarding Esther Trewartha.

2 MA, draft of letter to Helen MacMurchy, 15 July 1904, VUA, fonds 2067 (DOW), 90.141V, box 2, file 19.

3 William Westfall, *Two Worlds: The Protestant Culture of Nineteenth-Century Ontario* (Montreal: McGill-Queen's University Press, 1989), 7–8.

4 Report of James McBrien, Inspector for Ontario County, in *Report of the Minister of Education for 1891,* paper #11, Ontario Sessional Papers 24, no. 2: 140.

5 Rev. A.E. Griffith, "Education of Young Ladies," *Canada Christian Advocate,* 6 Dec. 1876.

6 Report to AHCOM, 15 Apr. 1926, VUA, fonds 2069 [Records relating to Women at Victoria University], series 2 [Records of University Councils and Committees], AHCOM, 90.064V, box 3, file 8.

7 Penina Glazer and Miriam Slater, *Unequal Colleagues: The Entrance of Women into the Professions, 1890-1940* (New Brunswick: Rutgers University Press, 1987), 31, 41.

8 MA, letter to Charlotte Addison, 30 Jan. 1915, VUA, MAP, 87.168V, box 1.

9 Annual report of 1907-08 to AHCOM, 90.064V, box 2, file 4.

10 For this term see, for instance, Alison Prentice et al., *Canadian Women: A History* (Toronto: Harcourt Brace Jovanovich, 1988), 170; and Wayne Roberts, "'Rocking the Cradle for the World': The New Woman and Maternal Feminism, Toronto, 1877–1914," in Linda Kealey, ed., *A Not Unreasonable Claim* (Toronto: Women's Press, 1979), 15–45.

11 MA, letter to Charlotte Addison, 5 Nov. 1925, MAP, 87.168V, box 1.

12 Glazer and Slater, *Unequal Colleagues,* 6–7. I have been unable to uncover any hint of a love affair in her life – neither heterosexual, to provide romantic interest; nor lesbian, to awaken scandal – and suspect that she was simply too preoccupied with other things.

13 MA, letter to Mrs Starr, 4 Aug. 1913, VUA, fonds 2051 [Alumni Association], 92.175v, box 2, file "General Correspondence 1905–26."

14 Entry for 9 June, dated by internal evidence to 1921, diary of 1920–21, MAP, 87.168v, box 1.

15 Report of 6 May 1926, in 90.064v, box 3, file 8 (marked "Prepared but not read").

CHAPTER ONE

1 Interview with Fred Griffin, *Star Weekly*, 15 Mar. 1924, 20.

2 Some of the stories recounted in the following pages are from the memoir written by Margaret's brother Arthur P. Addison, "An Account of the Addisons," preserved in the family archive, *The Book of the Addisons*, vol. 1 (in possession of Elizabeth McGregor).

3 Peter Addison, letter to Louise Addison, 9 June 1925, *Book of the Addisons*, vol. 1.

4 Obituary, *The New Outlook*, 28 Oct. 1925, 30.

5 Neil Semple, *The Lord's Dominion: The History of Canadian Methodism* (Montreal: McGill-Queen's University Press, 1996), 254–62.

6 John Webster Grant, "Theological Education at Victoria," in *From Cobourg to Toronto: Victoria University in Retrospect*, ed. Goldwin S. French and Gordon L. McLennan (Toronto: Chartres Books, 1989), 88. A theological course was introduced in 1870, and the department of theology was established in 1872.

7 VUA, Registrar's Office, Student records for Arts, 87.143v, box 3, file 1. The record indicates that he left before the end of his last term.

8 "An Account of the Addisons," 11.

9 Semple, *The Lord's Dominion*, 133.

10 A rather unedifying contemporary picture of a pioneer Methodist revival is given in W.F. Munro, *The Backwoods' Life* (Toronto: Hunter, Rose, 1869), 63–6; for a more sympathetic one, see William Withrow, *Life in a Parsonage; or, Lights and Shadows of the Itinerancy* (London: T. Woolmer, 1885), 50–9. Modern views may be found in J.W. Grant, *A Profusion of Spires* (Toronto: University of Toronto Press, 1988), 58–61, and Semple, *The Lord's Dominion*, 128–31.

11 See G.S. French, "The Evangelical Creed in Canada," in *The Shield of Achilles*, ed. W.L. Morton (Toronto: McClelland and Stewart, 1968), 25.

12 A contemporary description by William Proudfoot, quoted by Grant, *A Profusion of Spires*, 57.

13 *The New Outlook*, 28 Oct. 1925, 30.

14 Interview with F.W. Griffin, 20.

15 Wesley F. Campbell, "An Account of the Campbells," 5 (separately paginated), in *Book of the Addisons*, vol. 1.

16 A.P. Addison, "An Account of the Addisons," 7.

17 So runs the family tradition; however, her name does not appear among the teachers named in the local trustees' report for the town of Dundas in 1863–66, nor in that for Ancaster, Hamilton, Fergus (where her family lived), or Elora (AO, RG 2–17, reel MS 3526). So dates and place are not verified.

18 A.P. Addison, "An Account of the Addisons," 7; conversation with Louise Lewis.

19 I owe this formulation to the anonymous "Reader 2" of my manuscript.

20 Munro, *The Backwoods' Life*, 9. The book was published in 1869, while Peter Addison was a resident of Horning's Mills. Although in the book the settlement is called "Corning's Mills," it is known to be based on the real Horning's Mills.

21 Peter Addison, letter to S. Graham, 10 Aug. 1868, in *Book of the Addisons*, vol. 1.

22 "Historical Sketch of the Methodist, Presbyterian, and United Churches in Newcastle," typescript in UCA, local church files.

23 Mary Addison, letter to Margaret Campbell, Newcastle, 15 May 1875, MAP, 87.168v, box 1.

24 In MAP, 87.168v, box 1.

25 Pencilled addition to the letter to Margaret Campbell of 15 May 1875.

26 This picture of Ontario public schools is indebted chiefly to Robert M. Stamp, *The Schools of Ontario, 1876–1976* (Toronto: University of Toronto Press, 1982).

27 "Tell the Generation Yet to Come," 100th Anniversary booklet, UCA, local church files.

28 Stamp, *The Schools of Ontario*, 7.

29 R.D. Gidney and W.P.J. Millar, *Inventing Secondary Education* (Montreal: McGill-Queen's University Press, 1990), 309. The authors point out that, in 1888, 77 percent of high-school pupils were in Form 1 and only about 5 percent in Forms 3 and 4.

30 AO, High School Inspectors' Reports, RG2, series G2A, vol. 10 (1880).

31 Details of the Newcastle high school are taken from inspectors' reports in AO, RG2, G2A, vols. 12 (1882–83) and 13 (1884).

32 I owe this anecdote to Irene Rinch, niece of William Beman.

33 Mary Addison, letter to family, 7 July 1888, MAP, 87.168v, box 1.

34 MA, letter to Arthur, 9 Oct. 1898, MAP, 87.168v, box 1.

35 A.P. Addison, "An Account of the Addisons," 15.

36 Note dated Christmas 1899, in *Book of the Addisons*, vol. 1.

37 I have to thank William Addison (grandson of Margaret's brother Will) for letting me have a copy of his transcription of this work.

38 MA, letter to Arthur, 4 Dec. 1892, MAP, 87.168v, box 1.

39 "Rev. Peter Addison Calls it 'Lazy Age,'" undated clipping from
    Toronto *Star* (approx. 1920), MAP, 87.168v, box 2, file "Newspaper
    Clippings re. M. Addison's Relatives."

CHAPTER TWO

1 *Acta Victoriana* (*Acta*) 11, no. 5 (Feb. 1888): 19.
2 Ibid. 10, no. 1 (Oct. 1886): 7, 4.
3 Nathanael Burwash, *The History of Victoria College* (Toronto: Victoria
   College Press, 1927), 404. This work and *A History of Victoria University* by C.B. Sissons (Toronto: University of Toronto Press, 1952) give
   a detailed description of the negotiations leading to federation.
4 Arthur Addison, "An Account of the Addisons," 18.
5 Michael Gauvreau, "The Taming of History: Reflections on the
   Canadian Methodist Encounter with Biblical Criticism, 1830–1900,"
   Canadian Historical Review 65 (1984): 330–3. The year after Addison's
   graduation there was an "incident" in which Professor George Work-
   man, newly returned from five years of study in Germany, gave a lecture on the messianic prophecies that was considered unacceptable,
   and that ultimately led to his dismissal (Sissons, *History of Victoria
   University*, 193). The criticism, however, emanated from the Methodist
   Church, not from the college, and Burwash was on the liberal side,
   as he was later in the controversy over George Jackson in 1910.
6 Grant, *A Profusion of Spires*, 134.
7 "Scientific Morality or Conscientious Search for Truth," VCA, fonds
   2042, Nathanael Burwash Papers, box 14, file 367.
8 Speech of the 1850s, quoted in A.B. McKillop, *A Disciplined Intelligence*
   (Montreal: McGill-Queen's University Press, 1979), 89.
9 Reminiscence of Mary Bull (Margaret's niece), in *Book of the Addisons*,
   vol. 2.
10 The names of women appear in *Acta*, in lists of students in the calendar, and in mark books preserved in VUA, Registrar's Files, 87.219V.
   According to documents in VUA, fonds 2069, ser. 1 (Records relating to
   Women), 90.146v, box 1, file 1, a complete list of women at Victoria
   from 1887 to 1902 is sealed in the cornerstone of Annesley Hall.
11 Anne Rochon Ford, *A Path Not Strewn with Roses* (Toronto: University
   of Toronto Press, 1985), 26; Elsie Pomeroy, "Mary Electa Adams: a
   Pioneer Educator," *Ontario History* 41 (1949): 113; and cornerstone
   documents in 90.146v, box 1, file 1.
12 According to the 1886–87 calendar, Miss R.G. Ellis and Miss M.F.
   Libby were freshmen, and Miss Addison was a specialist (presumably
   because she had not matriculated in all the required subjects). But in

the freshman biographies of *Acta*, Ellis and Addison are said to be the two women in the class.

13 John Squair, *The Admission of Women to the University of Toronto and University College* (Toronto: University of Toronto Press, 1924), 13.

14 See Burwash, *History of Victoria College*, 61–2.

15 *Acta* 11, no. 2 (Nov. 1887): 13.

16 Barbara Ibronyi, *Early Voices: Women at Victoria* (Victoria University, 1984), 15. The story was told by Viola Whitney Pratt, who graduated from Victoria in 1913; perhaps she had heard it from Addison herself.

17 See, for example, M.E. Spence, "Eliza May Balmer" [first woman student at Toronto], *University of Toronto Monthly* 33, no. 5 (1933): 146–9; Margaret Gillett, *We Walked Very Warily: A History of Women at McGill* (Montreal: Eden Press Women's Publications, 1981), 93.

18 *Acta* 11, no. 2 (Nov. 1887): 18.

19 *Acta* 9, no. 1 (Oct. 1885): 19.

20 Reminiscences of Nellie Greenwood, vua, Nellie Greenwood Personal Papers, box 1.

21 *Acta* 10, no. 4 (Jan. 1887): 17.

22 *Acta* 12, no. 5 (Feb. 1889): 18.

23 *Acta* 12, no. 6 (Mar. 1889): 16.

24 *Acta* 9, no. 1 (Oct. 1885): 17.

25 *Acta* 12, no. 7 (Apr. 1889): 17. Oddly, she is described by the writer (who should certainly know) as the only lady to grace the class with her presence. Perhaps he means the only one who stayed throughout the four years. The calendar for 1889–90 lists three women as seniors in 1888–89: Addison, Ella Barber, and Emma Woods. Miss Woods is in the prize list, but for some reason she did not graduate and returned the next year. Miss Barber, however, appears both in the class photograph and in the list of B.A.'s of 1889.

26 Interview of the author with Julia Addison, 28 Apr. 1995.

27 *Christian Guardian*, 9 July 1890, 436; 4 Mar. 1891, 133. In 1892, first- and second-year honours university work was introduced (*Whitby Chronicle*, 24 June 1892, in Whitby Archives).

28 See comment in *Christian Guardian*, 28 Aug. 1889, 553.

29 Johanna Selles-Roney, "'A Realm of Pure Delight': Methodists and Women's Education in Ontario 1836–1925" (thesis, oise, 1993), 187.

30 Calendar for 1891–92, 40; ao, rg 2–109, box 2, file rg2–109–0–99.

31 This and other details are taken from Brian Winter, *Vox Collegii Centennial Edition, 1874–1974* (Ontario Ladies' College, 1974).

32 Johanna Selles [formerly Selles-Roney], *Methodists and Women's Education in Ontario, 1836–1925* (Montreal: McGill-Queen's University Press, 1996), 116. This book was based on the thesis cited in n29.

33 John G. Reid, "Mary Electa Adams," *DCB* 12:9.
34 All the quotations in this paragraph are from MA, letter to Arthur Addison, 15 Oct. 1889, MAP, 87.168v, box 1.
35 Calendar of 1891–92, 41.
36 Francis E. Clark, *World Wide Endeavour* (Toronto: Endeavour Herald Co., 1896), 57–8, 68–9, 640.
37 MA, letter to Arthur Addison, 15 Oct. 1889.
38 MA, letter to Arthur Addison, 18 May 1890, MAP, 87.168v, box 1.
39 MA, letter to Arthur Addison, 18 May 1890.
40 MA, letter to Arthur Addison, 9 Oct. 1890, MAP, 87.168v, box 1.
41 MA, letter to Arthur Addison, 18 May 1890.
42 MA, letter to Arthur Addison, 15 Oct. 1889.
43 MA, letter to Arthur Addison, 18 May 1890.
44 MA, letter to Arthur Addison, 15 Oct. 1889.
45 Ibid.
46 M.E. Adams, diary entry of 10 Oct. 1880, quoted in Selles, *Methodists and Women's Education*, 91.
47 See the portrait by J.W.L. Forster and the personal description in Pomeroy, "Mary Electa Adams."
48 Pomeroy, 115; Selles, *Methodists and Women's Education*, 90.
49 Elsie Pomeroy, "Salute to Valour," reprinted from *The Educational Record* (Quebec), Oct.-Dec. 1956 (VUL, Helena Coleman Papers, box 6, file 148).
50 Character sketch by Edith Laurie, aged 15, Mar. 1904, Helena Coleman Papers, box 4, file 118.
51 There is disagreement among authorities about the date of the opening, some (e.g., Charles E. Phillips, *The Public School in Ontario* [typescript, University of Toronto Library], 137) giving 1891, others (Stamp, *Schools of Ontario*, 44) saying 1890. It is more likely that it opened in 1891 and that Addison was in its first class. Its formation is announced in the Report of the Minister of Education for 1891, Paper #11 in Ontario Legislature, *Sessional Papers* 24, no. 2 (1892): xxvi.
52 See the discussion in Phillips, *The Public School in Ontario*, 134–47.
53 Arthur Addison, "An Account of the Addisons," 16.
54 Circular No. 9: Departmental Regulations for Provincial School of Pedagogy, 1892, AO, RG2, H-1, box 9, file "Memos re. School of Pedagogy."
55 W.G. Fleming, *Supporting Institutions and Services*, vol. 5 of *Ontario's Educative Society* (Toronto: University of Toronto Press, 1971), 80.
56 Herbert Spencer, *Education: Intellectual, Moral, and Physical* (New York: Appleton, 1862), 124–5.
57 Circular No. 9, quoting Regulation 66(1).
58 MA, letter to Arthur Addison, 6 Jan. 1893, MAP, 87.168v, box 1.

59 *Stratford Central Secondary School: its History, 1853–1979*, ed. K.D. Malvern (Stratford: n.p., [1979]), iv.

60 See Report of the Minister of Education for 1891, xxiii, where the average salary for assistant masters is said to be $804.

61 Details of salary are taken from the High School Inspectors' Reports, AO, RG2, G2A, vols. 22–36.

62 MA, undated letter to Arthur Addison, MAP, 87.168v, box 1, file "Undated or fragmentary correspondence."

63 In a booklet called "Testimonials of Margaret E.T. Addison, B.A.," including testimonials from Taylor, Mayberry, and William Forrest, MAP, 87.168v, box 2.

64 *Acta* 22, no. 8 (May 1899): 497.

65 Ibid., 498–9.

66 Ibid., 499.

67 MA, letter to Arthur, 4 Dec. 1892, MAP, 87.168v, box 1.

68 MA, letter to Arthur, 6 Jan. 1893, MAP, 87.168v, box 1.

69 MA, letter to Arthur, 11 June 1895, MAP, 87.168v, box 1.

70 MA, letter to Arthur, 30 Sept. 1895, MAP, 87.168v, box 1.

71 MA, letter to Arthur, 6 Jan. 1893.

CHAPTER THREE

1 Burwash, *History of Victoria College*, 451–2.

2 She had given birth to twelve children, including four girls, but eight had died. In the diphtheria outbreak of 1889 she lost four children: on June 20th one of her five-year-old twins, and on June 24th a ten-year-old girl, an eight-year-old boy, and the other twin.

3 Margaret Burwash, letter of 25 Feb. 1895, DOW, 90.141v, box 1, file 1.

4 Sissons, *History of Victoria University*, 210–12.

5 Burwash, *History of Victoria College*, 452.

6 G.S. French, "Barbara Heck Ruckle," DCB 5:728–9.

7 William Withrow, *Barbara Heck: A Tale of Early Methodism* (Toronto: Methodist Mission Rooms, 1895). See also Elizabeth G. Muir, *Petticoats in the Pulpit: The Story of Nineteenth-Century Methodist Women Preachers in Upper Canada* (Toronto: United Church Publishing House, 1991), 165 ff.

8 Letter from C.T. Currelly to Ned Burwash, Dec. 1897, VUA, Margaret Burwash Papers, 92.010v, box 1.

9 In June 1912 its name was changed again, to the Victoria Women's Association, and now it is generally called the VWA.

10 See the quotation from Fausta Danard Aikens (9T8), in *One Hundred Years: Women at Victoria*, Catalogue for an Exhibition in the E.J. Pratt Library, February 8 – March 30, 1984 (Victoria University, 1984), 5–6.

11 MA, letter to Mrs Burwash, 11 May 1897, DOW, 90.141V, box 1, file 1.

12 Ethel Bennett, address at the laying of the date stone of Margaret Addison Hall, 16 Oct. 1958, *Victoria Reports* 8, no. 2:21.

13 Undated address by Margaret Burwash on Annesley Hall history in 90.146V, box 1, file 17.

14 There was residential accommodation at St. Michael's College; however, this college was not yet part of the university, though it had been affiliated since 1881.

15 Speech of 8 Feb. 1901, reported in *Christian Guardian*, 13 Mar. 1901, 6.

16 Notes for a speech to a church group, Margaret Burwash Papers, box 1, file 18.

17 Margaret Burwash, "An Appeal to the Methodist Women of Canada," *Christian Guardian*, 7 Apr. 1897, 210.

18 MA, speech of 8 Feb. 1901.

19 Burwash, letter to Addison, 25 Feb. 1895.

20 MA, letter to Mrs Burwash, 10 Apr. 1899, DOW, 90.141V, box 1, file 1. With this letter Addison seems to be sending her presidential address, which she felt too ill to deliver herself.

21 Material on the formation of the association in AA, 92.175V, box 1, file "Minutes 1898–1935."

22 The inspector's report for 1900 (AO, RG2, G2A, vol. 36) says that Miss Marty, her successor, was appointed in 1900. However, the school history says that Miss Marty came in 1899, so possibly Addison had resigned earlier (*Stratford Central Secondary School*, ed. Malvern, 24).

23 Charlotte Addison, letter to Arthur Addison, Leipzig, 26 August 1900 (in possession of William Addison).

24 MA, letter to Arthur, 9 Oct. 1898, MAP, 87.168V, box 1.

25 See Margaret Addison, *Diary of a European Tour, 1900*, ed. Jean O'Grady (Montreal: McGill-Queen's University Press, 1999).

26 Ibid., 9.

27 Rough draft of essay in the back of the diary, MAP, 87.168V, box 1. This passage is not in the published version, for which see n41.

28 My chief source of information on the fair is Richard Mandell, *Paris 1900: The Great World's Fair* (Toronto: University of Toronto Press, 1967). See also Robert Burnand, *Paris 1900* (London: Hachette, 1951). For the art work, see the *Art Journal*'s special number, *The Paris Exhibition, 1900* (London: H. Virtue, 1901).

29 "Tours to Paris with Extensions," *The School World* 2 (July 1900): 255–6.

30 Addison, *Diary*, 11, 12.

31 All quotations in this paragraph are from Addison, *Diary*, 12–14.

32 Addison, *Diary*, 24, 19, 14.

33 Quotations on national pavilions are from Addison, *Diary*, 28, 30.

34 Addison, *Diary*, 18.

35 Burnand, *Paris 1900*, 149n.
36 MA, letter to Margaret Burwash, 30 Aug. 1900, DOW, 90.141V, box 1, file 2. This letter is the only surviving one of Addison's for the period; occupying more than five single-spaced pages when typed, its information supplements the gaps in the *Diary*.
37 MA, letter to Helen Kemp (later Frye), 4 Sept. 1925, VUL, Northrop Frye Fonds, 1990, box 1, file 1.
38 Addison, *Diary*, 38.
39 MA, letter to Mrs Burwash, 30 Aug. 1900.
40 Addison, *Diary*, 48.
41 "Glimpses of Education in Europe," *Acta* 24, no. 6 (1901): 301.
42 Addison, *Diary*, 45–6.
43 Ibid., 51.
44 MA, letter to Mrs. Burwash, 30 Aug. 1900.
45 Charlotte Addison, letter to Arthur Addison, 26 August 1900.
46 "Glimpses of Education in Europe," 302.
47 MA, letter to Louise Addison, 1 Dec. 1927, MAP, 87.168v, box 1.
48 Addison, *Diary*, 76.
49 Ibid., 97.
50 Ibid., 105.
51 Ibid., 82.
52 *Parliamentary Papers*, 1897, vol. 25.
53 Addison, *Diary*, 107–8.
54 Hugh Price Hughes, *Social Christianity: Sermons Delivered in St. James's Hall, London*, 2nd ed. (London: Hodder & Stoughton, 1889), xiii. Chapter 4 is entitled "Christ the Greatest of Social Reformers." For Hughes's influence, see Grant, *A Profusion of Spires*, 193.
55 Addison, *Diary*, 106–7.
56 The institution evolved into the East London College; it stood in the Mile End Road until destroyed by fire in 1931.
57 Asa Briggs and Anne Macartney, *Toynbee Hall: The First Hundred Years* (London: Routledge and Kegan Paul, 1984), 4.
58 MA, letter to Kathleen Coburn, 16 Sept. 1931, DOW, 90.141V, box 2, file 15.
59 Dean's Annual Report to AHCOM for 1907–08, in 90.064V (AHCOM), box 2, file 4.
60 Addison, *Diary*, 114.
61 Addison, *Diary*, 161.
62 MA, speech of 8 Feb. 1901.
63 Addison, *Diary*, 125, 124.
64 Ibid., 138.
65 Vera Brittain, *The Women at Oxford* (London: George Harrap, 1960), 86.
66 Addison, *Diary*, 158.

242 NOTES TO PAGES 76–82

67 Ibid., 118–19.
68 Ibid., 119.
69 Ibid., 135, 138.
70 Ibid., 117–18.
71 Though this quotation is not in the diary, it is taken from Sadler's chapter, "University extension," in J. Wells, ed., *Oxford and Oxford Life*, 2nd ed. (London: Methuen, 1899), 185, which Addison bought and read.
72 Addison, *Diary*, 162.
73 Ibid., 150.
74 *The Making of a Feminist: Early Journals and Letters of M. Carey Thomas*, ed. Marjorie Housepian Dobkin (n.p.: Kent State University Press, 1979), 265.

CHAPTER FOUR

1 Letter of Elizabeth Scoley Addison to her daughter Louise, 15 May 1928 (in possession of Ann Lewis).
2 Addison, *Diary of a European Tour, 1900*, 162.
3 Addison, *Diary*, 167.
4 See Carman Miller, *Painting the Map Red: Canada and the South African War, 1899–1902* (Montreal: Canadian War Museum and McGill-Queen's University Press, 1993).
5 Addison, *Diary*, 167.
6 Watson Kirkconnell, *A Canadian Headmaster: A Brief Biography of Thomas Allison Kirkconnell, 1862–1934* (Toronto: Clarke, Irwin, 1935), 81. Kirkconnell became principal in 1908.
7 Her diary for this period is in loose, unnumbered sheets in an envelope marked "Diary, Dec.–Apr. 1901," MAP, 87.168v, box 1.
8 MA, letter of 23 Nov. 1901, Margaret Burwash Papers, box 1, file 12.
9 Addison, *Diary*, 140–1. On physical education in American colleges, see Lulu Holmes, *A History of the Position of Dean of Women in a Selected Group of Co-Educational Colleges and Universities in the United States* (New York: Bureau of Publications, Teacher's College, Columbia University, 1939), 64–75.
10 For the career and ideals of Scott Raff, see Heather Murray, *Working in English: History, Institution, Resources* (Toronto: University of Toronto Press, 1996), 50–2, and "Making the Modern: Twenty-Five Years of the Margaret Eaton School of Literature and Expression," *Essays in Theatre/ Etudes théâtrales* 10, no.1 (Nov. 1991): 39–57, to which I am indebted.
11 Details on the early days of physical culture at Victoria may be gleaned from Minutes of the BHMA/VWREA, 1897–1903, VUA, fonds 2069, 90.066v, box 1, file 1, and Minutes of the Executive Committee of

the Board of Regents, 1901–03, VUA, fonds 2000, ser. 3, 87.126v, box 1, file 2.

12 MA, letter to Mrs Burwash, 23 Nov. 1901.

13 MA, letter to Mrs Burwash, 4 Feb. 1902, DOW, 90.141V, box 1, file 2.

14 Report of the Department of Expression, 10 Mar. 1903, Margaret Burwash Papers, box 1, file 16.

15 At the same time, Lady Edgar sold to Victoria, for $8,000, her interest in a block of property extending from the east side of Queen's Park to Bloor Street. Fortunately for the future prosperity of the college, the notion of reselling this was dropped.

16 See J.S. Mill's 1833 review of W.J. Fox's article "A Victim," in his *Newspaper Writings*, ed. Ann P. Robson and John M. Robson (Toronto: University of Toronto Press, 1986), *Collected Works of John Stuart Mill*, 23:556–8.

17 Leslie Maitland, *The Queen Anne Revival Style in Canadian Architecture* (Ottawa: published for the Ministry of the Environment, 1990), 13. For Annesley Hall, see 77, 213.

18 Maitland, *The Queen Anne Revival Style*, 111. The architect was Basil Champneys (1842–1935).

19 AA minutes of 11 Feb. 1902 (AA, 92.175V, box 1, file "Minutes 1898–1935").

20 MA, "Some Women's Colleges," *Acta* 28, no. 7 (May 1905): 516–18. Some of the alumnae's replies are found in AA, 92.175V, box 2, though they are not used in the rather impersonal finished paper.

21 For their business interconnections, see Michael Bliss, *A Canadian Millionaire: the Life and Business Times of Sir Joseph Flavelle, Bart, 1858–1939* (Toronto: Macmillan, 1978), esp. 64–79. I was not aware when writing this chapter that Bliss had originated the mafia joke; see "Better and Purer: the Peterborough Mafia and the Renaissance of Toronto," in *Toronto Remembered: A Celebration of the City*, ed. William Kilborn (Toronto: Stoddart, 1984), 194–205.

22 A.A. Chown, letter to Mrs Burwash, 1 Aug. 1901, Nathanael Burwash Papers, box 9, file 135. See also letter of Mabel Chown to Addison, 14 Aug. 1901, AA, 92.175V, box 2, file "Correspondence from Alumnae to M. Addison." Alice Chown was a cousin of Methodist superintendent Rev. Samuel D. Chown, and Mabel Chown (B.A. 1900) was her brother's daughter.

23 "Canadian Women in the Public Eye: Mrs G.G. Nasmith" [Scott Raff's name after her second marriage in 1916], *Saturday Night*, 11 Sept. 1920, 26.

24 Petition in Nathanael Burwash Papers, box 9, file 135.

25 VWREA minutes of May 29 1903, VWREA, 90.066v, box 1, file 1.

26 "The Women's Residence," *Acta* 25, no. 3 (Christmas 1901): 172.

27 W.H. Withrow, "From College Halls," *Onward*, 20 Dec. 1902, 414.
28 *Acta* 26, no. 8 (June 1903): 577.
29 Letter of Martha Bain, 8 May 1900, DOW, 90.141V, box 1, file 2. It is not likely at this date that the future headship of residence was being discussed, though the letter is not specific.
30 *Christian Guardian*, 13 Mar. 1901, 6.
31 Unnumbered loose sheets, Dec. 1900 – Apr. 1901. Florence Kenny had graduated from Victoria in 1893 and was vice-president of the BHMA in Ottawa; Miss Stover has not been identified.
32 Notebook of May to September 1903, MAP, 87.168V, box 1.
33 Letter from Mrs Burwash of 6 June 1903, DOW, 90.141V, box 1, file 3.
34 Notebook of May – Sept. 1903.
35 Carolyn Heilbrun, *Writing a Woman's Life* (New York: Norton, 1988), 23.
36 Notebook of May–Sept. 1903.
37 Ibid.
38 C. Armstrong and H.V. Nelles, *The Revenge of the Methodist Bicycle Company* (Toronto: Peter Martin, 1977).
39 MA, draft of letter to Helen MacMurchy, 15 July 1904, DOW, 90.141V, box 2, file 19.
40 On this area see John P.M. Court, "Out of the Woodwork: The Wood Family's Benefactions to Victoria University," *Canadian Methodist History Society Papers* 11 (1995 and 1996): 37. The Taddle was diverted underground in 1885.
41 The letters from Victoria girls can be found in DOW, 90.141V, box 1, file 4. Draft replies to them and to other prospective residents fill most of the 1903 notebook.

CHAPTER FIVE

1 The Royal Victoria College had opened in 1899. St. Hilda's began in 1888 in a small house with two resident students; it offered classes in pass subjects, but these had to be abandoned in 1894 because of a financial crisis. See *Sanctam Hildam Canimus*, ed. Barbara Sutton (Toronto: St. Hilda's College, 1988), xi.
2 Holmes, *History of the Position of Dean of Women*, 55.
3 See her Annual Report to AHCOM, 1906–7, Margaret Burwash Papers, box 6, file 98. These reports, an invaluable source of information, were given (sometimes in slightly different forms) to the committee, the senate, and the board of regents. Monthly reports were presented to the committee only.
4 Report of Annesley Hall Gymnasium 1905–6, Margaret Burwash Papers, box 6, file 97.

5 Letter from Scott Raff to Addison, 10 Sept. 1908, DOW, 90.141V, box 1, file 8. Dr Burwash's opposition was mentioned by Celia Corcoran in an interview with the author, 9 May 1995.

6 MA, draft of speech of 26 Feb. 1920 to consider rules and regulations, MAP, 87.168V, box 2, folder "Notes for Talks to ASGA."

7 William Butler Yeats, "A Prayer for My Daughter," in *Collected Poems of W.B. Yeats* (London: Macmillan, 1963), 214.

8 Letter from M. Burwash to Addison, 18 Apr. 1901, DOW, 90.141V, box 1, file 2.

9 MA, undated letter to Miss M.M. Costier, 1903 notebook.

10 The original rules are preserved only in the dean's descriptions: in her Nov. 1903 Report to AHCOM (90.064V, box 2, file 3), and Report before the Annual Meeting of the VWREA, 23 Mar. 1904, Nathanael Burwash Papers, box 9, file 132.

11 MA, undated letters to Miss M. Dickson and to Miss M.M. Costier, 1903 notebook.

12 MA, draft of a speech dated by internal evidence to approximately Nov. 1903, DOW, 90.141V, box 3, file 1.

13 "College Residence for Women," *Canadian Methodist Magazine* 51 (Jan. – June 1900): 444.

14 *Acta* 27, no. 7 (Apr. 1904): 436.

15 Annual Report to AHCOM of 1905–6, 90.064V, box 2, file 3.

16 Letters of 27 July 1904 and 31 Dec. 1904, DOW, 90.141V, box 1, file 5.

17 MA, letter of 2 July 1904, DOW, 90.141V, box 1, file 5.

18 Helen MacMurchy, "The University Women's Club, and University Residences for Women," *University of Toronto Monthly* 5 (1904–5): 143. The speech in question is probably the undated draft in VUA, 90.146V, box 2, file 7.

19 Annual Report to AHCOM for 1903–4, 90.064V, box 2, file 3.

20 Annual Report to AHCOM for 1904–5, 90.064V, box 2, file 3.

21 Annual report to AHCOM for 1903–4.

22 Letter of Prof. Bain, 3 May 1905, DOW, 90.141V, box 1, file 6.

23 Undated letter from Cartwright, DOW, 90.141V, box 2, file 10.

24 Petition in AA, 92.175V, box 2, file "General Correspondence, 1905–26."

25 MA, "Annesley Hall," *Torontonensis* 10 (1908).

26 Constitution in DOW, 90.141V, box 3, file 6.

27 See Selles-Roney, "A Realm of Pure Delight," 31–2.

28 Letter from Hockey to Chancellor Burwash, 4 Mar. 1912, VUA, fonds 2048 [Senate], 87.221V, "Records, especially re. Annesley Hall, 1906–23," file 1.

29 G.L. Rutherford, "Dean of Women," *United Church Observer*, 15 Jan. 1941, 22.

30 See requests for information on the ASGA constitution, and Addison's letters on the advantages of student government to other administrators, in DOW, 90.141V, box 2, files 13 and 14.

31 Report to AHCOM, 4 June 1931, 90.064V, box 2, file 2.

32 Sissons, *History of Victoria University,* 241–2.

33 *Acta* 27, no. 7 (Apr. 1904): 436.

34 Kathleen Cowan, *It's Late, and All the Girls Have Gone,* ed. Aida Farrag Graff and David Knight (Toronto: Childe Thursday Press, 1984). Quotations in this paragraph are from pp. 18, 94, 107–8, 174, 272, 310, 334, and 337.

35 MA, diary fragment dated only Fri. Oct. 2, MAP, box 1, file "Diary Fragment re. Annesley Hall rules." In this interesting fragment she talks of comforting one girl who felt guilty at leaving home, and of putting another who had a cold to bed with poultices and other remedies.

36 MA, "A Summer in Westmoreland," *Acta* 32 (1909): 394–400; letter of Charlotte Addison, 2 Aug. 1906, in possession of William Addison.

37 The version of this annual report sent to the senate and the board of regents (90.064V, box 2, file 4) does not contain these personal considerations found in the report to the committee of management in the Margaret Burwash Papers, box 6, file 98.

38 MA, draft of letter to Helen MacMurchy, 15 July 1904, DOW, 90.141V, box 2, file 19.

39 From a small notebook of 1907–8, MAP, box 1. This notebook is the source of several of the details regarding Addison's brief faculty career.

40 Meeting of the committee on faculty, 8 Nov. 1905, in "Minutes of the Executive Committee of the Board of Regents, 1896–1913," VUA, fonds 2000 [Board of Regents], ser. 3, 87.126V, box 1, file 2.

41 *Acta* 9, no. 8 (May 1886): 16.

42 Annual Report to AHCOM of 1905–6, dated 9 May 1906.

43 Letter from A.J. Irwin, 23 Apr. 1907, DOW, 90.141V, box 1, file 7.

44 Report to AHCOM, Feb. 1908, 90.064V, box 2, file 4.

45 MacMurchy, "The University Women's Club," 142.

46 "Interview: Kathleen Coburn," *Acta* 108, no. 2 (spring 1984): 21.

47 Letter from H. Oakeley, 12 Apr. 1907, DOW, 90.141V, box 1, file 7.

48 MA, draft letter to Mullin, 21 Aug. 1912, DOW, 90.141V, box 1, file 13.

49 Letter of J. Mullin, 16 July 1908, DOW, 90.141V, box 1, file 8.

50 Her close friend Helena Coleman, and Helena's niece Helen Coleman, were elected to an honorary membership of this body in 1908 (Minutes of 20 Apr. 1908 in AA, 92.175V, box 1).

51 For a brief history, see Margaret Foster, *The First Fifty Years, 1903–53* (Toronto: Hunter Rose, 1953).

52 For these and other considerations, see Maud Edgar, "The Higher Education of Women," *University of Toronto Monthly* 8 (1907–8): 225–30, and Jennifer Brown, *"A Disposition to Bear the Ills...": Rejection of a Separate College by University of Toronto Women* (Toronto: OISE, 1977), 9–15.
53 Letter of Cartwright to Addison, 27 Feb. 1908, DOW, 90.141v, box 1, file 8.
54 Dean's Annual Report to AHCOM, 1907–08, 90.064v, box 2, file 4.
55 Minutes of 29 Dec. 1908 and 12 Apr. 1909, AA, 92.175v, box 1.
56 Report to AHCOM, 11 Feb. 1909, 90.064v, box 2, file 5.
57 Annual Report to Senate, 1908–9, AHCOM, 90.064v, box 2, file 5.
58 "Report of a Committee Appointed to Enquire in regard to a Possible College for Women," reprinted in *University of Toronto Monthly* 9 (1908–9): 286–91.
59 G. Wrong, "A College for Women," *University of Toronto Monthly* 10 (1909–10): 4–7.
60 Mabel Cartwright, "A College for Women," *University of Toronto Monthly* 10 (1909–10): 1. See n52 for title of Jennifer Brown's pamphlet.
61 *Star*, 19 May 1909, cited in Wayne Roberts, "'Rocking the Cradle for the World'," 32.
62 AA, 92.175v, box 2, file "General Correspondence 1905–26."
63 *Dean of Women*; Report of Committee (nd, np), 12. The pamphlet, which according to the Alumnae minutes was in the hands of the printers in October 1909, is available in UTA.
64 Holmes, *History of the Position of Dean of Women*, 25–6.
65 Susie Chown was the sister of the Mabel Chown mentioned before. They were daughters of Kingston minister Edward Chown, cousin of Methodist general superintendent Rev. Samuel Dwight Chown.
66 See minutes of the United Alumnae Association, 1909–11, UTA, B65–0030, box 1, files 01, 03.
67 Ford, *A Path Not Strewn with Roses*, 44.

CHAPTER SIX

1 Annual Report of 1910–11 to the senate, 87.221v, "Records re. Annesley Hall," file 1.
2 Occupational and religious backgrounds are given sporadically in the annual reports from 1915–16 on, but there is no reason to believe they were drastically different in the years immediately preceding.
3 MA, undated draft of speech, probably of 1905, in 90.146v, box 2, file 7. Similar sentiments may be found in Report to AHCOM, 8 Feb. 1917, 90.064v, box 2, file 13.

4 President Hutton, address to VWREA, 27 Mar. 1907, in VWREA Annual Report 1906–7, 90.066v, box 2, file 6.

5 MA, speech "The Work of the Graduate at Home," 29 Dec. 1904, AA, box 1, file "Minutes 1898–1935."

6 Ethel Kirk, "What Residence Life Means to a University Woman," *Canadian Home Journal*, Feb. 1911, 40.

7 Dean's report to the VWA, 22 Nov. 1916, VWREA/VWA, 90.066v, box 2, file 18.

8 Entry for Mar. 1911 in a notebook marked "Record," MAP, 87.168v, box 1, envelope 1910.

9 MA, speech of 28 Sept. 1909, in the notebook marked "Record," p.17. Kathleen Cowan's diary refers to this talk, saying that "the dean had us in after dinner and spoke about wealth, feeds, and things all of which were very true" (*It's Late*, 251).

10 Talk of 27 Apr. 1916, AA, 92.175v, box 1, file "Minutes 1898–1935."

11 AA, minutes of Christmas 1904, 92.175v, box 1, file "Minutes 1898–1935."

12 Talk to VWREA of 13 Jan. 1909, VWREA/VWA Minutes, 90.066v, box 1, envelope 3.

13 MA, letter to family of 14 Nov. 1914, MAP, 87.168v, box 1. According to Sara Z. Burke in "Science and Sentiment: Social Service and Gender at the University of Toronto, 1888–1910," *Journal of the Canadian Historical Association* n.s. 4 (1993): 75–93, the university settlement had a strongly male orientation and originally accepted only men as volunteers. The Annesley record, however, suggests that this bias was rapidly overcome.

14 See Minutes of the Executive Committee 1895–1913, NAC, MG 28/I 198, vol. 9, passim. In the early years, this committee often met at Annesley Hall.

15 J.P. Harnshaw, *When Women Work Together: A History of the YWCA in Canada* (Toronto: Ryerson Press, 1966), 22. See also Diana Pedersen, "'The Call to Service': the YWCA and the Canadian College Woman, 1886–1920," in Paul Axelrod and John G. Reid, ed., *Youth, University, and Canadian Society* (Montreal: McGill-Queen's University Press, 1989), 187–215.

16 Interview with Ethel Granger Bennett in VUA biographical file. This was the Ethel Bennett who married Harold Bennett, future principal of Victoria. As Ethel Granger, she lived in residence from 1911 to 1915.

17 Burwash, address to graduates of 1889, Nathanael Burwash Papers, box 14, file 367.

18 John R. Mott, *History of the Student Volunteer Movement for Foreign Missions* (n.p., 1892), 45.

19 Grant, *A Profusion of Spires*, 172.

20 *Acta* 10, no. 1 (Oct. 1886): 18. At some point Kono left the class, graduating with the class of 1890.

21 On her work, see Margaret Prang, *A Heart at Leisure from Itself: Caroline Macdonald of Japan* (Vancouver: UBC Press, 1995). Addison had worked with Macdonald when the latter was city secretary for the national YWCA in 1903–4.

22 Report to AHCOM of 9 Feb. 1911, 90.064v, box 2, file 7.

23 Annotation in Addison's hand to her letter of 1 July 1904, DOW, 90.141v, box 1, file 5. Wong does not seem to have stayed for more than a year.

24 Bertha Herington, letter to MA, 4 Sept. 1913, DOW, 90.141v, box 1, file 16.

25 Ethel Wallace, letter of 11 June 1916, DOW, 90.141v, box 1, file 20.

26 MA, general letter of 18 Mar. 1916, MAP, 87.168v, box 1. These general letters were typed with carbons and sent to friends and family. Many of the letters cited in subsequent notes as "to Charlotte," "to Father," etc., are actually carbon copies with a blank space in which the recipient's name has been written.

27 Letter of Elizabeth Apps, 29 Jan. 1913, DOW, 90.141v, box 1, file 15.

28 Joan Sangster, "The 1907 Bell Telephone Strike," *Labour/ Le Travailleur* 3 (1978): 109–30.

29 MA, letter to M.E. Teats, Jan. 1914, DOW, 90.141v, box 1, file 17.

30 Speech of Viola Pratt at 75th anniversary meeting of VWA, 22 Nov. 1972, VWA, 90.066v, box 4, file 5.

31 See Ruth Hall, *Marie Stopes* (London: André Deutsch, 1977), 51, 56, 92. According to this account, MacMurchy was in love with her.

32 Report to AHCOM, 9 Oct. 1907, 90.064v, box 2, file 4.

33 Report to AHCOM, 9 Feb. 1911.

34 *Acta* 28 (1904–5): 55.

35 Report to AHCOM, 12 Sept. 1912, 90.064v, box 2, file 8.

36 Reports to AHCOM of 10 Nov. and 8 Dec. 1910, 90.064v, box 2, file 6.

37 Mrs Burwash, letter to MA, 17 July 1905, DOW, 90.141v, box 1, file 6.

38 *Acta* 31, no 6 (Mar. 1908): 397–8.

39 MA, letter to Mrs Rowell, 16 Oct. 1910, DOW, 90.141v, box 1, file 10.

40 Copy of letter from Dr. Burwash, DOW, 90.141v, box 1, file 11.

41 Mrs Lang, letter of 6 Apr. 1911, DOW, 90.141v, box 1, file 11.

42 Letter of Nettie Burkholder, 27 Feb. 1912, DOW, 90.141v, box 1, file 12.

43 Undated letter of A.J. Irwin, DOW, 90.141v, box 1, file 12. At that time all board of regents members such as Irwin were also members of the senate.

44 AA, 92.175v, box 1, file "Minutes 1898–1935."

45 Margaret Burwash Papers, box 6, file 99.

46 Notes of an interview in VUA, Ethel Mary Granger Bennett biographical file.

47 Margaret Eaton, letter of 18 Apr. 1912, Margaret Burwash Papers, box 4, file 67.

48 Letter of Margaret Proctor, 31 May 1912, ibid.

49 MAP, 87.168v, box 2, folder "Notes for Talks to ASGA."

50 Minutes for 3 Feb. and 4 Apr. 1911, VUA, fonds 2048 [Senate], 92.113v, box 1, file 1 [microfilm]. This standing joint committee had been set up after the establishment of ASGA to review disputes. It included Addison and Sheffield from the residences and Mrs Burwash, Mrs Lang, and Mrs Rowell from the committee of management, as well as representatives from the senate and ASGA.

51 Handwritten notes in Margaret Burwash Papers, box 6, file 99.

52 Minutes of AHCOM, 9 Mar. 1911, 90.064v, box 1, file 2.

53 Letter of J.C. Robertson, convener of the senate committee on Annesley Hall, to AHCOM, 22 May 1911, DOW, 90.141v, box 1, file 11.

54 MA, draft letter of 26 May 1911, DOW, 90.141v, box 1, file 11.

55 Senate minutes of 26 May 1911, 92.113v, box 1, file 1.

56 AHCOM minutes of 23 May and 13 June 1911, 90.064v, box 1, file 2.

57 *Acta* 35, no. 4 (Jan. 1912): 240–1.

58 Later printed in a booklet, "Documents for Use of Commission on Annesley Hall," 90.146v, box 1, file 8. This booklet, which assembles many relevant extracts and reports, was printed for the use of a commission appointed by the board of regents on 2 May 1912 (after the adoption of the new rules) to consider the supervision of both resident and non-resident women, probably with reference to the question of appointing a dean of women.

59 Robert Bruce Mantell (1854–1928) was a Scottish-born American actor, known for romantic roles and for what the *Oxford Companion to the Theatre* calls uninspired but careful studies of the leading Shakespearean characters.

60 Letter of Albert Carman to Dr Burwash, 13 Mar 1912, "Records re. Annesley Hall," 87.221.v, file 1. The same folder contains the replies from Cora Hewitt and others.

61 The letter is in DOW, 90.141v, box 2, file 1, as the date "March 24 1912" was read as "1918." Its immediate cause seems to have been a shadowy dispute concerning the payment of doctors and of Mrs Scott Raff, whose salary Mrs Burwash thought should be almost equal to that of Addison.

62 Letter of Margaret Eaton to Mrs Burwash, 18 Apr. 1912.

63 Memorial in "Documents for Use of Commission on Annesley Hall."

64 Minutes of meeting of 11 April 1912, AHCOM, 90.064v, box 1, file 2.

65 Sissons, *History of Victoria University,* 244.

66 Margaret Proctor, letter of 25 Nov. 1913, Margaret Burwash Papers, box 4, file 70.

67 *In Memoriam Margaret Addison, 1868–1940* (Toronto: Clarke, Irwin for Victoria University, 1941), 3.

68 Conversation with Louise Lewis, 24 Nov. 1995.

69 Interview of William Addison with Peter Addison ("Black Peter"), 27 Dec. 1992. He pointed out that the boys were only asked until they were about ten years old.

70 Report to AHCOM of 14 Oct. 1909, 90.064v, box 2, file 5.

71 Script for talk "Work of the Graduate at Home," AA, 92.175v, box 1, file "Minutes 1898–1935."

72 *The Times*, 3 July 1912, 6.

73 Ibid.

74 Quoted in general letter of 22 Dec. 1921, MAP, 87.168v, box 1.

75 For the congress program, see J.C. Robertson, "Congress of the Universities of the Empire," *U of T Monthly* 13 (1912–13): 60–8.

76 Toronto *Globe*, 24 Aug. 1912, 20. Besides reporting on the delegates' visits to northern universities, Young also reported on the congress for the *Globe* on the 10 and 17 of August. A printed copy of White's speech, "The Position of Women at Universities," is found in 90.146v, box 2, file 12. It has no satiric reflections on the University of Toronto; however, as delegates were given printed copies ahead of time, speakers offered informal summaries and comments rather than reading their papers.

CHAPTER SEVEN

1 Minutes of AHCOM, 21 Feb. 1913, AHCOM, 90.064v, box 1, file 2; see also letter of Nellie Langford, dated 1913 in pencil, DOW, 90.141v, box 1, file 16.

2 Unsigned draft of a letter, presumably from Mrs Sheffield, to Mrs Burwash, 20 Aug. 1910, DOW, 90.141v, box 1, file 10.

3 Report of Jan. 1914 to AHCOM, 90.064v, box 2, file 10.

4 Report of AHCOM for the year June 1913–June 1914, 90.064v, box 2, file 10.

5 Documents concerning Mrs Reid may be found in AHCOM, 90.064v, box 3, file 28.

6 MA, general letter of 6 Mar. 1915, MAP, 87.168v, box 1.

7 Report to AHCOM, Dec. 1913, 90.064v, box 2, file 9.

8 Report to AHCOM, 8 Oct. 1914, 90.064v, box 2, file 10.

9 Report to AHCOM for the year June 1913–June 1914.

10 Report to AHCOM, 14 Jan. 1915, 90.064v, box 2, file 11.

11 Vincent Massey, undated letter to George Wrong, quoted in Claude Bissell, *The Young Vincent Massey* (Toronto: University of Toronto Press, 1981), 80.

12 The anonymous article "The Canadian in Oxford," *Acta* 39 (1914–15): 70–4, questioning whether imported traditions have much meaning, and recommending Canadian honesty over Oxford polish, was evidently provoked by Massey's innovations.

13 *Acta* 39 (1914–15): 1.

14 Vincent Massey, "Victoria College and the War," in Burwash, *History of Victoria College*, 484.

15 MA, letter to Charlotte, 30 Jan. 1915, MAP, 87.168v, box 1.

16 MA, general letter of 29 Jan. 1916, MAP, 87.168v, box 1.

17 Report to AHCOM of 22 May 1916, 90.064v, box 2, file 12. The Victoria College *Bulletin* of 1919–20 also records the death of Ross's brother, Alfred Livingstone Taylor, at the Battle of Arras in August 1918.

18 See especially Reports to AHCOM of 14 Nov. 1912, in 90.064v, box 2, file 10, and 13 Mar. 1913, in "Records re. Annesley Hall," 87.221v, file 1.

19 *Varsity*, 20 Feb. 1914.

20 MA, letter to Charlotte, 30 Jan. 1915.

21 MA, letter to Miss Rouse, 21 Dec. 1914, DOW, 90.141v, box 1, file 18.

22 Report to AHCOM, 11 Nov. 1915, 90.064v, box 2, file 11.

23 MA, general letter of 6 Mar. 1915.

24 Addison's letters to father, 10 Oct. 1914, and to Charlotte, 17 Oct. 1914, MAP, 87.168v, box 1.

25 Undated letter "to the Girls of Victoria College," in VUA, fonds 2069, series 3 (Records of Student Organizations), 90.134v (Women's Literary Society), file 9.

26 MA, letter to Charlotte, 17 Oct. 1914.

27 See documents in VWREA/VWA, 90.066v, box 4, file 11, from which the ensuing statistics are taken.

28 MA, general letter of 6 Mar. 1915.

29 Letter of Bowles to MA, 18 July 1916, DOW, 90.141v, box 1, file 21.

30 Hilda R.B. Collins, "College Girls on Fruit Farms at Winona," *Canadian Home Journal*, Aug. 1917, 37–8 (clipping in 90.146v, box 1, file 23). For a less positive description of the experience of University College women, see Edith Alexander, "The University College Fruit-Pickers," *University Monthly* 18 (1917–18): 21–7.

31 Letter from Dominion Council of the YWCA, 90.146v, box 1, file 23.

32 Collins, "College Girls on Fruit Farms at Winona," 37.

33 Reminiscence of Edna Ash, relayed through the kindness of Celia Corcoran, 1995.

34 See *Canadian Annual Review* for 1917, 420.

35 MA, general letter of 12 Feb. 1916, MAP, 87.168v, box 1, the source for all the details about the meetings with labour.

36 MA, letter to J.D. Flavelle of Lindsay, 24 Feb. 1917, DOW, 90.141v, box 1, file 22.

37 MA, general letter of 10 Apr. 1915, MAP, 87.168v, box 1.

38 See, for example, draft of speech to ASGA, 26 Feb. 1920, MAP, box 2, folder "Notes for Talks to ASGA"; and letter of 27 Mar. 1915, MAP, 87.168v, box 1.

39 See, for example, Report to AHCOM of 15 Jan. 1920, DOW, 90.141v, box 3, file 3.

40 MA, letter to Charlotte, 27 Mar. 1915, MAP 87.168v, box 1.

41 Letter of Hare to MA, 26 Apr. 1915, DOW, 90.141v, box 2, file 14.

42 MA, general letter of 6 Mar. 1915.

43 MA, general letter of 17 Jan. 1915, MAP, 87.168v, box 1.

44 When it opened in 1919, the Massey Foundation offered $125,000 towards a matching building for women; the plans, however, did not come to fruition (Ford, *A Path Not Strewn with Roses*, 67).

45 Memorial of 23 Jan. 1913, UTA, B65–0030, box 1, file 5.

46 United Alumnae minutes, UTA, B65–0030, box 1, file 6. A more extensive course in physical education had also been urged by the Toronto Local Council of Women, of which Addison was naturally a member: see resolution of April 1913, VUA, 90.146v, box 1, file 27.

47 Minutes of VWA, 90.066v, box 2, file 19. The university calendar, however, registers no change at this time. Victoria and Trinity women were still under the aegis of their individual colleges with regard to physical education.

48 MA, letter to Charlotte, 27 Mar. 1915.

49 Ibid.

50 Senate minutes of 5 Nov. 1915, 92.113v, box 1, file 1.

51 See report of Miss Skinner to the VWA, Nov. 1917, VWA, 90.066v, box 2, file 18.

52 Report to AHCOM, 8 Feb. 1917, 90.064v, box 2, file 13.

53 MA, general letter of 5 Dec. 1914, MAP, 87.168v, box 1.

54 MA, letter to Charlotte, 27 Mar. 1915.

55 MA, general letter of 6 Mar. 1915.

56 MA, general letter of 11 Dec. 1915, MAP, box 1.

57 MA, general letter dated by internal evidence, MAP, 87.168v, box 1, file "Undated and Fragmentary."

58 MA, general letter of 5 Oct. 1918, MAP, 87.168v, box 1.

59 Dated simply Fri. Oct. 2, MAP, 87.168v, box 1, file "Diary Fragment re. Annesley Hall Rules."

60 MA, general letter of 13 May 1915, MAP, 87.168v, box 1.

61 Ibid.

62 Information from interview of author with Irene Rinch, 24 Nov. 1995.

63 Information from Addison's nephew George Addison, and from Judith Skelton Grant.
64 MA, letter to T.E. Robertson (Massey's secretary), 3 Dec. 1917, NAC, Massey Papers, MG 32 A1, vol. 22, microfilm reel C-9213. The earlier bill of 11 Nov. 1916 is also here.
65 MA, letter to Charlotte, 20 Feb. 1915, MAP, 87.168v, box 1.
66 Report to AHCOM of 8 Feb. 1917.
67 Ibid.
68 Ibid.
69 Report to Senate for 1916–17, dated 8 Mar. 1917, "Records re. Annesley Hall," 87.221v, file 1.
70 Report to AHCOM, Sept. 1912, 90.064v, box 2, file 8.
71 Report to AHCOM, 8 Feb. 1917.
72 Report to Senate for 1916–17.
73 MA, draft of a letter of 30 Mar. 1918, DOW, 90.141v, box 2, file 1.
74 Information from Louise Lewis (who entered college that year).
75 Report to AHCOM of 14 Nov. 1918, DOW, 90.064v, box 3. There was another serious outbreak in February 1920 in which one girl hovered between life and death, but eventually she recovered.
76 Report to the Senate for 1919–20, 87.221v, file 1.
77 Notes in MAP, 87.168v, box 2, folder "Notes for Talks to ASGA."
78 For the meeting with Falconer on 6 Feb. 1919, see 90.146v, box 2, file 18. For the resolutions of 1 Feb., see UTA, A67-0007/051a (file Abbot-Av) and DOW, 90.141v, box 3, file 3.
79 Report to AHCOM, 13 Feb. 1919, 90.064v, box 3, file 2.
80 1919–20 Report to Senate.
81 Ibid.
82 Report to AHCOM, 15 Jan. 1920.

CHAPTER EIGHT

1 Addison, "Sketch of the History of the Committee of Management," MAP, 87.168v, box 2.
2 1919–20 Report to Senate, 87.221v, file 1.
3 See p. 179 below.
4 Annual Report to Senate, 1908–9, AHCOM, 90.064v, box 2, file 5.
5 The chief sources for this rearrangement are the Report of the Committee re. the Women's Student Union and Women's Residences, in Minutes of the Board of Regents, 20 May 1920, 87.125v, box 2, file 1 [microfilm reel 2]; letter of R.P. Bowles, 90.141v, box 2, file 3; and Addison's letters of 5 May, 28 Oct., and 20 Dec. 1920, MAP, 87.168v, box 1.

6 Alison Prentice, "Bluestockings, Feminists, or Women Workers? A Preliminary Look at Women's Early Employment at the University of Toronto," *Journal of the Canadian Historical Association* n.s. 2 (1991): 248.

7 Report for 1912–13, in *VWA Annual Report, 1912–13*, VWA, 90.066V, box 2, file 6.

8 MA, general letter of 28 Oct. 1920.

9 Entry of 14 May 1921 in diary of 1920–21, MAP, 87.168v, box 1.

10 Claude Bissell, *The Young Vincent Massey*, 31.

11 The remark on mediocrity is from a diary entry of 4 Mar. 1910, quoted in Bissell, *The Young Vincent Massey*, 43. The commission examined secondary schools and secondary "colleges," such as OLC, not post-secondary institutions such as Victoria.

12 Bissell, *The Young Vincent Massey*, 106.

13 MA, letter to Charlotte, 27 Mar. 1915, and general letter, 6 Mar. 1915, MAP, 87.168v, box 1.

14 MA, letter to Charlotte, 27 Mar. 1915.

15 MA, general letter of 13 May 1915, MAP, 87.168v, box 1.

16 Alice Massey to Vincent Massey, 5 June 1917, NAC, Massey papers, vol. 33, microfilm reel C-9217.

17 Bissell, *The Young Vincent Massey*, 58.

18 Alice Massey, letter of 29 Oct. 1921, AHCOM, 90.064v, box 3, file 31.

19 See Addison's diary entry of 14 May 1921 for this point.

20 MA, loose pages of a letter beginning November 11, "the third anniversary of the peace" [i.e., 1921], MAP, box 1, file "undated or fragmentary."

21 MA, general letter of 22 Dec. 1921, MAP, 87.168v, box 1.

22 Dean's Report to AHCOM, 9 Nov. 1922, 90.064v, box 3, file 5.

23 MA, general letter of 28 Oct. 1920, MAP, 87.168v, box 1.

24 MA, draft of a speech to ASGA, 26 Feb. 1920, MAP, box 2, folder "Notes for Talks to ASGA."

25 MA, notes for "A Speech on Chicken Dinners," 3 Dec. 1923, ibid.

26 Hannah Fudger, letter of Nov. 1921, AHCOM, 90.064v, box 3, file 31.

27 Ruth Lawson later became Ruth Staples, wife of Professor Staples of Orientals. Anecdote courtesy of Elizabeth McLeod, her daughter.

28 Conversation of the author with Jean Cameron, 27 Apr. 1998.

29 See DOW, 90.141v, box 2, file 3.

30 MA, letter to alumnae of 20 Dec. 1920.

31 MA, entry for 6 Sept. 1920, diary of 1920–21.

32 Dean's Report to AHCOM, 10 Mar. 1921, 90.064v, box 3.

33 The relevant correspondence is found in UTA, Massey papers, B87–0082, box 140, file 7.

34 VUA, fonds 2060 [R.P. Bowles Papers], 96.128v, Correspondence file B-V, 1921–25.

35 Carroll Smith-Rosenberg, *Disorderly Conduct: Visions of Gender in Victorian America* (New York: Oxford University Press, 1986), 275–81. According to the author, college administrators in the years before World War I were adopting restrictive policies in women's dorms to counter such accusations. See also Nancy Sahli, "Smashing: Women's Relationships Before the Fall," *Chrysalis* 8 (1979): 17–27.

36 MA, diary of 1920–21, entry for 12 Mar., MAP, 87.168v, box 1.

37 MA, diary of 1920–21, entry of 21 Mar.

38 Ibid., entry for 31 Mar.

39 AA, 92.175v, box 1, file "Minutes 1898–1935."

40 All preceding quotations in this paragraph are from the description of the meeting of 12 May in Addison's diary of 1920–21, entry for 14 May.

41 Entry for 9 June, filed with 1920 papers but dated by internal evidence to 1921; diary of 1920–21.

42 Bowles, confidential letter to Massey, 10 May 1921, UTA, Massey papers, B87–0082, box 140, file 7.

43 All quotations in this paragraph are from the entry for 14 May in Addison's diary of 1920–21.

44 Northrop Frye, diary of 1952, entry for 27 Jan., VUL, Northrop Frye Fonds, 1991, box 50.

45 Minutes of the board of regents for 14 Feb. 1919, 87.125v, box 2 [microfilm reel 2].

46 MA, general letter of 13 Dec. 1919, MAP, 87.168v, box 1.

47 MA, general letter of 20 Dec. 1920.

48 Minutes of the board of regents for meeting of September 1920. This is the last time that this particular new building is mentioned, though new buildings are again in prospect in 1923, 1925, and 1929 (see pp. 185 and 196–7 below). In truth the question was a chronic one until Margaret Addison Hall opened in 1959.

49 Minutes for 13 Oct. 1921, AHCOM, 90.064v, box 2, file 1. See also Addison, "Sketch of the History of the Committee of Management."

50 Letter from Mrs Massey to Mrs Burns, 29 Oct. 1921.

51 Report to AHCOM, 11 Dec. 1924, 90.064v, box 3, file 6.

52 Report on the Conference of the National Association of Women Deans, 9 Mar. 1922, AHCOM, 90.064v, box 3, file 5. For another of the few references Addison makes to American halls of residence she has inspected, see her comments on Whittier Hall, attached to the School of Practical Arts at Columbia, in letter of 12 Feb. 1914, MAP, 87.168v, box 1.

53 Report to AHCOM, 9 Nov. 1922, 90.064v, box 3, file 5.

54 Booklet *St. Wolfgang, 1922* (np, nd), p. 13, NAC, YWCA papers, MG28 I 198, vol. 37.

55 Isabelle Bronk, "The Second Conference of the International Federation of University Women," *School and Society* 16 (16 Sept. 1922): 322–6.
56 MA, letter to Louise Addison, 18 Feb. 1922, MAP, 87.168v, box 1.
57 MA, letter to *Varsity*, 14 Feb. 1924.
58 MA, general letter of 16 Feb. 1924, MAP, 87.168v, box 1.
59 Report to AHCOM of 14 Feb. 1924, 90.064v, box 3, file 6.
60 MA, general letter of 16 Feb. 1924, MAP, 87.168v, box 1.
61 "Fine Harmony Marks Meeting," *Globe*, 25 Sept. 1922, in UTA, Margaret Addison clipping file, A73–0026/002 [83].
62 See A.A. Perry, "Our Women Magistrates," *Chatelaine*, July 1929, in Toronto Public Library Biographical Scrapbooks, 15:576; and Dorothy E. Chunn, "Maternal Feminism, Legal Professionalism and Political Pragmatism: the Rise and Fall of Magistrate Margaret Patterson, 1922–1934," in *Canadian Perspectives on Law and Society Issues in Legal History*, ed. W. Wesley Pue and Barry Wright (Ottawa: Carleton University Press, 1988), 91–117. Chunn points out that Patterson espoused a "rehabilitation" model of justice – seeking to correct wrongs rather than to punish – in the service of an old-fasioned moralism.
63 MA, letter to Charlotte, 27 Apr. 1925, MAP, 87.168v, box 1.
64 MA, letter to family, 1 Mar. 1924, MAP, 87.168v, box 1.
65 MA, general letter of 15 Mar. 1924, MAP, 87.168v, box 1.
66 All quotations in this paragraph are from letter to Charlotte of 5 Nov. 1925, MAP, 87.168v, box 1.
67 For the senate involvement, see its minutes of 29 Feb., 3 Oct., and 17 Oct. 1924, as well as 3 Apr. 1925, in senate minutes, 92.113v, box 1, file 1 [microfilm].
68 Report to AHCOM, 14 Feb. 1924, 90.064v, box 3, file 6.
69 See Report in "Records, especially re. Annesley Hall," 87.221v, file 2.
70 See Minutes of Dean's Council, 90.141v, box 2, file 20. Mary Rowell was not the lecturer in French but a fourth-year student in the pass course. The sorority at this time included Ruth Jenking and Marion Hilliard.
71 Report to AHCOM, 8 Oct. 1925, 90.064v, box 3, file 7.
72 See minutes of committee of management, AHCOM, 90.064v, box 2.
73 See undated press clipping [Mar. 1925] in AHCOM Minute Book, 1925 section, 90.064v, box 2.
74 Report to AHCOM, 9 Nov. 1922, 90.064v, box 3, file 5.
75 Lucy Booth Martyn, "Wymilwood," in *Aristocratic Toronto: Nineteenth-Century Grandeur* (Toronto: Gage, 1980), 198. John P.M. Court in "Out of the Woodwork: The Wood Family's Benefactions to Victoria University" describes the negotiations which, in 1949, resulted in Wymilwood's being transferred to the university in exchange for Victoria's acquiring the lease on other university lands it occupied, p. 43.

76 Undated clipping from *Christian Guardian* pasted into AHCOM minute book, 1925 section.

77 MA, letter to Charlotte, 8 Oct. 1925, MAP, 87.168v, box 1.

78 Gertrude Pringle, "Wymilwood," *Saturday Night* 41 (6 Feb. 1926): 32.

CHAPTER NINE

1 Northrop Frye, Convocation Address at the University of Saskatchewan, *Wascana Review* 3, no. 2 (1968): 84.

2 Gertrude Rutherford, "Dean of Women," *United Church Observer*, 15 Jan. 1941, 22.

3 *In Memoriam Margaret Addison, 1868–1940*, 7–8.

4 MA, general letter of 16 Feb. 1924, MAP, 87.168v, box 1.

5 MA, undated letter fragment [11 Nov. 1921], MAP, 87.168v, box 1.

6 Interview of author with Ottelyn Addison, 28 Dec. 1995.

7 MA, general letter of 16 Feb. 1924.

8 MA, general letter of 4 Dec. 1924, MAP, 87.168v, box 1.

9 "Good Qualities Balance Faults of Modern Girl," Toronto *Star*, 9 Jan. 1926.

10 Report of 4 June 1931, AHCOM, 90.064v, box 3, file 12.

11 Report of 29 May 1930, AHCOM, 90.064v, box 3, file 11.

12 MA, speech of 26 Feb. 1920, MAP, 87.168v, box 2, folder "Notes for Talks to ASGA."

13 Report to AHCOM, 15 Apr. 1926, 90.064v, box 3, file 8.

14 "Canadian Women in the Public Eye: Miss M.E.T. Addison," *Saturday Night* 40 (4 Apr. 1925): 27. The article is unsigned, but Addison's letter of 1 Dec. 1924 reveals that it was written by "a lady from *Saturday Night*" whom Addison would have liked to have sent away, as she despised being interviewed. The *Report of the Consultative Committee on Differentiation between the Sexes in the Curricula of Secondary Schools* was a non-Parliamentary publication of HMSO in 1923.

15 Benjamin Kidd, *The Science of Power*, 8th. ed. (London: Methuen, 1919), esp. 199. Addison quoted from this book in a speech of 26 Feb. 1920, MAP, box 2, file "Notes for Speeches to ASGA."

16 Lorine Pruette, "The Flapper," in *The New Generation*, ed. V.F. Calverton and S.D. Schmalhausen (London: George Allen and Unwin, 1930), 587.

17 Geraldine Jonçich Clifford, ed., *Lone Voyagers: Academic Women in Coeducational Universities 1870–1937* (New York: Feminist Press at the City University of New York, 1989), 31. Martha Vicinus in *Independent Women* (Chicago: University of Chicago Press, 1985), 147, notes the same phenomenon in the United Kingdom.

18 *Toronto Star Weekly*, 9 Apr. 1927.

19 MA, general letter of 10 Nov. 1923, MAP, 87.168v, box 1.

20 MA, letter to Charlotte, 2 Apr. 1927, MAP, 87.168v, box 1.

21 Dorothy Forward, reminiscence in *U of T Graduate* 4, no. 3 (1977): 22.

22 MA, letter to family, 1 Mar. 1929, MAP, 87.168v, box 1.

23 MA, letter to Charlotte, 25 Oct. 1924, MAP, 87.168v, box 1.

24 See unheaded, undated clipping in Addison's scrapbook, p. 77, MAP, 87.168v, box 3. The minutes of ASGA provide no clue as to the date.

25 Report to AHCOM, 9 Sept. 1929, 90.064v, box 3, file 10. For a listing of books on sex in the early twentieth century such as she may have been reading, see the notes to the chapter "The New Woman as Androgyne" in Smith-Rosenberg's *Disorderly Conduct*, 342–9.

26 For her views, see Kathleen McConnachie, "Methodology in the Study of Women in History: a Case Study of Helen MacMurchy, M.D.," *Ontario History* 75, no. 1 (1983): 67–9.

27 MA, circular letter entitled "Leaves from a Dean's Diary 1928," MAP, 87.168v, box 1.

28 MA, draft of letter to Rev. D.N. McLachlan, 6 Feb. 1928, DOW, 90.141v, box 2, file 8. The request from Rev. D.N. McLachlan, secretary of the Board, is in file 7.

29 Marguerite Van Die, *An Evangelical Mind: Nathanael Burwash and the Methodist Tradition in Canada, 1839–1918* (Montreal and Kingston: McGill-Queen's University Press, 1989), 146ff.

30 MA, general letter, 8 Oct. 1929, MAP, 87.168v, box 1.

31 MA, letter to Charlotte, 2 Apr. 1927.

32 Sissons, *History of Victoria University,* 287.

33 Minutes of VWA, 21 Jan. 1930, 90.066v, box 1.

34 A copy of the proposals is located in Trinity College Archives, Cartwright Family Papers, Mabel Cartwright, box 10, file "St. Hilda's College Correspondence 1921–35" (undated but dated by internal evidence to about 1929).

35 Report to AHCOM, 4 June 1931, 90.064v, box 3, file 12.

36 Minutes of 8 Dec. 1927, AA, 92.175v, box 1.

37 MA, letter to Charlotte and Mary, 14 Feb. 1928, MAP, 87.168v, box 1.

38 Personal information from Elizabeth McLeod; see also letter of 29 Nov. 1926, MAP, 87.168v, box 1. Addison's written references to Miss Manning are few and non-committal.

39 Addison, though praising the artist, confessed that she was a poor subject for a portrait and that she "[did] not really think much of the lady." Letter to Charlotte, 8 Oct. 1925, MAP, 87.168v, box 1.

40 Interview of the author with Laure Rièse, 17 January 1996.

41 MA, letter to Charlotte, 11 Oct. 1926 and general letter of 6 Nov. 1927, MAP, 87.168v, box 1.

42 "Memories of Annesley," *Victoria Reports*, Dec. 1963, 30.

43 A brief history of the committee may be found in its notebook, VUA, 90.148v, box 1, file 3.

44 *Acta* 52, no. 2 (Nov. 1937): 34.

45 MA, letter to Louise Addison, 24 Mar. 1926, MAP, 87.168v, box 1.

46 Minutes of AHCOM, 15 Sept. 1927, 90.064v, box 2, file 1.

47 MA, letter to Louise Addison, 6 Nov. 1927, MAP, 87.168v, box 1.

48 MA, letter to Arthur and Lizzie Addison, 15 Feb. 1928, MAP, 87.168v, box 1.

49 MA, letter to Louise Addison, 9 Mar. 1928, MAP, 87.168v, box 1.

50 MA, letter to Louise Addison, 6 Nov. 1927, MAP, 87.168v, box 1.

51 Report to AHCOM, 11 Oct. 1928, 90.064v, box 3, file 10.

52 MA, letter to Louise Addison, 18 Feb. 1928, MAP, 87.168v, box 1.

53 Minutes of 9 Sept. 1929, AHCOM, 90.064v, box 2, file 2.

54 Minutes of the board of regents, 21 Oct. 1930, 187.125v, file 2, box 2 [microfilm reel 2].

55 MA, letter to Kathleen Coburn, 16 Sept. 1931, DOW, 90.141v, box 2, file 9.

56 Report of 12 Mar. 1931, AHCOM, 90.064v, box 3, file 12.

57 MA, letter to Kathleen Coburn, 16 Sept. 1931.

58 Letter to Northrop Frye, 19 Nov. 1936, in *The Correspondence of Northrop Frye and Helen Kemp, 1932–1939*, ed. Robert D. Denham (Toronto: University of Toronto Press, 1996), 2:642.

CHAPTER TEN

1 MA, circular letter to Victoria alumnae, 7 Dec. 1929, in possession of Ann Lewis.

2 Interviews of author with Julia Addison, 28 Apr. 1995, and Irene Rinch, 24 Nov. 1995.

3 Interview of author with Ottelyn Addison, 28 Dec. 1995. The Cowans (Janie's mother's family) were dyed-in-the wool Scots.

4 MA, letter of 29 Nov. 1926, MAP, 87.168v, box 1.

5 A.N. Whitehead, *The Aims of Education and Other Essays* (London: Ernest Benn, [1959]), 23. The book is mentioned in Addison's letter to alumnae of 7 Dec. 1929.

6 MA, general letter of 1 Mar. 1927, MAP, 87.168v, box 1.

7 MA, letter to Charlotte, 2 Apr. 1927.

8 Minutes of annual meeting of Board of Education, 1930, UCA, 83.003C, box 1, file 1.

9 MA, letter to Charlotte, 2 Apr. 1927.

10 Report of the Commission on Secondary Education, 1929, UCA, 83.003C, box 2, file 11.

11 Olive Sparling, "The United Church of Canada Board of Christian Education, 1925–1971," UCA, doc. BX 9881 S75, 13.

12 Report of Committee to Study the Place and Function of Secondary Schools in the United Church, in *Reports and Agenda, Second Annual Meeting of the Board of Christian Education*, UCA, 83.051C, box 3, file 4, 133, 140, 133.

13 MA, undated note of reply, Board of Education, 83.003C, box 1, file 3.

14 *The First Fifty Years, 1895–1945: the Training and Work of Women Employed in the Service of the United Church of Canada*, published by the Committee on the Deaconess Order & Women Workers, the United Church Training School, and the WMS of the United Church, p. 8, in UCA, WMS, 83.058C, box 24, file 19; John D. Thomas, "Servants of the Church: Canadian Methodist Deaconess Work, 1890–1926," *Canadian Historical Review* 65 (1984): 371.

15 Unattributed quotation in *The First Fifty Years*, 5.

16 Mary Anne MacFarlane, "A Tale of Handmaidens: Deaconesses in the United Church of Canada, 1925 to 1964" (MA thesis, University of Toronto, 1987, in UCA), 1.

17 Ibid., 23.

18 Letter of M. Eadie to G. Rutherford, 1 Oct. 1936, UCA, Women Workers, 82.292C, box 1, file 7.

19 Report of Committee on Employed Women Workers, *United Church of Canada Year Book*, 1928, 254–60.

20 The uniform was a navy-blue dress with white collar and cuffs and a neat row of buttons down the front.

21 Committee on Women Workers, minutes of 14 June 1927, 82.292C, box 1, file 2.

22 Autumn Newsletter to Deaconesses, 1928, 82.292C, box 1, file 1.

23 "Report of the Study Group Appointed by the Inter-Board Committee on Women's Work to Consider Questions Vital to its Work," 7 Feb. 1936, 82.292C, box 1, file 7.

24 Ibid., and also MA, Memorandum of 15 Apr. 1937, 82.292C, box 1, file 5.

25 *The First Fifty Years*, 19.

26 Lydia E. Gruchy, "Far-Seeing Church Leader," *United Church Observer*, 15 Jan. 1941, 22.

27 *The First Fifty Years*, 27.

28 Documents regarding the house are in 82.292C, box 3, file 1.

29 Alison Prentice, *et al.*, *Canadian Women: a History, 172*.

30 *Re-Thinking Missions: a Laymen's Inquiry after One Hundred Years*. (NY and London: Harper & Brothers, 1932), 107–8.

31 Addison is presumably referring to this commission when she complains, of a published report, "How can people get at the great realities of life–spiritual life–by 'fact-finding' and appraisal of facts!" Letter to President Wallace, 4 Dec. 1932, VUA, President's office, 89.130V,

box 34, file 1. See also the criticism of James Endicott, *New Outlook*, 30 Nov. 1932, 1114.

32 Minutes of the Dominion Board, 1929–33, 84, WMS, 83.058C, box 1.

33 MA, circular letter to alumnae of Victoria, 7 Dec. 1929.

34 Minutes of the Interim Executive Board, 1926 and 1927, esp. Sept. 1927, 83.058C, box 1.

35 MA, general letter of 1 Mar. 1927.

36 See, for example, minutes of 12 May 1926, 83.058C, box 1.

37 See notes of the scholarship department, 83.058C, box 132, file 2.

38 Ideals described in Diana Pedersen, "'The Call to Service': the YWCA and the Canadian College Woman, 1886–1920," 187–215.

39 MA, letter to Charlotte, 12 Mar. 1915, MAP, 87.168v, box 1.

40 Minutes of the Executive Committee, 1923–25, NAC, YWCA, vol. 10, file 5. All further references to "YWCA" are to these YWCA papers in the National Archives of Canada, MG 28, I 198.

41 YWCA, box 1, file 6.

42 *YWCA Notes* 3 (July 1924): 3, YWCA, box 47, file 4.

43 On membership requirements see Pedersen, "'The Call to Service'," 203; Harshaw, *When Women Work Together: a History of the YWCA in Canada*, 41–3; and Membership Commission, minutes of 16 Jan. 1925, YWCA, box 16, file 5.

44 *YWCA Notes* 3 (July 1924). See also review of the membership commission at the 1929 convention, YWCA, box 16, file 9.

45 MA, letter to fellow workers, 25 Jan. 1927, YWCA, box 16, file 8.

46 Report at Banff Convention, 28 May 1927, YWCA, box 16, file 8.

47 MA, letter of 25 Jan. 1927, YWCA.

48 Minutes of 30 Dec. 1926, YWCA, box 16, file 8.

49 MA, letter to Arthur and Lizzie, 15 Feb. 1928, MAP, 87.168v, box 1.

50 Interview with Peter Addison by William Addison, 27 Dec. 1992.

51 Minutes of the board of regents, 12 Mar. 1936, 187.125v, box 2, file 2 [microfilm reel 2].

52 Interview of author with Celia Corcoran, 9 May 1995.

53 Celia Corcoran, sketch of cottage life on 3–5 Aug. 1940, in possession of Ann Lewis.

54 Emma Kaufman, "Exponent of International Friendship," *United Church Observer*, 15 January 1941, 22.

55 *New Outlook*, 28 Sept. 1932.

56 "Our Work in Japan, An Appreciation," *YWCA Notes* 12 (June 1933): 5, YWCA, box 47, file 13.

57 *Missionary Monthly*, Jan. 1933, 9–11; Mar. 1933, 105–7; Apr. 1933, 157–9; May 1933, 200–2.

58 Some notes on this school may be found in the Japanese visit folder in MAP, 87.168v, box 2.

59 *Missionary Monthly,* May 1933, 201.
60 Ibid., 202.
61 Ibid., 202.
62 Ibid., 202.
63 Helen Frye, *Letters of Northrop Frye and Helen Kemp, 1932–1939,* 2:642–3.
64 MA, letter to Louise Addison, 24 Mar. 1926.
65 MA, letters to Louise and to Arthur and Lizzie Addison, 13 and 15 Feb. 1928, MAP, 87.168v, box 1.
66 MA, letter to Louise, 1 Dec. 1927, MAP, 87.168v, box 1.
67 MA, letter to Kathleen Coburn, 16 Sept. 1931.
68 Toronto *Globe and Mail,* 20 May 1935. The purpose was to approve of the House of Commons' support of the Kellogg-Briand pact, which renounced war as a means of settling disputes.
69 Letter to Peter Addison (Arthur's son), 29 Oct. 1939, in possession of Christine Dow.
70 The series begins in the *Missionary Monthly* of Oct. 1936 and extends irregularly through 1940; the last article appeared posthumously in January 1941. Although the series title varies between "Times" and "Time," the quotation is presumably a play upon the inscription in the Venice arsenal, "Happy is that city which in time of peace thinks of war."
71 "In Time of War Prepare for Peace," *Missionary Monthly,* Oct. 1939, 436. Nielson was a radical who subsequently defended the "agitators" and "Reds" who had been interned under the defence of Canada regulations: *House of Commons Debates* 1940, 1:59–61, and 1941, 1:187–92.
72 *Missionary Monthly,* Oct. 1940, 437.
73 For her leadership of the Philathea Class of young women here, see the Golden Jubilee booklet (1939), 3, in UCA, Simpson Avenue Church file.
74 MA, letter to Peter Addison, 29 Oct. 1939.
75 *In Memoriam Margaret Addison, 1868–1940,* 2.
76 See pp. 158, 166 of this volume.
77 MA, letter to President Wallace, 4 Dec. 1932.
78 Typescript address, MAP, 87.168v, box 2, folder "Memorial Addresses by Gertrude L. Rutherford."
79 Kathleen Coburn, *In Pursuit of Coleridge* (Toronto: Clarke, Irwin, 1977), 59.

Index